THE FOUNDING

A Dramatic Account of the Writing of the Constitution

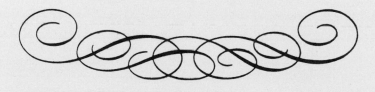

Fred Barbash

THE LINDEN PRESS / SIMON AND SCHUSTER
1987

Copyright © 1987 by Fred Barbash
All rights reserved
including the right of reproduction
in whole or in part in any form
Published by The Linden Press/Simon and Schuster
A Division of Simon & Schuster, Inc.
Simon & Schuster Building
Rockefeller Center
1230 Avenue of the Americas
New York, New York 10020
THE LINDEN PRESS/SIMON AND SCHUSTER and colophon are trademarks
of Simon & Schuster, Inc.
Designed by Eve Kirch
Manufactured in the United States of America

10   9   8   7   6   5   4

Library of Congress Cataloging-in-Publication Data

Barbash, Fred.
   The founding.

   Bibliography: p.
   Includes index.
   1. United States. Constitutional Convention (1787)
2. United States—Constitutional history. I. Title.
KF4520.B37   1987   342.73'0292   87-4078
ISBN: 0-671-55256-2   347.302292

To Jack and Kate Barbash

ACKNOWLEDGMENTS

Rebecca Rogers provided invaluable and skillful assistance in researching and writing this book.

Professor Walter Dellinger of the Duke University Law School provided inspiration, guidance and criticism of the manuscript in draft form. I was privileged to sit in on Professor Dellinger's brilliantly taught course in constitutional history while spending a month at Duke University in 1984, courtesy of a joint *Washington Post*–Duke University visiting-journalist program. My thanks to Duke University and its Law School.

I am indebted to Dr. James Hutson, Chief of the Manuscript Division of the Library of Congress and a noted scholar of the Constitution, for advice, for allowing me access to the United States Constitution Collection he was compiling in honor of the Bicentennial, and for reading and criticizing portions of the manuscript.

John C. Armor, of the Commission on the Bicentennial of the United States Constitution, was also kind enough to review an early draft of the book.

I alone am responsible for any errors.

I would also like to thank: archivist Leonard Rapport for assistance with documents; the Independence National Historical Park for access to its collection of documents; Independence Park Chief Historian David C. G. Dutcher and Park Historians Robert K. Sutton and David A. Kimball for advice and a wonderfully vivid tour of Independence Park; Paul Chestnut of the Library of Congress; Professor Donald L. Robinson of Smith College; David M. Ludlum for assistance in gathering weather data; and Mary Ellen Waller, historian and friend, for encouragement.

Rhoda Weyr, my agent, Allen H. Peacock, my editor at Simon and Schuster, Vera Schneider, who copyedited the manuscript, and Marjorie Williams and T. R. Reid of the *Washington Post* deserve special thanks for professional and moral support.

I am grateful to the *Washington Post* for financial support and leave time while I worked on the book and to those at the *Post* who made my sabbatical possible, including Publisher Donald Graham, Executive Editor Benjamin C. Bradlee, Managing Editor Leonard Downie, Jr., Deputy Managing Editor Peter Silberman, Assistant Managing Editors Tom Wilkinson and Robert G. Kaiser, and Molli Martin. Many of my colleagues at the *Post*, too many to mention, were wonderfully generous in their tolerance and encouragement.

Special personal thanks to Serena Gray Simons, Susan Osborn and Carrie Barbash.

CONTENTS

PREFACE

In 1983, in search of material to help me prepare a news analysis on the Supreme Court for the *Washington Post*, I consulted James Madison's *Notes of Debates in the Federal Convention of 1787*. As I started reading them, I quickly lost interest in the task before me and was lured instead into a wonderful and suspenseful political story. It was a story with which I was largely unfamiliar. I recalled being taught fleetingly in high school about the convention. I remembered it being portrayed as a rather scholarly gathering of philosopher-statesmen, all of whom knew the Great Books by heart, who sat down in a room in Philadelphia and designed the perfect form of government. I remembered being left with the impression that the convention and its outcome was kind of inevitable, an obvious next step following the Declaration of Independence in a grand parade of historic documents. They made us memorize the preamble to the Constitution, but I have no recollection of being asked to read any further. By the time I reached college, more sophisticated teachers were exposing the philosopher-statesmen as plutocrats, driven by self-interest, and the convention itself as a dark conspiracy. Most of our attention was directed to the financial interests of the delegates; little or none to the meaning and origin of the operative clauses of the document. Later on in the sixties and seventies, in the era of civil rights and civil liberties, interest seemed to shift exclusively to the Bill of Rights as the part of the Constitution that really counted. By the time of graduate school, scholars and students were subjecting the debates and the votes of the convention to computerized analysis, showing how the Constitution actually evolved through the formation and dissolution of various factions within the convention.

As I read through the *Notes* again and again, and later through the notes of other delegates and then through the correspondence of James Madison, George Washington, George Mason and others who planned and attended the convention, I decided that this was a story I would like to tell. My purpose was to write a small, accessible book that would tell the story accurately but as simply as possible. To further this end I have taken a single liberty. The most complete account of the debates in the convention are Madison's *Notes*. But they are not a conventional transcript of dialogue; they report what he and others have said in the third person. I have treated the *Notes* as dialogue in the first person. For example, Madison reports Edmund Randolph saying that "he took a step which might be the most awful of his life." I have changed this to read: "I take a step which might be the most awful of my life."

The Convention of 1787 does not yield a single, simple theme; it was far more interesting than that, and the motivations and intentions were far more varied and complicated. The Constitution was ·the work of politicians, sweating it out for nearly four months in a sealed room in Philadelphia. Each delegate brought with him an agenda shaped by local, regional and personal interests, by his state of mind at that particular moment, by philosophy, theory and a vision of what America would become. Beyond this, each state and each region represented in Philadelphia had certain conditions for participation in the Union that had to be met.

There were fifty-five voices in the convention. To be sure, they were united on some broad issues—faith in republican government, the critical need for a checks and balances—but the delegates held splendidly diverse views of what a government should do and how it should do it. Contrast, for example, Roger Sherman's desire for an extremely limited government with the expansive government sought by Alexander Hamilton and James Madison. Compare Alexander Hamilton's disdain for state sovereignty with Luther Martin's emotional attachment to the rights of the states. All the conflicting currents are reflected in the Constitution, and it is possible to find supporting quotes in the debates for all but the most outlandish interpretations of some of the document's clauses.

Add to this the fact that many of the premises and prejudices on which the convention decisions were based have vanished. The country is no longer torn over the propriety of paper money. Conflict between small states and large is no longer part of our political landscape. Indeed, one of the "miracles" of Philadelphia is that a document with considerable potential to become irrelevant remains vital two hundred years later.

All this raises questions about a view of the convention current in the 1980s, as an oracle from which something called "the Intent of the Framers" may be confidently discerned. Whose intent? Sherman's? Madison's? Hamilton's? The problem, among many others, is that one can take one's pick. If the Framers collectively believed that their intent, as enunciated in the convention, should guide future generations of judges and lawmakers, one wonders why they insisted on keeping convention proceedings secret for fifty years after they were completed.

This is not to say the convention is useless as a guide to constitutional interpretation. Many broad principles of government attracted a clear consensus in Philadelphia. Among them was the conviction that no branch of government should exercise power unchecked, and that power exercised ought to be derived from the Constitution itself. These principles, many delegates felt, made a Bill of Rights unnecessary, for they believed that the government they founded, if properly managed, would both protect the rights of individuals and be a continuing source of national strength.

I often wondered as I researched this book what the delegates of 1787 would find most surprising were they to be miraculously transported to the year 1987. In my opinion, it would not be the power wielded by the Supreme Court, as some have suggested; or the extent of congressional involvement in foreign policy, as others believe. They would be most shocked by the power assumed every day in a hundred different ways by the executive and legislative branches of government without serious reference to whether the Constitution provides the authority for the exercise of such power. The operating principle of government today seems to be that authority may be exercised until someone proves to the satisfaction of a court that it violates a right. Thus courts address the aggrieved party and say: show us what constitutional right has been breached.

They should be addressing their question more often to government and they should be saying: show us, if you please, by what constitutional authority you act.

Many of the conflicts of the eighteenth century on which parts of the Constitution are based have indeed disappeared. But, as Madison pointed out, conflict itself would always be prevalent in a country so large and so diverse. Their great gift of the convention to future generations was a structure of government that recognized this, controlled it, and, to a remarkable extent, converted it into energy.

FRED BARBASH

Washington, D.C.
January 1987

BOOK ONE

"A Critical Minute"

CHAPTER ONE

Prelude to the Convention

From our perspective of two hundred years, it would be nice to say that all early Americans viewed the Constitutional Convention of 1787 as a great and solemn event and that everyone who was anyone vied to participate in it. Perhaps that spirit was there in 1776, when patriots assembled in the same room in Philadelphia to declare independence. But 1787 was different. Only a handful of enthusiasts organized the convention. Dozens of those who were asked to attend begged off. The New Hampshire delegation arrived two months late. Rhode Island boycotted the convention entirely. And it got started eleven days late because of tardiness.

Part of the problem was Philadelphia itself. It took courage to go to Philadelphia for the summer, especially not knowing when you would leave. The city was dirty, noisy, known for its unbearable summer heat and its flies. Thomas Jefferson once joked that the Declaration of Independence was signed so quickly in Philadelphia because of the flies biting through the silk stockings of the signers. "I dare not think of residing in Philadelphia during

17

the Summer," wrote one Marylander who was planning on being late.

The city was chosen not because it was a good place in which to pass the season, but because it was centrally located, had enough rooming houses and a fine building to meet in, and was not New York, where the political climate was less favorable.

Among the reluctant was George Washington himself.

When the Virginia legislature chose him to be a delegate to the convention, he told them to take his name off the list.

Choose someone else, he said, firmly.

Your name cannot be spared, they pressed.

I have served my country, said Washington, and "it is not my business to embark again on the sea of troubles."

We will keep the door open, they responded, in case you change your mind.

Washington had retired after the Revolutionary War at age fifty-two to tend to Mount Vernon, his seven-thousand-acre farm along the Potomac. Those who saw him there—and there were visitors aplenty to this place of pilgrimage—were surprised to see this stiff and formal man, who had rarely smiled during the war, so utterly relaxed, stripping off his coat to work on the land with his men, laughing and talking and sipping champagne with friends in the evening.

He looked remarkably well, reported Robert Hunter, Jr., a British traveler who visited Mount Vernon in the fall of 1785.

> The General is about six foot high, perfectly straight and well made, rather inclined to be lusty. His eyes are full and blue and seem to express an air of gravity. His nose inclines to the aquiline; his mouth small; his teeth are yet good; and his cheeks indicate perfect health. His forehead is a noble one, and he wears his hair turned back, without curls (quite in the officer's style) and tied in a long queue behind. Altogether, he makes a most noble, respectable appearance, and I really think him the first man in the world . . .

The first man in the world had made a promise to himself after the war to "glide gently down the stream of life," and he fully intended to keep it.

The convention's planners knew that the convention was suspect in many eyes, and that Washington's presence would give it badly needed credibility and attract others. They pressed him for months. Each time he was asked why he was reluctant, Washington gave a slightly different reason.

He had made something of a show of withdrawing from public life after the war, so how would it now look to take center stage once again? He had declined an invitation to attend another convention in Philadelphia, he said on another occasion, a reunion of Revolutionary War officers belonging to the Society of the Cincinnati that was to take place at the same time—how embarrassing to beg off from one convention only to turn up at another. He had worried that the convention was not strictly legal. How would it look if that turned out to be so?

But the heart of the matter was Washington's grave doubt that the convention would succeed. The delegates would come so fettered by timidity or by parochial interests that they would produce nothing. Worse, they would hold the convention and nobody would come. He valued his reputation too much to associate himself with a debacle.

More than that, a failure could further demoralize the nation and foreclose any future attempt to forge a new government—an attempt made when the time was right. America was in bad shape, Washington believed, but it might not have suffered enough to make the changes necessary.

A small group of men, led by fellow Virginian James Madison, were the ones pressing Washington, and the very fact that they were so dependent on the participation of a single man was the best evidence of their own uncertainty. As late as February 1787, with the convention less than three months away, Madison could only say that it was "probable' that a meeting would take place. But, he added, "What the issue of it will be, is among the other arcana of futurity, and nearly as inscrutable as any of them."

Madison, thirty-six, was in every respect the opposite of Washington. Washington, the elder, was a commanding presence. Madison was five foot six and seemed even smaller because of his slight build and his short legs. He was bald on the top of his head, bookish, obsessively punctual, immersed in theory. Washington dominated any crowd he chose to grace; Madison tended to get lost in crowds, was often described as unsociable and was so lacking in confidence about his public-speaking abilities that he had sat through whole sessions of the Virginia legislature in silence. Washington was a war hero; Madison had considered himself too frail to fight.

In appearance Madison was "little and ordinary," said Fisher Ames of Massachusetts, who served with him in Congress a few years later. "He speaks decently, as to manner, and no more. His language is very pure, perspicuous, and to the point. Pardon me, if I add, that I think him a little too much of a book politician . . ."

Madison was to bring ideas to Philadelphia; Washington was to bring only himself.

This is not to say that Washington did not know what he wanted for a new government: it should be very strong, very energetic, "well guarded and closely watched . . ." In short, what Washington wanted was precisely the opposite of the government the country now had under the Articles of Confederation. The existing Congress of the Confederation, a single house consisting of delegates chosen by each state, was weak and lethargic. There was no need for it to be well guarded or closely watched, for without any real power there was nothing to be guarded and nothing to be watched.

It was Washington's wish that "the convention may adopt no temporizing expedient, but probe the defects of the constitution to the bottom, and provide radical cures, whether they are agreed to or not." But he was long on adjectives and short on detail.

Madison had created a new government in his mind many times and an elaborate theory to back it up. No one else had thrown himself into the subject as he had.

Indeed, Madison had thought of little else for a year, holing up for the winter of 1785 at his family home, Montpelier, at the foot of the Blue Ridge Mountains in Virginia. Montpelier was the perfect retreat, isolated by "the winter blockade," as he called it, through which no one could pass and disturb him. He worked solidly there, occasionally glancing to the tops of the mountains that were tipped with snow until early spring. The winter was altogether strange that year at Montpelier, warm when it was supposed to be cold and unseasonably cold in March as spring arrived. On the first day of April 1786, Madison later reported to Jefferson, it "snowed and hailed the whole day in a storm from the northeast and the thermometer stood at four oclock at twenty six degrees. If the snow had fallen in the usual way it would have been eight or ten inches deep, at least; but consisting of small hard globules, mixed with small hail, and lying on the ground so compact and firm as to bear a man, it was less than half that depth."

Beforehand, Madison had asked Jefferson, who was in Paris representing America, to send him a "literary cargo" for his winter's reading. Madison buried himself in the books. One can picture him there in his modest house, bundled up against the cold, surrounded by books, earnestly dissecting the history of nations, taking his usual careful and voluminous notes. The study of history was never academic with Madison. Even as a student, he had waded through it with an extraordinarily practical eye, extracting the essence, storing it in his Commonplace Book for future use. One of those lessons he had copied was now especially compelling. "There is a Critical Minute in every thing, and the masterpiece of Good Conduct is to perceive it and take hold of it. If it is miss'd chiefly in revolutions of State, 'tis odds if it can be met with or perceived again."

By the time he came down from Montpelier, he must have

believed that the critical minute had arrived, for it wasn't long
before he began planning the convention at Philadelphia and the
grand scheme of government he would propose there. Soon thereafter, he and his allies began working on Washington.

With two months left before the convention, Washington was
still refusing to attend, but his resistance had weakened because
of Shays' Rebellion, the armed insurrection of hard-pressed farmers that had engulfed New England for a year and had threatened
for a time to spread. It had peaked and had finally been sup-
pressed, but not with the help of Congress, which had stood by
helplessly throughout.

Madison and the others had made sure Washington was kept
informed, painting the situation—bad as it was—in the darkest
and most ominous tones possible and suggesting that at a time
like this his excuses sounded feeble indeed.

Washington's greatest fear was that in response to the disorder
America might turn in desperation to a monarchy—the monarch
most often mentioned being none other than himself. Madison
played on this fear. There are indeed men who favor a monarchic
form of government for America, he reported to Washington,
without specifying who these men are. And there is one way
to prevent it: "Those who may lean towards a Monarchical Government, and who I suspect are swayed by very indigested ideas,
will of course abandon an unattainable object whenever a prospect opens of rendering the Republican form competent to its
purpose."

Washington was as disgusted with the incapacity to suppress
Shays' Rebellion as he was with its perpetrators, reserving his
most withering disdain for those who asked him to use his "influence" to help restore the peace. "You talk, my good Sir, of
employing influence to appease the present tumults in Massachusetts," he wrote to Virginian Henry Lee. "I know not where that
influence is to be found, or, if attainable, that it would be a proper
remedy for the disorders. Influence is no government."

In the months before, Washington had always asked himself

how bad it might look if he chose to attend. Now he asked how bad it would look if he did not. Congress had by now endorsed the convention. Would public opinion regard him as negligent? Might people believe he actually wanted republican government to fail, and that he had some nefarious motive for wishing it?

"A thought . . . has lately run through my mind, which is attended with embarrassment," he wrote to his trusted friend Henry Knox. "It is, whether my non-attendance in this Convention will not be considered as dereliction to Republicanism, nay more, whether other motives may not (however injuriously) be ascribed to me for not exerting myself on this occasion. . . . Under these circumstances, let me pray you, my dear Sir, to inform me confidentially what the public expectation is on this head, that is, whether I will, or ought to be there."

By the time Knox replied to the letter, Washington had already made up his mind. In late March 1787, he sat down and wrote a letter to Edmund Randolph, Governor of Virginia: "As my friends, with a degree of solicitude which is unusual, seem to wish for my attendance on this occasion, I have come to a resolution to go, if my health will permit it."

Randolph, delighted, responded: The date is May 14. When it comes, "it is my purpose to take you by the hand."

By mid-April, Madison reached the peak of anxiety. "The nearer the crisis approaches, the more I tremble for the issue. The necessity of gaining the concurrence of the Convention in some system that will answer the purpose, the subsequent approbation of Congress and the final sanction of the States, presents a series of chances, which would inspire despair in any case where the alternative was less formidable," he wrote to his friend Edmund Pendleton.

After all the effort to get the great man to Philadelphia, the thought now flashed through Madison's mind that perhaps he should tell Washington to stay put for a while, until it was certain that the convention would get off the ground. "It ought not to be wished by any of his friends that he participate in any abortive undertaking." By then, the decision had been made to make Washington president of the convention, and Madison thought better of it, advising him to wait.

Washington had hoped to leave Mount Vernon on May 8, but a spring squall in the valley had made travel impossible, so he postponed his departure until the next day. How tempting it must have been during the night to go to his study and write to them again, saying he wasn't coming, telling them once again to count him out. But having run out of excuses, he got up before it was light on May 9, dressed, put on his coat against the damp morning, and stepped into his carriage bracing for the long journey. He crossed the Potomac just as the sun came up.

Washington noted every miserable step of the journey in his diary, as if to say to himself, "Why on earth am I doing this?"

On the first day, he progressed no farther than to twenty miles south of Baltimore, where he stayed the night with a friend and, "feeling very severely a violent head ache and sick stomach," went to bed early.

The following day, Thursday, he felt better, but his departure was delayed by rain, and he wound up spending the night in Baltimore.

By late Friday, he was still in Maryland, attempting to catch the ferry at Havre de Grace, "where I dined but could not cross, the wind being turbulent and squally."

Finally, on Saturday, he crossed the Susquehanna "with difficulty (on account of the wind)" and began the approach to Philadelphia, arriving in the outskirts on May 13.

A few miles south of town, he was met by a party of old army confederates, former colonels and majors, who escorted him toward the city. This was more like it. At Gray's Ferry, along the Schuylkill, troops appeared to greet him, the City Light Brigade standing at attention, saluting Washington as he rode the final few miles into the heart of Philadelphia, where a large crowd hailed him and followed him as he went to call on the President of Pennsylvania, Benjamin Franklin. As America's two most celebrated men met, the bells of the city chimed.

Washington was then whisked away to the grand mansion of Robert Morris, one of the wealthiest men in town, where he would lodge until the end of the convention.

"The American Fabius arrives," gushed one newspaper. "The hero comes. . . . All hail! Great man!"

"Yesterday," said *The Pennsylvania Packet,* "His Excellency General Washington, a member of the grand convention, arrived here. . . . The joy of the people on the coming of this great and good man was shewn by their acclamations and the ringing of bells."

Madison had arrived in Philadelphia from New York (where he had been attending the Congress) three days before Washington had even left Mount Vernon, a full eleven days before the date set for the convention to begin. It was freezing when he climbed down from the Flyer, the coach from New York, celebrated for being able to make the trip in a full day provided the horses didn't collapse from exhaustion. Madison's arrival, it seems, went unnoticed, for he was not the sort to be recognized on the streets or to be greeted by delegations of notables. No troops assembled and no bells chimed. With his bags, Madison went quietly to Mrs. House's inn, a traditional lodging for Virginians in Philadelphia, where he could unpack and pore once again over the outline of the new constitution, the plan he had shared only with his closest allies, his plan for a new republic.

The second Monday in May, the fourteenth, arrived. Washington, revived by his grand reception the day before, got up early after a night's rest at Morris' mansion, strode out into streets moist from three straight days of rain, and made his way over to the State House, home of the government of Pennsylvania and site of the signing of the Declaration of Independence. Madison, confident that his eleven days of nervous waiting in Philadelphia were over, composed himself, gathered together all the notes and pa-

pers he had brought for the occasion, and walked the few blocks
from his rooming house.

The State House—where the convention was to meet—was
the finest building on the continent, but there was something
distinctly republican about it, for, unlike the seats of government
in Europe, this was no grand-scale classical edifice. Two stories
high, brick and wood, with gabled roof and with chimneys on
either end, it resembled an exceptionally fine mansion. Passersby
could stare directly into the Assembly Room, where the convention was to meet, and their representatives could stare right back
at them, eye to eye. There would be no staring at the convention,
for the Virginians had hired sentries to keep the people away and
guard against eavesdropping.

To the north, east and west were block after dense block of
houses, private stables and covered markets, a couple of smelly
tanyards, a soap factory and, about five blocks to the east, the
Delaware River and the harbor.

Washington and Madison entered the building, took their
places and waited for the others. They waited in vain that day,
for only a few more Virginians and the Pennsylvania delegation,
all of whom lived in Philadelphia, showed up. That was it. They
sat in the room alone for some time, a dozen or so men surrounded
by tables draped in green baize and by forty or fifty empty chairs,
before getting up and leaving, vowing to return the next day. On
the following morning the scene was repeated—the Virginians
and the Pennsylvanians sitting alone, waiting, staring at one
another.

The third day was equally disappointing, as well as the day after
that and the day after that. Each day, the few additional delegates
who had trickled in went to the State House, waited for others to
arrive on the floor and left disappointed. A full week passed and
still no convention.

If Madison's spirits were low, he didn't let on. He had served
in the Confederation Congress long enough to be accustomed to
such tardiness. He was sure that it was just the bad weather.

Washington was another matter. In public, he kept up appearances, making the rounds of teas and dinners, of meetings of the Society of Cincinnati, which had gotten its convention off the ground, his every movement noted by the newspapers. Privately, he was fretting. Gouverneur Morris of Pennsylvania, one of the little band of men in waiting, later described Washington's mood as time wore on: "His countenance had more than [the] usual solemnity. His eye was fixed, and seemed to look into futurity."

"Not more than four states were represented yesterday," Washington wrote to a friend. "If any have come in since, it is unknown to me. These delays greatly impede public measures, and serve to sour the temper of the punctual members, who do not like to idle away their time."

Madison, for his part, never idled away time. During the delay, he convened the Virginia delegation for two to three hours each day, explaining his plan of government. It was, after all, to be offered in the name of Virginia, even though it was mostly his.

One delegate from Pennsylvania in particular—the oldest one of all—never wavered in his optimism. The very sight of him, a squat old man in Quaker dress, bald except for white fringes, riding through the streets in a sedan chair like a potentate: Ben Franklin was Philadelphia's biggest attraction.

Though he had been preparing for the end for years, life, and great events, had kept interfering. "I seem to have intruded myself into the company of posterity," he said, "when I ought to have been abed and asleep." He was eighty-one and had made something of an art of adjusting to it. He had brought the sedan chair back from Paris because an intensely painful gallstone made a carriage ride through the bumpy streets of town excruciating. He became dizzy when he tried to climb the ladder to reach books atop his floor-to-ceiling shelves. So he had recently invented something he called the "long arm," a stick of pine, eight feet long, fitted on the end with a tweezerlike contraption controlled by a string from the bottom, with which he could stand on the floor, grab the book he wanted, and bring it down.

These practical talents and his scientific achievements were recognized by all, but of what use they would be in the convention remained to be seen. His name, on the other hand, would be extremely useful, for Franklin was relatively neutral in the great political controversies of the day—so much so that he was the only man the warring political factions in Pennsylvania had been able to settle on as chief executive of the state; thus this world-famous and legendary man occupied a job ordinarily reserved for a relatively obscure politician. Franklin groused about the constant demand for his services: "They engrossed the prime of my life. They have eaten my flesh, and seem resolved now to pick my bones." But he rarely turned anyone down, and when the call came for the convention, Franklin served once more.

On or about the twentieth of May, the mood of the city began to change. Delegates were arriving six and seven a day now, by coach and by ship—from New York, New Jersey, Delaware, from Massachusetts, from the far-off Carolinas—each new arrival bringing news of others on the way. The inns filled up, and those delegates who found themselves alone from their region, realizing that the convention would indeed take place, fired off dispatches urging others to get to Philadelphia.

"I am mortified that I alone am from New England," Rufus King of Massachusetts wrote to Jeremiah Wadsworth of Connecticut. "The backwardness may prove unfortunate—Pray hurry on your Delegates—some personal sacrifices perhaps may stand in the way of their immediate attendance—But they ought not to yield to such considerations—Believe me it may prove most unfortunate if they do not attend within a few days."

On the morning of May 25, 1787, twenty-nine men converged on the State House, filing into the Assembly Room, taking their places at the tables assigned to each state. Madison had decided in the interest of posterity to keep careful records of everything that was said in the convention, and so he took a seat front and center to better hear all that passed. As the roll of states was called, he wrote down each one and took a count: Massachusetts, New York, New Jersey, Pennsylvania, Delaware, Virginia, North Carolina, South Carolina, Georgia. Finally, more than half the states were represented.

The elusive quorum was achieved.

Washington was immediately and unanimously elected president of the convention, as planned. Robert Morris of Pennsylvania and John Rutledge of South Carolina came to his side and, with the convention on its feet, escorted Washington to the chair. As he addressed the house, Madison took down Washington's words.

"[I]n a very emphatic manner, he [Washington] thanked the Convention for the honor they had conferred on him, reminded them of the novelty of the scene of business in which he was to act, lamented his want of better qualifications, and claimed the indulgence of the house towards the involuntary errors which his inexperience might occasion."

A few days later, Washington wrote to Jefferson to tell him he had changed his mind about the convention: "Much is expected from it by some; not much by others; and nothing by a few. That something is necessary, none will deny; for the situation of the general government, if it can be called a government, is shaken to its foundation, and liable to be overturned by every blast.

"In a word, it is at an end. . . ."

CHAPTER TWO

America in Crisis

"I am mortified beyond expression when I view the clouds that have spread over the brightest morn that ever dawned upon any country."

George Washington had good reason to despair in October 1786 when he wrote those words: the unity of the war years had collapsed; troops had mutinied; the currency had lost its value; the states feuded bitterly; the national treasury was empty; Barbary pirates were preying on American shipping; and a violent insurrection had broken out and was threatening to spread.

It all stood out sharply against the romantic backdrop of the previous decade, when Americans were bursting with pride and high expectations. Had the morn been less bright, perhaps the clouds would have appeared less dark. In the tenth year of independence America was in deep trouble.

The government had not caused all the problems—it was simply helpless in the face of them. The Confederation Congress, the direct descendant of the illustrious Continental Congress that blessed America with the Declaration of Independence, had fallen on hard times. In 1783 it had fled Philadelphia in fear, not of the British, who were long gone, but of its own troops demanding their unpaid wages. From thereon in, the "United States in Congress Assembled," as it called itself, wandered the East from city to city like some nomadic tribe. Whole months went by with no quorum, leaving Congress capable only of opening its mail each day and recessing until the next. Its acts "were as little heeded as the cries of an oysterman," as one Congressman said.

It wasn't Congress' fault. Some of its members—including Madison, James Wilson of Pennsylvania and Alexander Hamilton of New York—had struggled desperately to do something about Congress' "imbecility," the standard deprecation. But the states were in control, and, having thrown off one central government, the Crown, they were loath to replace it with another by granting Congress authority to cope.

It was also hard to blame the states. They took seriously the words of the Declaration of Independence that had declared America not a free and independent nation, but a nation of "Free and Independent States." Ten years before the Federal Convention, most of the states had held their own conventions and drafted their own constitutions, complete with separated powers, checks and balances, and bills of rights, documents that would serve as models for years to come. For the first (and last) time in American history, they were truly, exuberantly, sovereign. They intended to make the most of it.

The legislatures drafted, passed, repealed and reenacted more laws than they had in all their previous years combined. Their capitals vibrated with politics and became power centers, where men learned the art of lobbying, logrolling and patronage; where the foundations of political parties and political machines were built.

Popular politics was being born, too. During most of America's history, the affairs of government had been in the hands of a tiny elite, men of wealth and education. The masses of the people, the landless, the artisans, the mechanics, "the lower sort," as they were called, had appeared content to leave governance to "the better sort," as they were called. They took it for granted that the better sort was, indeed, better. Because of the Revolution, all this was changing. For the first time, ordinary people began participating in politics, electing representatives who were more like them, men truly of their own choosing.

America was thirteen small democratic republics, with their own interests, their own currencies, their own little armies and even their own foreign policies. When Jefferson spoke of "my country," he meant the commonwealth of Virginia, not the United States.

The states did not view the Confederation Congress as their government, but as an assembly of nations, which was what it was. There was no president and no judiciary. Congress passed no laws truly binding on individuals or states. Its delegates were elected not by the people, but by the state governments, which told them how to vote and when to vote and told them often. The members of Congress were the states' ambassadors.

The greatest symbol of Congress' status as a diplomatic assembly and of the sovereignty of the states was the equality each enjoyed in the body. Regardless of size or population, each state wielded a single vote.

On paper, it was idyllic. Americans had been taught by great European philosophers that the best governments were small and close to the people, ruling over a manageable land area. In reality it didn't work, for America had come of age with independence, assuming the obligations of a nation with three million people whether it liked it or not, while possessing none of the attributes needed to behave like one.

Behaving like a nation meant paying national debts, of which America had more than its share. It was indebted to the foreign allies who had helped finance the war, to the citizens who had loaned money for it, and to the men and the widows and children of the men who had fought it. The government could meet none of these obligations, because the states denied it the power to tax.

The states made Congress beg them for money, and then they were ungenerous in response.

Behaving like a nation meant keeping the national word, meeting American obligations under the treaty of peace with Great Britain, which required payment of prewar debts owed to Englishmen. The authority to enforce the treaty lay with the state legislatures and the state courts, and many simply refused to comply. In response, the British breached the treaty as well, keeping their troops menacingly in frontier outposts they had agreed to abandon.

At the same time, Britain launched another kind of war against America, a trade war, closing to American commerce what had once been lucrative ports in the West Indies. Being a nation meant retaliating, but the Congress could not, for it had no authority to impose its own retaliatory tariffs or trade restrictions. Simultaneously, American shipping was driven from the Mediterranean by the Barbary pirates of North Africa—and America could do nothing. The matter of trade was not simply a matter of domestic prosperity. The ability to wage international commerce —to trade on a free and equal footing with other powers—was as important to America's standing as a nation as the ability to wage war.

The list of obligations unmet was endless. The most ominous of all, however, were those that threatened to break the loose confederation into pieces. There was nothing new about the many feuds among the states, though it had been easy to forget about them in the patriotic fervor of the war. When the war ended they reared up with a vengeance.

The greatest bone of contention was land. Two to three million people lived in America in the 1780s, with the vast majority in the narrow stretch along the Atlantic coast where they had always been. It wasn't expected to stay that way for long, however, for Americans were looking west now, to the unsettled territory across the Appalachians to the Mississippi. There were tens of millions of acres there, and money to be made for the states and the speculators who held title to them. Under old British "sea-to-sea" charters, the West supposedly belonged to six of the thirteen states: Virginia, Massachusetts, Connecticut, New York, Georgia and North Carolina. The landless states—Maryland, New Jersey, New Hampshire, Rhode Island, Delaware and South Carolina—were intensely jealous. There were claims, counterclaims, counter-counterclaims and even outbreaks of violence over these lands, as well as over lands closer to home.

Another conflict simmered over trade. Only a handful of the states, New York, Massachusetts and Pennsylvania, had good harbors, and the others were dependent on them for their imports— foreign and domestic, staples and luxuries. The port states exploited their advantage mercilessly, slapping heavy taxes on the goods needed by neighboring states, driving up their prices while fattening their own treasuries. New York was the worst offender, and its neighbor New Jersey the most offended.

The Congress could do nothing, for it was denied the power to regulate commerce.

The slave trade was potentially the most explosive issue. While all the states had some slaves, those south of Maryland had hundreds of thousands of them and depended on them for economic survival. Southerners had already beaten back an attempt to denounce the slave trade in the Declaration of Independence. They expected and feared further assaults, and with reason. Many Northerners were convinced that a slave rebellion was imminent; it was costing enough to fight off the Indians.

The fact was that one region of America was quite prepared to sell any other region down the river. New England congressmen recently had generously offered Spain permanent control over the Mississippi River in exchange for commercial access to the immense Spanish appetite for fish. To Southerners, the Mississippi was the future commercial lifeline for their westward-expanding population, and New England's proposed treaty with Spain was greeted in the South as a near act of war. Talk of

splitting the country into three separate confederacies reached
its peak.

A few advanced thinkers, like Ben Franklin, believed as early
as the 1750s that some useful purpose might be served by forging
a more permanent national union. But sentiment for a convention was slow to galvanize, even in the face of the growing problems of the 1780s. It took two additional bitter and emotional
disputes to convince enough influential men finally that something drastic must be done.

A "chain of debt" stretched from the subsistence farmers in the
remotest western regions of New England to the small merchants
who sold them goods, to the importers and financiers of the cities
to the great banking houses of London. Everyone owed money,
and the only money that really counted was hard money—gold
and silver—of which there was precious little in America. Those
on the bottom of the heap, especially the farmers, suffered the
most as one by one their farms were seized for unpaid debts. They
clamored for help, and in state after state the newly responsive
legislatures complied, enacting laws forstalling debt payments and
printing wagonloads of paper money for the relief of their people.
The value of the money, backed mostly by hope, plummeted
dramatically even as it came off the presses. Within a month or
two, a dollar might be worth thirty cents or ten cents or nothing
in some states. It was nevertheless offered in payment of debt,
and when creditors balked some states enacted laws making it a
crime to refuse paper money.

The sanctity of the contract was at stake. Breaching contracts,
in the view of "the better sort" at least, was every bit as vile as
religious oppression or taxation without representation. "My
countrymen, the devil is among you," thundered Noah Webster.

Make paper as much as you please; make it a tender in all future
contracts, or let it rest on its own bottom, but remember that past
contracts are sacred things; that legislatures have no right to inter-

fere with them; they have no right to say a debt shall be paid at a discount, or in any manner which the parties never intended. . . . My countrymen . . . : mankind detest you as they would a nest of robbers.

Of course those who were forced to use paper money or lose their land regarded their opponents as selfish aristocrats, antidemocratic, the old order struggling to preserve itself.

Soon, virtually every state was torn apart and divided into factions over the issue, with those opposing paper money increasingly on the losing side.

A strange reversal of traditional roles was the result. The men most offended by paper money were a privileged lot, many living grandly on plantations or in fine city houses in Philadelphia, Boston or New York, or in manors like Liberty Hall (the Livingstons), Morrisania (the Morrises), Fairhill (the Dickinsons) and Bohemia (the Bassetts)—the traditional ruling class. By 1787, they had come to see themselves as an oppressed minority—victims of democracy-run-wild. The people had gotten "far too much political knowledge. . . . They will not sit down contented in their proper line . . . till they possess the reins of Government, and have divided property with their betters . . . ," said Stephen Higginson, surveying the scene in New England.

The Revolution had gotten out of hand. Before the war for independence, some had warned of this. "When the pot boils, the scum will rise," James Otis had said.

"The mob begin to think and reason," Gouverneur Morris of Pennsylvania had written in 1774, wondering whether revolution was such a good idea after all. "Poor reptiles: It is with them a vernal morning, they are struggling to cast off their winter's slough, they bask in the sunshine, and ere noon they will bite, depend upon it."

The greatest shock of all was the rebellion of farmers that swept New England, also precipitated by debt. It began when the British tugged on their end of the chain, demanding payment from American debtors—wholesalers—and demanding it in hard money. These businessmen, in turn, called in their own debts from small merchants, who then demanded payment from the farmers. Many farmers took up arms rather than lose their property or go to prison —and thus was born Shays' Rebellion, named for one of its leaders, former Revolutionary War Captain Daniel Shays. They shut down the courts, beat lawyers and judges and merchants, and staged raids across the Northeast.

Congress, with no army and no money, was unable to stem the rebellion and looked on helplessly while a militia financed by businessmen finally put it down. The fear Shays instilled was profound: "The present," wrote Joel Barlow the poet,

> is justly considered an alarming crisis, perhaps the most alarming that America ever saw. We have contended with the the the most powerful nation and subdued the bravest and best appointed armies; but now we have to contend with ourselves, and encounter passions and prejudices more powerful than armies, and more dangerous to our peace. It is not for glory, it is for existence that we contend.

"The flames of internal insurrection were ready to burst out in every quarter," Pennsylvanian James Wilson said later, "and from one end to the other of the continent, we walked in ashes concealing fire beneath our feet."

The chaos in the land seemed to support the sneering claims in Europe that America would never make it on her own, that her people were incapable of ruling themselves. Ridicule from abroad was not simply offensive to American pride. It could have real consequences. "All respect for our government is annihilated on this side of the water, from an idea of its want of tone and energy," Jefferson wrote from France. "It is a dangerous opinion to us, and possibly will bring on insults which will force us into war."

The condescension from abroad went hand in hand with the "degeneracy" theories propounded by French philosophers like Abbé Raynal and Georges-Louis Leclerc, Compte de Buffon, which declared that the North American climate stunted both human and animal development. The idea was infuriating to Madison and Jefferson—who consumed many hours measuring and comparing American and European weasels, woodchucks and other four-legged creatures in an effort to disprove the theories.

Humiliation was as powerful an impetus toward reform as anything else, and probably more powerful than most.

Madison had come to Congress as a young man in 1781 bursting with enthusiasm about serving in that great and honored body. In a matter of months, he was appalled and disillusioned, and he resolved early on that when the time was right, if he could, he would drag America into the future.

In September 1786, the state of Virginia, largely at his urging, called on all the states to send delegates to a convention at Annapolis, Maryland, to consider a solution to the country's growing trade crisis. Only twelve delegates from five states showed up, however, and, unable to conduct business, the delegates, Madison and New Yorker Alexander Hamilton among them, issued a call for another convention to meet in Philadelphia on "the second Monday of May next." The stated purpose of the convention was vague: the delegates at Annapolis declared that they had been "induced to think, that the power of regulating trade is of such comprehensive extent, and will enter so far into the general system of the foederal government, that to give it efficacy, and to obviate questions and doubts concerning its precise nature and limits, may require a correspondent adjustment of other parts of the Foederal System."

But even at the time there were those who suspected that Madison and Hamilton had in mind something much grander than a "correspondent adjustment" as they rode together from Annapolis en route to New York. The Annapolis delegates "had no hope, nor even desire, to see the success" of their meeting, wrote Louis Otto, the French chargé d'affaires and a shrewd observer of American politics. The Annapolis Convention was intended only to pave the way for something "much more important than that of commerce."

The resolution from Annapolis went to Congress for its endorsement and sat there for months, eyed suspiciously, particularly by New Englanders, who wondered what the Virginians were up to. On February 21, 1787, reeling from the latest news of Shays' Rebellion, and mindful that seven states already had endorsed the meeting, the Congress finally granted its own carefully limited endorsement:

> RESOLVED, That in the opinion of Congress it is expedient that on the second Monday in May next a Convention of delegates who shall have been appointed by the several states be held at Philadelphia for the sole and express purpose of revising the Articles of Confederation and reporting to Congress and the several legislatures such alterations and provisions therein as shall when agreed to in Congress and confirmed by the states render the federal constitution adequate to the exigencies of Government & the preservation of the Union.

Madison was in the Congress when it debated and passed the resolution, and he recorded his impressions in his notes: "It appeared from the debates & still more from the conversation among the members that many of them considered this resolution as a deadly blow to the existing confederation."

CHAPTER THREE

The Delegates: A Kind of Brotherhood

Madison took soundings as the delegates arrived in Philadelphia, and he was pleased with what he heard. They might not yet agree on a solution, he found, but there was no doubt they shared his view of the severity of the problem. "In general," he wrote to his friend Edmund Pendleton, "the members seem to accord in viewing our situation as peculiarly critical and in being averse to temporising expedients."

Looking at the list of delegates, he had every reason to be satisfied, even to gloat over what was really his first major victory.

In Pennsylvania a powerful and tremendously popular party called "radicals" held considerable political sway, particularly among ordinary people. But this group was unrepresented in the state's delegation, which was dominated by their archenemies: Robert Morris, Gouverneur Morris, James Wilson—wealthy businessmen and lawyers.

Massachusetts too had a significant popular party, strongest in the western reaches of the state. But its delegation came entirely from Boston and the East, from the "codfish aristocracy."

The South Carolinians came exclusively from Charleston, representing the state's low-country planters, the famous South Carolina "oligarchy," but not the restless people of the outlying reaches. All of the delegates chosen by South Carolina were related to one another, by blood or marriage.

The same was true of virtually all the delegations. Absent were the names of many strong leaders identified with paper money or with the rights of the states, men whose views differed sharply from Madison's brand of nationalism; men like Patrick Henry of Virginia, Erastus Wolcott of Connecticut, Abraham Clark of New Jersey, Governor George Clinton of New York, Samuel Chase of Maryland, John Hancock of Massachusetts and Willie Jones of North Carolina. These men were formidable adversaries, skillful politicians, powerful orators, any one of whom was capable of affecting the course of events in Philadelphia.

No conspiracy in the selection process was evident, though perhaps if these men had known what Madison's plan of government contained they might have thought again about staying home. The lopsidedness was the result of self-selection: many of these men had had the chance to attend and turned it down.

In fact, the one state that might have really caused trouble boycotted the convention. Rhode Island. Rogue Island, its many enemies called it. Fools' Island. For most of the delegates, Rhode Island was the single best reason for having a convention in the first place. The state, in addition to craving paper money, was suspected of harboring fugitives from Shays' Rebellion. Right-thinking men from Rhode Island felt compelled to apologize for their state, as in this letter from James M. Varnum to Washington on the eve of the convention:

Permit me, Sir, to observe that the measures of our present legislature do not exhibit the real character of the state. They are equally reprobated, & abhor'd by Gentlemen of the learned professions, by the whole mercantile body, & by most of the respectable farmers and mechanicks. The majority of the administration [of the state] is composed of a licentious number of men, destitute of education, and many of them, void of principle. From anarchy and confusion they derive their temporary consequence, and this they endeavor to prolong by debauching the minds of the common people, whose attention is wholly directed to the abolition of debts both public & private. . . . Their paper money system, founded in oppression & fraud, they are determined to support at every hazard. . . .

All told, there were during the course of the convention fifty-five delegates in attendance—though never at one time.

From Massachusetts:

Elbridge Gerry, forty-three, merchant.

Nathaniel Gorham, forty-eight, businessman, president of the Congress.

Rufus King, thirty-two, lawyer, congressman.

Caleb Strong, forty-two, lawyer.

From New Hampshire:

Nicholas Gilman, thirty-one, congressman.

John Langdon, forty-five, businessman, former President of New Hampshire, congressman.

From Connecticut:

Oliver Ellsworth, forty-two, lawyer.

Roger Sherman, sixty-six, lawyer, mayor, congressman.

William Samuel Johnson, fifty-nine, lawyer, congressman.

From New York:

Alexander Hamilton, thirty or thirty-two, lawyer, former congressman.

John Lansing, Jr., thirty-three, lawyer, mayor of Albany.

Robert Yates, forty-nine, lawyer.

From New Jersey:

David Brearley, forty-one, chief justice, New Jersey Supreme Court.

Jonathan Dayton, twenty-six, lawyer, legislator.

William C. Houston, about forty-one, lawyer, former congressman.

William Livingston, sixty-three, lawyer, writer, governor of New Jersey.

William Paterson, forty-two, lawyer, former congressman.

From Pennsylvania:

George Clymer, forty-eight, merchant, legislator, former congressman.

Thomas Fitzsimons, forty-six, businessman, former congressman.

Benjamin Franklin, eighty-one, President of Pennsylvania, scientist, diplomat.

Robert Morris, fifty-three, businessman, former legislator, congressman and superintendent of finance of the Confederation.

Gouverneur Morris, thirty-five, lawyer, former congressman.

James Wilson, forty-four, lawyer, congressman.

Jared Ingersoll, thirty-seven, lawyer, former congressman.

Thomas Mifflin, forty-three, businessman, speaker of the Pennsylvania legislature.

From Delaware:

Richard Bassett, forty-two, lawyer.

Gunning Bedford, Jr., forty, attorney general of Delaware.

Jacob Broom, thirty-five, businessman.

John Dickinson, fifty-four, lawyer, former congressman, former President of Pennsylvania and Delaware.

George Read, fifty-three, lawyer.

From Maryland:

Daniel Carroll, fifty-seven, merchant, president of the Maryland Senate.

Daniel of St. Thomas Jenifer, sixty-four, planter, former president of the Maryland Senate and former congressman.

Luther Martin, about thirty-nine, lawyer, attorney general of Maryland.

James McHenry, thirty-four, physician, former congressman.

John F. Mercer, twenty-eight, congressman.

From Virginia:

John Blair, fifty-five, lawyer and judge.

James McClurg, physician.

James Madison, thirty-six, congressman.

George Mason, about sixty-two, planter.

Edmund J. Randolph, thirty-three, lawyer, Governor of Virginia.

George Washington, fifty-five, farmer.

George Wythe, about sixty-one, lawyer, judge.

From North Carolina:

William Blount, thirty-eight, businessman, congressman.

William R. Davie, about thirty-one, lawyer.

Alexander Martin, about forty-seven, lawyer.

Richard D. Spaight, twenty-nine, Speaker of the North Carolina Assembly.

Hugh Williamson, fifty-two, scholar, lawyer, congressman.

From South Carolina:

Pierce Butler, forty-three, planter.

Charles Pinckney, twenty-nine, lawyer, congressman.

Charles Cotesworth Pinckney, forty-one, lawyer.

John Rutledge, forty-seven, lawyer, judge.

From Georgia:

Abraham Baldwin, thirty-two, lawyer, congressman.

William Few, thirty-eight, congressman.

William Houstoun, about thirty-two, lawyer.

William L. Pierce, about forty-seven, businessman, congressman.

The titles and occupations said little about them. There were fifty-five names, but there were a hundred or two hundred answers to the questions "What do you do?" and "Where do you come from?" Roger Sherman of Connecticut, for example, was a merchant, an almanac writer, a judge, a mayor, a surveyor and, once upon a time, a shoemaker. William Churchill Houston was a lawyer, a professor of mathematics and a member of the Continental Congress. Hugh Williamson of North Carolina had been variously a Presbyterian minister, a professor of mathematics and a physician. Charles Cotesworth Pinckney of South Carolina, in addition to being a lawyer and a general in the Continental Army, was an accomplished botanist.

As a group, they were extremely well educated, far more so than the population as a whole, and in those days educated meant educated: admission to the best American colleges required young men at the age of fourteen or fifteen to translate works of Greek and Latin. The schools most heavily represented were Princeton (eight including Madison), Yale (four), William and Mary (four), Harvard (three) and Columbia (two).

They were the sons of cobblers, the sons of lords, the sons of clothiers, planters, blacksmiths and barristers; the children of patriots, loyalists and royalists. Almost all were wealthy or at least comfortable, and those who hadn't started out that way had become so, for all of them were constantly looking to improve their lot. Whether they chose land speculation, trade, manufacture or law, they subscribed to the tenet that in improving themselves they would also improve the country. Ambition was patriotic.

They were speculators in public securities, in "certificates" of one kind or the other, in money itself, and, above all, in land. Millions of acres in the West could be traced back into this room, to Franklin, William Blount, Jonathan Dayton, Wilson, Mason and the others. Sometimes the lines between improving themselves and improving their country blurred, but it was not something one apologized for.

Some politicians, such as William Blount, a delegate from North Carolina, had carried this notion to an extreme: As a member of the North Carolina assembly, Blount consumed most of his energy unabashedly pushing legislation to line his own pockets with profits from land in the western part of the state.

But many, especially Hamilton, believed that avarice was extremely useful, even a key to national strength. One of the great weaknesses of the existing Confederation, in Hamilton's view, was that influential Americans had little to gain from it and thus withheld their affection. The greater the benefits a government could deliver—whether through a national bank or through payments to holders of public securities or through protection of private property—the greater the loyalty that government would inspire.

They had come to Philadelphia to frame a constitution. For this task they were unquestionably qualified. Thirty of them had done this sort of thing at least once before, as participants in conventions called to draft state constitutions, and all but a few had served in state legislatures. They had no need for aides to tell them what to say and think. There would be no need for a staff.

Service in Congress was *the* unifying experience. At least forty-one of the fifty-five had served some time in the Congress, and many had devoted years to it. This was the place where they first encountered men from different states and different regions; this was the place where men became continentalists. This was the place that brought together characters as different as the pious New Englander Sherman and the high-living and exceedingly impious Gouverneur Morris; the self-confident and brash Hamilton and the shy and scholarly Madison. Over the years, though they disagreed on many points, the men devoted to the Congress had become a kind of brotherhood.

Many had been there in '76, for the break with England, and for the tension before the Declaration while Jefferson, Franklin, Sherman and the others went behind closed doors to draft it. Many had left Congress to fight the war. Others had stayed to help manage it, for there was no vast bureaucracy to do it for them. They personally gave Washington his orders; they personally had to figure out how to find the tents, the blankets, the powder and the troops. Nor was there such a thing as a safe distance: they fled for their lives during the battle for Philadelphia in '77 as the British captured the city.

Never would any of them forget the day the courier arrived

with news of the surrender at Yorktown. The doorkeeper of Congress, an aged man, died suddenly, Dr. Benjamin Rush later reported, "immediately after hearing of the capture of Lord Cornwallis's army. His death was universally ascribed to a violent emotion of political joy . . ."

They wept in '83, the last time some of them had seen Washington, when with his hands trembling and his voice faltering he retired as commander in chief. "Having now finished the work assigned me," he said, "I retire from the great theater of action, and bidding an affectionate farewell to this august body, under whose orders I have so long acted, I here offer my commission and take my leave of all the employments of public life."

Victory deprived Congress of its mission and its will. A lot of men lost interest, leaving the rest an even more select fraternity —a fraternity of frustration. The appointment to Congress carried no particular prestige and certainly no particular remuneration. Yet it required leaving behind comfortable homes, expectant wives, children, law practices and businesses for journeys lasting a few days to weeks, by choppy sea or rutted road, with the relief at the end being only a small boardinghouse room.

Congress could spend weeks, months, doing nothing, and when finally it did something the accomplishment could be dashed by a single recalcitrant state exercising its veto power.

Some lost faith and dropped out. Others, like Madison, became nationalists.

The three in addition to Madison who emerged from the experience most prominently as nationalists were Gouverneur Morris and James Wilson of Pennsylvania and Hamilton of New York.

Gouverneur Morris had as great a capacity for doing good, and for doing wrong, as any man in America, and it was often challenging to determine which of the two he was doing at any particular time, since he was sometimes doing both at once. Morris, for example, had helped stir up a near-rebellion among army officers seeking back pay and pensions in March 1783, just a few months before the rank-and-file troops had laid siege to the State House.

It had been Morris' way of pressuring Congress to do something about its fiscal mess, but only the personal intervention of Washington had headed off a dangerous upheaval or even a coup. Despite a wooden leg, Morris was a dashing figure, over six feet tall, blue eyes, prominent nose—and known for being "daily employed in making oblations to Venus," as his friend John Jay once described Morris' legendary lustfulness. When Morris lost his leg following a carriage accident in 1780, rumors circulated that he had actually suffered the injury jumping from the window of a married woman's bedroom to escape her husband. After the accident, Jay quipped that he was "almost tempted to wish he [Morris] had lost something else."

Morris had a unique outlook on life. While others of his generation declaimed constantly against high living, he celebrated it openly. "With respect to our taste for luxury, do not grieve about it," Morris wrote. "Luxury is not so bad a thing as it is often supposed to be, and if it were so, still we must follow the course of things, and turn to advantage what exists . . ."

Morris, of course, could afford to talk this way. He was born rich, in one of New York's great manors—Morrisania. He moved to Philadelphia to practice law and go into business because that was where the action was.

Hamilton exceeded Morris, and probably everyone else in the convention, in personal ambition, having promised himself even as a teenager to devote his life to elevating his station. And how well and how quickly he had succeeded. Born out of wedlock in the West Indies, he had, with the help of a few patrons and marriage into a prominent New York family, made his way from counting-house clerk to aide-de-camp to Washington to lawyer to New York political power before his thirtieth birthday. His great flaw was the shortness of his attention span. His great wish was that life were longer. "Let us both erect a temple to time," he had once written to Gouverneur Morris, "only regretting that we shall not command a longer portion of it to see what will be the event of the American drama."

Wilson was part politician, part theorist and part wild-eyed capitalist—a combination not uncommon in the convention. As a politician he was one of the leaders of the conservative party in Pennsylvania engaged in perpetual warfare with the radicals. Wilson's home in Philadelphia had taken on the name "Fort Wilson" when a bloodthirsty mob laid siege to it in 1779, precipitating a gun-blazing battle that cost four lives. As a theorist, Wilson was probably the only man in the convention who had thought as deeply about government as had Madison.

And as a capitalist, he was already badly overextended in land speculation and other ventures, usually in concert with his close friend and political ally, Robert Morris, said to be among the richest men in America. Robert Morris was so rich that his personal notes—"Morrisnotes"—served as currency on the streets of Philadelphia. He was so skillful with money that Congress had made him, for a time, the financier of the government—its secretary of the treasury, such as it was. Morris' financial empire was shaky when the convention opened, and he was preoccupied with it.

Many of the delegates had shared powerful and indelible experiences. But each man brought with him his own political calculus. Every proposal, every clause, every semicolon and comma, would be scrutinized for its impact on region, on state, on class, and this would determine the outcome of the convention. For these men were politicians, and the convention, whatever else it was to be, was, above all, about politics.

The calculation began in earnest even before the first item of business was brought to the floor. Gouverneur Morris and Robert Morris (they were not related) approached the Virginians to convince them to cut the small states down to size in the convention by having votes cast according to the size of each state, rather than giving all states equal votes. Madison stifled the idea. He wanted to soften up the small states, not enrage them.

Meanwhile, some of the small-state delegates in town had caught a glimpse of one of the proposals for a new government. It wasn't Madison's, but it might as well have been, for, like Madison's plan, it proposed a Congress based not on equality of the states but on the size of the states. The principle by which each state had one vote in the government would be replaced by proportional representation, allowing the large states to dominate.

Upon reading it, George Read of Delaware immediately wrote to Dickinson, who had not yet arrived:

> I am in possession of a copied draft of a federal system intended to be proposed. . . . By this plan our state may have a representation . . . of one member in eighty. . . . I suspect it to be of importance to the small states that their deputies should keep a strict watch upon the movements and propositions from the larger states, who will probably combine to swallow up the smaller ones by addition, division or impoverishment. . . . If you have any wish to assist in guarding such attempts, you will be speedy in your attendance.

Read had known instinctively that this was coming and had already taken defensive measures, making sure that the official instructions of the Delaware delegates included a provision requiring them to walk out of the convention if it aimed to wipe out state equality.

On opening day, as the instructions of each state from its legislature were read, Delaware's stood out ominously.

CHAPTER FOUR

The Plan: "One Supreme Power"

The setting was intimate. The room where they would be confined five, six or seven hours a day for nobody knew how long was small, some forty feet square, no bigger than a large schoolroom or a church. The delegates sat close enough to reach out and touch one another, or to lean over and whisper a wise comment or a dry observation. One need not bellow to be heard here; a civilized, conversational tone would do.

At the outset, the delegates made a pact that made the convention even more intimate. Before getting down to business, they decided to let no outsider observe the convention, to tell no one what had passed until it was done, and to never repeat to anyone the words spoken.

They wanted to be free to speak their minds—and to change their minds—without fear of political retribution. Those who had served in Congress had been besieged there with "instructions" from their state legislatures, telling them what to do, how to vote, at every turn. The secrecy would insulate the convention from outside interference.

Early on, Washington put everyone on notice that the oath of secrecy was to be taken seriously. One morning a delegate carelessly dropped a convention document in the State House. Another delegate picked it up and gave it to Washington, who placed it in his pocket, saying nothing. At the end of the day, he rose from his chair and spoke to the convention in his sternest manner. William Pierce of Georgia later reported Washington's words:

"Gentlemen. I am sorry to find that some one member of this body has been so neglectful of the secrets of the convention as to drop in the State House a copy of their proceedings, which by accident was picked up and delivered to me this morning. I must entreat the gentlemen to be more careful, [lest] our transactions get into the newspapers and disturb the public repose by premature speculations. I know not whose paper it is, but there it is. Let him who owns it take it."

Putting the paper on the table, Washington bowed, picked up his hat, and "quitted the room with a dignity so severe that every person seemed alarmed."

According to Pierce, no one ever claimed the paper as his own.

The flow of meaningful information from Philadelphia ceased. Fathers would not tell their sons or wives what was happening; the newspapers satisfied themselves with rumor; Madison cut off the flow of information to Jefferson, sending him a list of delegates but nothing more.

In furnishing you with this list of names [Madison wrote], I have exhausted all the means which I can make use of for gratifying your curiosity. It was thought expedient in order to secure unbiassed discussion within doors, and to prevent misconceptions & misconstructions without, to establish some rules of caution which will for no short time restrain even a confidential communication of our proceedings. The names of the members will satisfy you that the States have been serious in this business. The attendance of Genl. Washington is a proof of the light in which he regards it. The whole community is big with expectation. And there can be no doubt that the result will in some way or other have a powerful effect on our destiny.

Now, sealed in, they could begin.

On May 29, Randolph of Virginia took out a copy of a plan of government completed by the Virginia delegation. It was Madison's idea to have Randolph do the talking. Randolph, unlike Madison, was a fine orator and it was only right that the plan of Virginia be presented by the Governor of Virginia. As Madison had used Washington to polish the image of the convention, so he had chosen Randolph to present the plan in its best light. Madison was tainted as an extreme nationalist. Randolph was known as a moderate.

Madison had encountered some difficulty from Randolph on this score. Randolph's idea for the convention was to preserve the existing system with a few amendments "grafted on" to make it stronger. Ever so delicately, Madison had nudged him. "I think with you that it will be well to retain as much as possible of the old Confederation," Madison responded. But "I doubt whether it may not be best to work the valuable articles into the new System, instead of engrafting the latter on the former." Randolph was malleable as always and agreed to present the plan, though it was understood among all the Virginians that none of them were bound to support it.

The preparations for the convention had been healthy and distracting for Randolph. For months he had been in a deep depression caused by the deaths of his infant and of his aunt, who had been a mother to him. He had ignored his law practice as well as his official duties, leaving his mail "unanswered and probably unread." The convention flurry had revived him.

Randolph rose to speak.

What were the purposes of a great government? he asked. To secure the country from foreign invasion. To check quarrels among the states. To prevent rebellions within the states. To raise revenue. To make the nation competitive commercially. Our present government, he said, as if it needed saying, does none of those things.

Those who had framed the existing Confederation (many were

sitting in the room listening) were to be congratulated. They had
done what they could, a noble effort. Perhaps nothing better had
been possible then, for the "science of government" had been in
its infancy.

But now the crisis had arrived. Now we must prevent "the
fulfillment of the prophecies of the American downfall."

Then Randolph unveiled the Virginia Plan.

It was sparse on details, with the many blanks to be filled in by
the convention.

● It called for a two-house "national legislature" to replace the
old one-house Confederation Congress. The first, or lower,
branch would be elected directly by the people. The second, the
upper house, would be chosen by the lower house, from lists of
candidates submitted by the state legislatures.

● Seats in both houses would be allocated according to the *size*
of each state, so that the larger a state was in population (or
wealth), the more votes it would enjoy in the new national legislature.

● The new legislature would have the broad authority to "leg-
islate in all cases to which the separate states are incompetent, or
in which the harmony of the United States may be interrupted by
the exercise of individual legislation." It could strike down "all
laws" passed by any state legislature if it believed that those laws
violated the Constitution, and it could "call forth the force of the
union against any member of the union failing to fulfill" its obligations and duties.

● A national executive, a totally new office, would be created,
with "general authority to execute the national laws." The national executive (the plan did not specify whether there would be
one, two or three people occupying the position) would be chosen
by the national legislature and would be ineligible for a second
term.

● A national judiciary, consisting of "one or more supreme
tribunals" and "inferior tribunals," would also be chosen by the

national legislature. The judges would have life terms and jurisdiction to rule on cases involving foreigners, crimes on the high seas, captures from an enemy, "the collection of the national revenue," "impeachments of any national officers," and issues vaguely described as "questions which may involve the national peace and harmony."

● The national executive and a "convenient number of the national judiciary" would join together in a "Council of Revision," similar to those in several state constitutions, which could veto acts of the national legislature. The national legislature could override the veto.

● State legislators, state governors and state judges would be "bound by oath" to support the new constitution.

● The whole plan, the new articles of union, would take effect after approval by the Congress and ratification by special assemblies "to be expressly chosen by the people."

The plan was embodied in fifteen resolutions, the first of which blithely contradicted all those that followed it. "Resolved," it said, "that the Articles of Confederation ought to be so corrected and enlarged as to accomplish the objects proposed by their institution; namely, 'common defence, security of liberty, and general welfare.' " The Virginia Plan was much more than any "enlargement" or "correction" of the Articles. It was a new form of government entirely. (The first resolution was probably a concession to Randolph, the one part he could call his own.)

True, the three-branch structure of the proposed government was familiar, modeled after the state governments: there would be a legislative branch consisting of two houses, which would appoint both the executive and the judiciary.

But the powers of the Virginia Plan's government were new, radically new. In the existing system, the states chose and controlled the delegates to Congress. In the Virginia Plan, the states were stripped of both prerogatives. The people, not the state legislatures, would choose the members of the lower house; the lower house would choose the members of the upper house from lists submitted by each state—a token nod to the states.

In the existing government, each state had an equal vote in the Congress. In Madison's scheme, the notion that the states were equal and that Congress represented states instead of people vanished: representation would be proportional in both houses.

Madison's new Congress would have real authority. It would be able to veto any act of any state legislature that contravened the Constitution; acts by the states disrupting treaties, or trade, or oppressive laws violating property rights or religious freedoms, could simply be stamped out. The Congress would be able to pass laws binding on the people and enforce those laws by force.

Suddenly a government with no power was to become all-powerful. Suddenly a government utterly dominated by the states was to dominate them. Suddenly the states, which made and unmade delegates to the existing Congress, would be denied any real say over them.

America would undergo a change of identity.

Perhaps some of the delegates had seen the plan before, but for most it was a revelation, for Madison had carefully kept it secret until this moment. Thus one can imagine them sitting rapt as they listened, contemplating its audacity. This was indeed a radical cure.

The Virginia Plan would mean nothing less than a second American revolution. And as the delegates began to understand this in the days that followed, they began to react.

Do you mean "to abolish the state governments altogether?" said Charles Pinckney.

Are we even authorized to talk about such a change? said his elder cousin, Charles Cotesworth Pinckney. Would it be legal?

It doesn't square, said Gouverneur Morris, pointing out to Randolph that in light of the rest of the plan, the first of his resolutions made no sense.

Morris, who disliked euphemism, knew exactly what the plan

meant and said so. With this plan, he said, America would no longer have federal government but a *"national, supreme,* Government" (his emphasis). A federal government was "a mere compact resting on the good faith of the parties," Morris said. The power of a supreme national government was "complete and compulsive. . . . In all communities there must be one supreme power, and one only." That one, in the Virginia Plan, was national.

In the face of Morris' challenge, Randolph crumbled, withdrawing the first resolution without argument. He must have been prepared for this, for he immediately took out three resolutions to replace it.

The first declared the Articles of Confederation to be a failure: "That a Union of the States merely federal will not accomplish the objects proposed by the articles of confederation, namely, common defence, security of liberty, & general welfare."

The second explained why the current system had failed: "That no treaty or treaties among the whole or part of the States, as individual sovereignties, would be sufficient." A treaty among states was, indeed, what the Articles of Confederation were.

The third was the remedy, and it went to the heart of the Virginia Plan:

"That a national Government ought to be established consisting of a supreme Legislative, Executive & Judiciary."

A total change of identity was indeed just what Madison had in mind, for the Virginia Plan was much more than a scheme of government: it was meant by Madison to create a new political culture. The cause of the country's problems, of course, was the state governments. But the force that had led them astray was factionalism, the proliferation of self-interested political interest groups which ganged up to form majorities and imposed their will —the tyranny of the majority—on others.

The existence of competing factions—poor against rich, debtor against creditor, religion against religion, merchant against manufacturer—was an inevitable result of human nature. In a land that cherished liberty, there was nothing that should or could be done to suppress them. But there might be a way to make it difficult or impossible for one or the other of these factions to impose its will, and Madison was convinced he had found the way.

The states were small political spheres, where proximity, ease of communication and lack of diversity made it easy for a faction or a coalition of factions to band together and rule. But if the sphere were enlarged, dramatically enlarged, there would be so many competing groups that they would all be reduced in power, with no one of them capable of dominating. In this vast new political arena, factions would neutralize one another as they sought influence over the government and be forced to compromise. By pitting interest against interest, the government would be rendered safe for all.

James Madison's Virginia Plan would remove the states as centers of power and contention, and create a newer, larger theater: the "extended republic."

His theory defied the current wisdom, the notion that republicanism could flourish only in small, manageable states, close to the people. To be free, according to this idea, a republic must be small.

James Madison's republic had to be large to be free.

Madison explained his theory best in the Federalist Papers after the convention:

> The smaller the society, the fewer probably will be the distinct parties and interests composing it; the fewer the distinct parties and interests, the more frequently will a majority be found of the same party; and the smaller the number of individuals composing a majority, and the smaller the compass within which they are placed, the more easily will they concert and execute their plans of oppression. Extend the sphere, and you take in a greater variety of parties and interests; you make it less probable that a majority of the whole will have a common motive to invade the rights of other citizens; or if such a common motive exists, it will be more

difficult for all who feel it to discover their own strength, and to act in unison with each other. . . .

The influence of factious leaders may kindle a flame within their particular States, but will be unable to spread a general conflagration through the other States; a religious sect, may degenerate into a political faction in a part of the Confederacy; but the variety of sects dispersed over the entire face of it, must secure the national Councils against any danger from that source; a rage for paper money, for an abolition of debts, for an equal division of property, or for any other improper or wicked project, will be less apt to pervade the whole body of the Union, than a particular member of it; in the same proportion as such a malady is more likely to taint a particular county or district, than an entire State;

In the extent and proper structure of the Union, therefore, we behold a Republican remedy for the diseases most incident to Republican Government.

The transfer of power to a national arena had a double purpose. Not only would it secure Americans from invasions of their rights, it would permit the nation to speak and act as a nation—with one voice instead of thirteen. Nothing less was required for America to assume its rightful place on the world's stage and to fulfill its mighty destiny. The certainty that they were acting for generations yet unborn was among the great inspirations for the convention, as it had been for the Revolution itself. America's eighteenth-century political leadership was convinced to a moral certainty of America's future expansion and power and the important role it would play as a seafaring nation in world commerce and world politics. They even had a good guess as to how large the country would grow, thanks to Franklin's calculation in 1751, when 1.3 million people inhabited the colonies, that the population would at least double every twenty years.

Britain had stood in the way and brought on a revolution. Now Americans were standing in their own way; they had no one to blame but themselves. And to themselves they would now look.

Madison's scheme reflected two sometimes contradictory assumptions about human nature. On the one hand, the idea that individuals and combinations of individuals always dedicated themselves to the pursuit of narrow self-interest was a dark and depressing vision. On the other hand, the belief that this tendency could be controlled, if not stamped out, reflected the strong Enlightenment faith that a disciplined, rational analysis of a situation—however desperate it might seem—could yield a cure.

It was no accident that he and other thinkers of his generation spoke of "diseases" of the body politic and of "radical cures" and "remedies," and that his plan was preceded by a painstaking diagnosis of symptoms. A "science of government," as Randolph said, did indeed exist; it needed only to be properly understood and properly applied.

The fact that Madison's remedy was a republican remedy was crucial, for never before in history had such a large nation placed its future in the hands of a government based on popular consent. Many thought it impossible.

CHAPTER FIVE

Prelude to Conflict

The first few days of debate on the Virginia Plan went well. In hindsight, they went too well, and Madison should have known that something was wrong.

The convention glided over the resolutions with amazing speed: the monumental resolution calling for a supreme national government breezed through; the staggering provision allowing the new Congress to veto state laws passed without dissent. The most explosive proposal of them all, the proposition calling for an end to equality of the states in the Congress, drew only one objection, from Delaware, which forced its postponement by threatening to "retire" from the convention if it passed.

There was debate and disagreement, but much of it was unfocused, disengaged, laconic, and some of it literally had to be pried loose.

One day, for example, they took up the question of establishing a national executive. Profound as the subject was, no one seemed to have anything to say about it.

Come, now, gentlemen, said Franklin. This is a "point of great importance." Should not the gentlemen "deliver their sentiments on it" before taking a vote? Why the "shyness"? asked South Carolina's John Rutledge.

The convention went on like this for more than a week. If Delegate Pierce Butler of South Carolina was any indication, some of the members were having trouble with their attention spans. Butler, trying manfully to take notes, lapsed into doodling one afternoon. He wrote the letter "R" as if to begin a word. Then he gave the letter a nose and a mouth; then he drew it again, this time with hair and eyes and an ear; and again, this time with nose, mouth, hair, eyes and ear and long hair. Then, apparently roused by something he had heard, he started again on a word, "Elector," only to go through the same routine with the letter "E" until it too took on the appearance of a person.

To be sure, everything the convention did at this stage was tentative. Before it began taking up the Virginia Plan, the convention had decided that, to encourage freewheeling debate, it would proceed at the outset as an informal "committee of the whole" that would take nonbinding votes and submit a report to the full convention, which would then reconsider everything and flesh out the final details. The approach would provide a "sense of the convention" on every aspect of the new government before forcing delegates to make final decisions. The convention had chosen the Massachusetts merchant Nathaniel Gorham to chair this portion of its proceedings. Gorham was an experienced parliamentarian, having served as speaker of the Massachusetts House of Representatives and, at the time of the convention, president of the Confederation Congress. The convention didn't know it, but he had quietly written to Prince Henry of Prussia suggesting that he become king of the United States. Had the delegates been aware of how much Gorham pined secretly for a monarchy, he would likely not have been the choice. In any case, he replaced Washington at the speaker's platform.

Tentative or not, could it be that they were so casually undoing a century of tradition? Could it be that the small states had suddenly seen the light and were so graciously letting go their equality in the Union?

It couldn't be. Nevertheless Madison came away brimming with confidence, certain that his plan to substitute proportional representation for one state, one vote would easily pass. Even Franklin, who had been around long enough to know better, wanted to be taken in. The delegates, he told a friend, "will soon finish their business, as there are no prejudices to oppose, nor errors to refute in any of the body."

The convention was not confronting reality, at least not openly, for the delegates must have known what was coming, and that they could not construct a government without first determining the distribution of power in it. Debating the powers of the Congress without understanding how the votes in it would be counted was an exercise in abstraction. How could they seriously agree on a manner of electing a President in a political vacuum? This was not a scholarly seminar in the philosophy of government; this was a gathering of politicians, and without real numbers they could not perform their calculus. While everything they were saying and doing in the convention might be relevant later, for now it was premature. The issue of representation, as Gouverneur Morris pointed out along the way, was "fundamental."

And even as they spoke, a sheet of paper was circulating among the delegates from the small states with the numbers on it, and though it only confirmed the obvious, the tabulation made the obvious more vivid. At the top of the paper were the names of ten states. Beside each name was a number—a projection of the number of representatives each would have in a new Congress based on proportional representation.

Georgia—1.
Delaware—1.
Rhode Island—2.
New Hampshire—3.
New Jersey—5.

South Carolina—6.
North Carolina—6.
New York—8.
Connecticut—8.
Maryland—6.

At the bottom were the names of the other three states—
Massachusetts, Pennsylvania and Virginia. Beside each of those,
as well, was a number, also representing the state's potential
strength in the new government:

Massachusetts—14.
Pennsylvania—12.
Virginia—16.

The implication was clear to everyone. Under the Virginia
Plan, Massachusetts, Pennsylvania and, of course, Virginia would
have the controlling interest in the new Congress. Voting together, these three states, with one or two allies, could tax as they
pleased, regulate trade to their liking, dispose of the Western
lands as it suited them and veto any state laws that got in the
way. Under the Virginia Plan, they could also control the choice
of the President and of the judges.

In the existing Confederation, Delaware and Georgia each had
one vote of thirteen in the Congress. In the new Congress these
states would each command one vote of eighty-eight. The same
math produced a similar contraction of power for all the small
states and a similar expansion for the big three—the behemoths
of the new republic. In one respect, these small states like Delaware, Connecticut and New Jersey were potentially the most na-
tionalistic in the room, for they stood to benefit greatly from a
union which would hold exclusive authority to tax commerce and
would sell off those Western lands for the benefit of all Americans
rather than of the states that claimed ownership over them. On
the other hand, if they entered such a union on the wrong terms
things might actually get worse for them.

The small states had always said they would be "swallowed up" if they lost their equality. The phrase evoked much more than a loss of power in the union: it reflected a deep concern for their sovereignty and their identities and their rights and liberties.

Equality of the states was the heart of federalism.

Madison was equally intense on the subject. Of all the characteristics of the old order, none so interfered with his vision of nationhood as the principle of one state, one vote.

It was impure: As he saw it, this was to be a government constituted by the people, not by states, and the people rather than states should be represented.

It was unjust: Why should the power of 700,000, the population of Virginia, equal the strength of 59,000, the population of Delaware?

And it was impolitic: Instituted in the Continental Congress at a time of crisis, when no one wanted a fight, it had burdened the government and obstructed progress ever since, a monument to the tyranny of the states. The large states would never go along with the establishment of a national government with enhanced power if it was to be operated under this oppressive principle. Proportional representation was not only right; it was the price to be paid to get the new constitution accepted.

The proposition for proportional representation was, indeed, the heart of the Virginia Plan.

Madison, who had done some pre-convention vote-counting, believed he had the votes. Massachusetts, Virginia and Pennsylvania, the most populous states, would, of course, favor it. The Carolinas and Georgia, filling up with settlers, expected vast population increases in the near future. They too could expect to benefit by proportional representation. They too would be "gainers," as he had put it. "If a majority of the larger states concur, the fewer and smaller states must finally bend to them."

The small states had no intention of bending.

In truth, the delegates knew they were in for a long and bitter confrontation. On June 6, Edmund Randolph wrote: ". . . the prospect of a very long sojournment here has determined me to bring up my family."

Brearley of New Jersey wrote to his fellow New Jersey Delegate Jonathan Dayton, still not arrived, to get down to Philadelphia at once. "We have been in a Committee of the Whole for some time, and have under consideration a number of very important propositions, none of which, however, have as yet been reported. My colleagues, as well as myself, are very desirous that you should join us immediately. The importance of the business really demands it."

The North Carolina delegates wrote home to their Governor for more money. "By the date of this you will observe we are near the middle of June and though we sit from day to day, Saturdays included, it is not possible for us to determine when the business before us can be finished, a very large Field presents to our view without a single Straight or eligible Road that has been trodden by the feet of Nations. . . . Several Members of the Convention have their Wives here and other Gentlemen have sent for theirs. This Seems to promise a Summer's Campaign."

By June 9, the small-state men had had enough. Whatever else the convention might do, whatever the outcome of all these other matters, they were not about to go back to their states with a constitution that stripped them of power. There was no point in going any further. It was time to get serious, to let the others know that the future of the convention depended on the resolution of this issue.

William Paterson of New Jersey moved that the convention return to the subject of suffrage in the national legislature.

On cue, David Brearley of New Jersey seconded Paterson and then rose to speak.

He was "sorry that any question on this point was brought into view. It had been much agitated in Congress at the time of forming the Confederation and was then rightly settled by allowing to each sovereign state an equal vote. Otherwise the smaller states must have been destroyed instead of being saved."

The substitution of proportional representation, he said, might appear fair on its face, but on a deeper examination it was "unfair and unjust. . . . Virginia would have sixteen votes, and Georgia but one. . . . There will be three large states and ten small ones. . . . Massachusetts, Pennsylvania and Virginia will carry everything before them. . . . Virginia with her sixteen votes will be a solid column indeed, a formidable phalanx. While Georgia with her solitary vote, and the other little states will be obliged to throw themselves constantly into the scale of some large one, in order to have any weight at all."

Brearley, a judge and not much of an orator, was unaccustomed to the role of combatant, but the longer he spoke the more he was convinced of the injustice of the plan and the more incensed he grew. He had come there to be useful, he declared. But "when the proposition for destroying the equality of votes came forward, I was astonished, I was alarmed. . . ."

Paterson, a squat man with a bulbous nose, a receding chin and traces of his native Ireland in his voice, now rose to speak. He had listened closely to the words of Madison and the other large-state delegates; he had considered the Virginia Plan at length, putting his own thoughts on paper days ago in preparation for this moment. There was anger in his words, but it was premeditated anger and controlled, as he always was.

The proposition for proportional representation, he declared, struck "at the existence of the lesser states. . . . Give the large states an influence in proportion to their magnitude, and what will be the consequence? Their ambition will be proportionally increased and the small States will have everything to fear."

What's more, the whole subject of a national government was off limits. It was not authorized by the congressional resolution or by the states. "The idea of a national government as contradistinguished from a federal one never entered into the mind of any of them, and to the public mind we must accommodate ourselves. We have no power to go beyond the federal scheme, and if we had, the people are not ripe for any other. We must follow the people; the people will not follow us."

As to the large states, "Let them unite if they please, but let them remember that they have no authority to compel the others to unite. New Jersey will never confederate on the plan before the committee. She would be swallowed up. I would rather submit to a monarch, to a despot, than to such a fate. I will not only oppose the plan here but on my return home do everything in my power to defeat it there."

The message was loud and clear and uncomplicated and drew from Wilson of Pennsylvania an uncomplicated response.

So be it, he said to Paterson. "If the small states will not confederate on this plan, Pennsylvania and," he presumed, "some other states will not confederate on any other. . . . If New Jersey will not part with her sovereignty it is in vain to talk of government."

The convention recessed for the weekend.

The rising temperature of the words coincided with a change in the weather in Philadelphia. At the start of the week, it had been cold enough to make Philadelphians long for the warmth of fires in their homes. By the end of it, by Saturday, a heat wave had begun.

CHAPTER SIX

The Alternative

It was easy to underrate Roger Sherman of Connecticut, and exceedingly foolish to do so.

He came off as a bumpkin, a caricature of the pious and unsophisticated New Englander. His eccentricities, his large body and even larger head, his awkwardness, were a source of great amusement to those who had served with him in the Congress. Sherman was "the reverse of grace," John Adams had said of him. "There cannot be a more striking contrast to beautiful action than the motions of his hands; generally [when he speaks] he stands upright, with his hands before him, the fingers of his left hand clenched into a fist, and the wrist of it grasped with his right. . . . It is stiffness and awkwardness itself, rigid as starched linen or buckram; awkward as a junior bachelor or a sophomore."

William Pierce of Georgia, self-appointed critic of convention manners, who was recording his judgments in little character sketches, said this of Sherman: "Mr. Sherman exhibits the oddest shaped character I ever remember to have met with. He is awkward, un-meaning, and unaccountably strange in his manner. But in his train of thinking there is something regular, deep and comprehensive; yet the oddity of his address, the vulgarisms that accompany his public speaking, and that strange New England cant which runs through his public as well as his private speaking make everything that is connected with him grotesque and laughable. . . ."

Sherman was, to be sure, an unpretentious man.

But "laughable" he was not. Born of humble stock, he had worked his way up on his own from shoemaker to lawyer to one of Connecticut's most eminent political leaders. Connecticut had sent him to the Continental Congress, where he participated in drafting the Declaration of Independence, and to the Confederation Congress, where he helped draft the Articles of Confederation.

In Connecticut they knew better than to underestimate Sherman. "If you attack him you ought to know him well," Jeremiah Wadsworth of Connecticut wrote by way of warning to a friend in the Massachusetts delegation. "He is not easily managed. . . . If he suspects you are trying to take him in, you may as well catch an eel by the tail."

Sherman was a last-minute substitute in the Connecticut delegation, taking the place of Erastus Wolcott. Sherman, Oliver Ellsworth, a square-jawed Princeton-educated lawyer, and William Samuel Johnson, a worldly scholar and lawyer steeped in theology and philosophy, made up the Connecticut delegation. As a delegation, they had a narrow but refreshingly pragmatic quality about them. While Madison, Wilson and Hamilton brought radical solutions to Philadelphia, the men from "the Land of Steady Habits" saw the convention as a means of solving particular problems: the problems of trade, taxes, Western lands, and, of course, paper money. If the convention could do something about these problems, in a framework that preserved Connecticut's equality, they would be satisfied. On the other hand, if the convention had to go a bit farther than this in order to accomplish these goals, they might be satisfied, too. They were not purists and not out to transform the world. Sherman and Ellsworth, in particular, were devotees of small government—a government powerful enough to achieve certain limited ends, but no more powerful than that.

Sherman had another quality; when he latched onto an idea, he never let go of it. In 1777, when the Congress was beginning to frame the Articles of Confederation, Sherman had applied his practical mind to finding a way to govern America that suited reality. He believed that America was and should be a federation of equal states, with a Congress that gave each state an equal vote. He recognized, however, that the acts of such a Congress would lack wide public support, since they might not represent the sentiment of the majority of America's people. What was necessary was a mechanism by which acts of Congress would reflect the will of a majority of the states *and* of a majority of the people. Sherman tried to come up with a scheme in 1777; with the country in the crisis of war, he got nowhere.

Now, ten years later, at another time of crisis, he and Ellsworth dreamed up a proposal and saw an opening to try it as a compromise between the two sides.

On Monday, June 11, Sherman offered it on the floor of the convention: Let the vote in the lower house be proportional, so as to reflect the will of the majority of the people. But let each state have an equal vote in the upper house, so as to express the sentiments of the majority of the states.

In addition to the sound governmental principles embodied in Sherman's proposal, he thought it might be just what the convention needed to avert deadlock.

Characteristically, Sherman delivered no oration and little explanation in support of his idea but simply threw it into the pot, where, judging by the lack of response, it sat, barely noted.

Seeing this, Ben Franklin, who had kept his silence until now, decided it was time to speak up. Franklin had spent the weekend worrying about the hot words he had heard during the previous week, and what they portended. If there was any role for him in

this convention, he knew it was the same one he was playing in
Pennsylvania's fractious politics: as the conciliator, or at least as
a calming elder voice amid the stridency of his younger colleagues.
He had put his thoughts on paper, and, unable to stand on his
feet because of his gout, he handed the paper to Wilson, who rose
and read Franklin's words for him:

" 'It has given me great pleasure to observe that till this point
. . . our debates were carried on with great coolness and temper.
If any thing of a contrary kind has . . . appeared, I hope it will
not be repeated; for we are sent here to consult, not to contend,
with each other; and declarations of a fixed opinion, and of determined resolution never to change it, neither enlighten nor convince us. Positiveness and warmth on one side naturally beget
their like on the other. . . .' "

The speech rambled on for a few minutes. Franklin was acknowledged to be a great man, and he always found a respectful
audience, but his ideas about government were thought to be
eccentric and were often dismissed. The convention listened re-
spectfully once again, and then rushed ahead with a vote.

Sherman had not put his proposal in the form of a motion, but
there were two propositions on the floor that would suffice. The
first called for proportional representation in the lower house of
the new Congress. The second concerned representation in the
upper house. The outcome of both, in combination, would measure the receptiveness of the convention to Sherman's or anybody
else's idea of compromise.

First came the vote on proportional representation in the lower
house.

In favor: Massachusetts, Connecticut, Pennsylvania, Virginia,
North Carolina, South Carolina and Georgia.

Opposed: New York, New Jersey, Delaware.

Divided: Maryland.

The motion passed.

Connecticut had voted in the affirmative, with the large-state
bloc, signaling *its* willingness to compromise.

Next came the vote on Sherman's proposal for equal suffrage in the Senate. Would the large states reciprocate Connecticut's concession? "Everything depended on this," Sherman said just before the vote. "The smaller states would never agree to the plan on any other principle than an equality of suffrage in this branch."

The question: Would each state have an equal vote in the upper house?

The roll was called:

Massachusetts: No.
Connecticut: Aye.
New York: Aye.
New Jersey: Aye.
Pennsylvania: No.
Delaware: Aye.
Maryland: Aye.
Virginia: No.
North Carolina: No.
South Carolina: No.
Georgia: No.

Sherman's compromise proposal had failed by the vote of a single state. The large states held fast to their position.

And why not? There was no reason for Madison and the large states to compromise: everything was going their way. The convention had completed nearly two weeks of work and, in between the skirmishes over representation, had debated and taken tentative votes on the full skeleton of the government, resolution by resolution. They had approved the establishment of three branches, with a legislature of two houses, popular elections for the first, the state legislatures to choose the second (an alteration of Madison's plan). They had—with little struggle—given the new Congress a veto power over state laws, the right to elect a national executive, and, to the upper house, the power to appoint the judges.

Despite the novelty of Madison's scheme, there had been strikingly little quarrel over its broad principles. So little threatened was Madison by Sherman's proposal, the Virginian hadn't even thought to challenge it.

From events so far, Madison could draw the illusion of momentum.

Life was taking on a rhythm for the delegates. Up in the morning. Out for a walk or a ride. Breakfast. Over to the State House by ten. Meet until three or four. Gather in small parties for dinner, at one of the inns or a private home, and then back to their rooms for the night.

Their quarters were sparse, but acceptable. The Indian Queen, where many stayed, was "a large pile of buildings, with many spacious halls, and numerous small apartments," each equipped with field bed, bureau, a table with drawers, a looking glass, and one or two chairs. Some of the rooms, those at the top of the three-story inn, offered views of the river and the Jersey shore. A staff of black servants, with ruffled shirts and powdered hair, blue coats and red capes, waited on the delegates, bringing them reading material, summoning barbers and bowls of water for washing.

The Indian Queen set aside private sections for the members of the convention, who formed themselves into a little club. "The Gentlemen of the Convention at the Indian Queen in 4th Street Present their Compliments . . . ," the invitations to dinner said. They would invite some guest to drink and dine and talk, someone like Franklin or the chief justice of Pennsylvania or some friendly face from home who happened to be in town.

In the presence of outsiders, convention business was off limits. But when they were alone, delegates could caucus, formally or informally, trying out ideas. Would this or that work? Was it worth bringing to the floor? Would you support it? Do we have the votes?

The conventioneers were themselves regularly invited to parties at the homes of Philadelphians, who welcomed the return of the sociability they had missed since Congress' departure in 1783. None was more elegant than the parties thrown by Robert Morris and his wife ("Queen Morris," as she was called behind her back), especially with the guaranteed presence of the Morrises' celebrated house guest, George Washington. Morris, an amiable, expansive and portly host, presided over forty or more guests, perhaps a harpsichord recital, playing and singing by the ladies, lemonade served in silver urns, "a profusion of iced creams" and a table "more resplendent" than any other in Philadelphia. The popular pre-dinner drinks were Madeira, burgundy, claret and rum punch. Dinners among the wealthy ran to fourteen courses and might include beef, ham, pork, mutton, lamb, duck, chicken, game, oysters, herring, mackerel and shad.

The best anecdote to emerge from one of these social gatherings concerned Washington, Gouverneur Morris and Alexander Hamilton and captured the essence of all three of them.

At an interview between Hamilton, the Morrises, and others, the former remarked that Washington was reserved and aristocratic even to his intimate friends, and allowed no one to be familiar with him. Gouverneur Morris said that was a mere fancy, and he could be as familiar with Washington as with any of his other friends. Hamilton replied, "If you will, at the next reception evenings, gently slap him on the shoulder and say, 'My dear General, how happy I am to see you look so well!' A supper and wine shall be provided for you and a dozen of your friends." The challenge was accepted. On the evening appointed, a large number attended; and at an early hour Gouverneur Morris entered, bowed, shook hands, laid his left hand on Washington's shoulder, and said, "My dear General, I am very happy to see you look so well!" Washington withdrew his hand, stepped suddenly back, fixed his eye on Morris for several minutes with an angry frown, until the latter retreated abashed, and sought refuge in the crowd. The company looked on in silence. At the supper, which was provided by Hamilton, Morris said, "I have won the bet, but paid dearly for it, and nothing could induce me to repeat it."

For quieter amusement, after the sessions of the convention members would go on long solitary walks, or ride into the country, or shop for horses or china, or inspect one of the curiosities with which Philadelphia abounded. "My curiosity was highly gratified the other day," Ellsworth wrote, "by clasping the hand of a woman who died many hundred years ago. The ancient Egyptians had an art, which is now lost out of the world, of embalming their dead so as to preserve the bodies from putrification many of which remain to this day. From one of these an arm has lately been cut off and brought to this city. The hand is entire. The nails remain upon the fingers and the wrapping cloth upon the arm. The flesh which I tried with my knife, cuts and looks much like a smoked beef kept till it grows hard. This will be a good story to tell Dr. Stiles, which is all the use I shall probably make of it. His avidity for food of this kind you know is strong enough to swallow the arm and body whole."

For additional entertainment, there were the newspapers, a mix of correspondence from abroad, advertisements, propaganda and pressing items of local news, such as this report in *The Pennsylvania Mercury*:

A few days ago in Third street a young coxcomb who had made too free with the bottle having staggered after a lady of delicate dress and shape for some distance, at length laid hold of her hand and peeping under her large hat, told her that he did not like her so well before as behind, but notwithstanding he would be glad of the favour of a kiss; to which the lady replied: "With all my heart, Sir, if you will do me the favour to kiss the part you like the least."

Some of the Massachusetts gentlemen spent their idle hours in a library of heraldry, looking up the coats of arms of families they knew.

But every weekday morning, without fail, they would all rise again, breakfast, and head off to the State House. And again that sight—every morning between 9:30 and 10, thirty or forty of the most famous and important men in America emerging from their doors and converging on this one place: Franklin being carried in his sedan chair; the towering Washington with his long stride; the small men Madison and Paterson, with their little steps; the corpulent Gunning Bedford; James Wilson, his glasses on the end of his nose; rail-thin Elbridge Gerry; the determined Hamilton, always in a hurry; all of them making their way through the crowds in the covered markets, past the work gangs of convicts in the bright green and red rags that identified them for what they were, past the sentries at the State House and the litigants and lawyers and judges gathered for the court, past the curious onlookers, and into the Assembly Room to work in utter secrecy.

The outside world knew nothing. "Such circumspection and secrecy mark the proceedings of the foederal convention," said *The Pennsylvania Herald* on June 2, that the members

> find it difficult to acquire the habit of communication even among themselves, and are so cautious in defeating the curiosity of the public, that all debate is suspended upon the entrance of their own inferior officers. Though we readily admit the propriety of excluding an indiscriminate attendance upon the discussions of this deliberative council, it is hoped that the privacy of their transactions will be an additional motive for dispatch, as the anxiety of the people must be necessarily encreased, by every appearance of mystery in conducting this important business.

"I enclose some small extracts from the papers by which you will be amused to learn all we yet know of the convention," Dr. William Shippen of Philadelphia wrote to his son. "Much is hoped for from their wisdom and patriotism. Aristocracy is said to be the Idea of almost all of them. I shall not call it a miracle if G.W. is seen living in Philadelphia as Emperor of America in a few years. The eastern men hold these principles as strongly as the southern. Glorious future prospects for you my boy."

Sometime early in the week of June 10, 1787, somewhere in the city of Philadelphia, a small group of delegates in search of a strategy sat down together in a room. There is no evidence that they went out of their way to keep the meeting secret—that would have been well near impossible living so closely with one another—but also no evidence that Madison and the others were aware of what was happening.

Luther Martin of Maryland was there. So were Brearley and Paterson and Livingston of New Jersey, John Dickinson of Delaware, Yates and Lansing of New York, Sherman of Connecticut, and perhaps others. Their purpose: to come up with a counter-thrust to the Virginia Plan. Of course they should have done this earlier. They should have anticipated the intransigence of the large states and made common cause beforehand, but when the convention began some hadn't even left home. Had they met before, perhaps they too would have had a plan to put on the table; perhaps their plan, not Madison's, would have set the agenda. At the very least, they might not have found themselves so badly outflanked and outnumbered.

It was a tenuous coalition with only one wish in common: to stop the convention's headlong drive toward a government based exclusively on proportional representation. Beyond that, their missions in Philadelphia varied widely. Some, like Yates and Lansing, simply opposed any change in the status quo. They had been sent to Philadelphia by their political boss, Governor George Clinton of New York, whose state was doing quite well, thank you, with things as they stood. Nearly a third of New York's revenue came from the taxes it imposed on imports destined for New Jersey and Connecticut, levies that the state might lose to a new government empowered to regulate commerce. The money New York raised kept taxes down for the farmers and the artisans who formed a large part of Clinton's constituency, and keeping taxes down meant keeping the peace, keeping Shays' Rebellion out of New York.

Closest to Yates and Lansing in sentiment was Luther Martin, the attorney general of Maryland, who like them was tied to a political organization committed to preserving the rights of the states. Unlike them, he brought passion and volatile temper to Philadelphia: he was already convinced that the convention was nothing short of a secret conspiracy to annihilate the states and, with them, the liberties of all Americans. Men such as Martin did not share the near-pathologic hostility of many of the nationalists toward the states and their governments. Their creed was the reverse of Madison's. Madison saw the state governments as a threat to individual rights and looked to an "extended republic" to protect them. They saw big government as threatening, and looked to the states as the bulwark to protect individual rights.

The New Jerseyans and the men from Connecticut and Delaware, on the other hand, wanted a stronger national government and felt that their states would gain by it. But as representatives of states often regarded as mere satellites of larger neighbors, they wanted some guarantee against being swallowed up. For them equality in the Congress was a condition of participation.

New Jersey was particularly illustrative. New Jersey had an uncommonly large debt and had been forced to impose heavy taxes on land to pay it. A national government, armed with the power to tax imports and to sell Western lands, could relieve New Jersey's burden by assuming that debt. At the same time, New Jersey had felt the consequences of being dominated by large states like Pennsylvania and New York—which used their port to exact tribute from New Jersey—and needed a means of self-defense that proportional representation would not provide.

Despite the differing motives among its members, the caucus was united in its desperation for a tactic to slow the momentum of the convention and to break the large-state dominance. As its vehicle, it chose to prepare its own plan of government, an alternative to Madison's.

Each man proposed something. Ideas were considered and discarded, others accepted. Some were lifted from the Virginia Plan, others from the Articles of Confederation. Still others were cooked up on the spot. The theme, when it was complete, was the status quo—with a few improvements. It began with some of

2 THE FOUNDING

the same words Randolph had first used to introduce the Virginia
Plan: "Resolved, that the Articles of Confederation ought to be
so revised, corrected and enlarged, as to render the federal Constitution adequate to the exigencies of government, and the pres-
ervation of the Union." Only this time, the words more
accurately described the propositions which followed.

The Congress, of course, would remain exactly as it was—one
house with an equal vote for each state. Congress would be given
the power to raise and collect revenue and to regulate trade and
commerce. The executive of the government would be several
persons rather than one, and they would be removable by the
governors of the states. Finally, the new plan declared that the
Constitution and the laws of the Congress should be supreme,
overriding any state law conflicting with them. On its face, this
notion of national supremacy appeared radical. But there was an
intentional omission. The clause gave national law supremacy
over state laws but not state constitutions. The omission was
critical, a massive and intentional loophole which would allow
the states to go on doing as they pleased.

William Paterson of New Jersey would be the spokesman for
the counterplan. Unlike Randolph (or Madison and the other
Virginians), Paterson hadn't been born to leadership: he had
climbed to it. Paterson was born in County Antrim, Ireland, in
1745. His father, Richard Paterson, a tinplate worker, followed
his two brothers to America in 1747, earning his living peddling
pots and pans until opening a general store in Princeton, not a
hundred yards from the site of Nassau Hall, home of the new
College of New Jersey. The store, which prospered, included
among its customers all the students at the college, including,
eventually, young James Madison.

William attended Princeton, where Martin and Ellsworth were
classmates. Like them, he dedicated himself to financial and political advancement, and to his own admission into what he called
"polished society." He read law, set up a law practice and from
1775 to 1782 served as attorney general of New Jersey. Though

Paterson was once chosen as a delegate to the Continental Congress, his duties in New Jersey prevented him from devoting much attention to it and he remained essentially a statebound politician.

Paterson now readied himself for the most important moment of his political career.

CHAPTER SEVEN

The Alternative Rejected

The emergence of an organized opposition seems to have shaken Madison rather badly. Until the fourteenth of June his notes reflect nothing short of supreme confidence. On the fifteenth, when Paterson took the floor and presented what was now called "the New Jersey Plan" to the convention, the tone of Madison's notes changed immediately and for the first time we have a sense of a man on the defensive.

It wasn't so much the plan itself that did it, but the determination of its sponsors, their sudden unity and perhaps the little lecture Madison got that morning from John Dickinson of Delaware, who wanted to make sure the Virginian understood what was happening, and that he had brought this on himself with his intransigence and impatience.

"You see the consequence of pushing things too far," Dickinson said to Madison as Paterson presented his plan. "Some of the members from the small states wish for two branches in the general legislature, and are friends to a good national government; but we would sooner submit to a foreign power than submit to be

deprived of an equality of suffrage in both branches of the legislature, and thereby be thrown under the domination of the large
states."

Madison recorded his own thoughts at the bottom of a page of
his notes: "The eagourness displayed by the members opposed to
a National Government from these different motives began now
to produce serious anxiety for the result of the Convention."

On the floor, he reacted equally defensively, objecting vehemently but unsuccessfully when Lansing of New York demanded
that the convention recess for another day so that the delegates
could take copies of the new plan and study it overnight.

What may have really been bothering Madison was the loss of
momentum the debate over the New Jersey Plan would cause.
From the very beginning, his side had been the best organized and
the best prepared and had exploited the advantage effectively.
Now everything would grind to a halt while they contended over
a patchwork scheme of government.

As a debate, it wasn't a fair match. Wilson, Madison and Gouverneur Morris had prepared for such a combat for years, not days.
Their opponents were learned, but they lacked flair—as did their
New Jersey Plan itself. No one ever described Sherman as "brilliant." Solid, yes. Persevering, a pillar, but not brilliant. Ellsworth was a big plodder, six foot two, broad-shouldered, a good
lawyer but a plodder no less, who once had confessed that "the
key to his success in life was his ability to overcome his lack of
imagination and culture by exhaustive and painstaking study."

The Paterson plan itself—though parts had merit—was an easy
target. The increased powers it granted were insufficient to get
the job done, but sufficient to be dangerous if not internally
checked, which they were not. Without popular elections, the
plan increased governmental authority without anchoring it in a
popular base. The absence of any popular voice in the Confederation Congress was one of the reasons some were reluctant to
enhance its powers. Without a serious executive, without a sec-

ond house of congress, there was little check at all in the New Jersey Plan. All the power was vested in a single branch of the legislature.

There is evidence as well that the authors of the New Jersey Plan themselves did not take it terribly seriously as an outline of government, for they hardly mentioned it in their defense, which began on the sixteenth of June. The best argument they could muster—amid the greatest crisis since the war—was an appeal to the convention to go slowly, to hold back, to be timid.

The convention was illegal, they claimed. Look at the acts authorizing the convention, said Lansing, the lead-off speaker. Look at the act of Congress. "Is it probable," he pleaded, "that the states would adopt and ratify a scheme which they had never authorized us to propose, and which so far exceeded what they regarded as sufficient? . . ."

"If the Confederacy was radically wrong," Paterson said, "let us return to our states and obtain larger powers, not assume them of ourselves. I came here not to speak my own sentiments, but the sentiments of those who sent me. Our object is not such a government as may be best in itself, but such a one as our constituents have authorized us to prepare, and as they will approve. . . ."

There was a measure of truth in these words. The convention of 1787 was a runaway, probably far ahead of public opinion. But it was the wrong argument, at the wrong time and at the wrong place. Sherman and Ellsworth didn't even join in. Paterson and Lansing were asking the convention to yield to popular sentiment.

From Randolph came the answer: "When the salvation of the Republic is at stake, it would be treason to our trust not to propose what we found necessary. . . . There are seasons certainly of a peculiar nature where the ordinary cautions must be dispensed with; and this is certainly one of them. . . . The present moment is favorable, and is probably the last that will offer. . . . After this select experiment, the people will yield to despair."

On that same day, the sixteenth of June, Wilson took aim at the weakest strand of the Paterson plan. The New Jersey Plan's

Congress had only one house, he said. "Despotism comes on mankind in different shapes, sometimes in an executive, sometimes in a military one. Is there no danger of a legislative despotism? Theory and practice both proclaim it. If the legislative authority be not restrained, there can be neither liberty nor stability. . . . In order to control the legislative authority, you must divide it" into two houses, he said.

The convention rested on Sunday, June 17.

Alexander Hamilton took the floor on the eighteenth and held it all day.

Of all the deputies to the convention, he was the one man capable of making Madison look tame. He was the country's leading proponent of "high-mounted" or "high-toned" government, meaning powerful centralized national rule. (Once, legend has it, while visiting Jefferson in his rooms, Hamilton noticed three portraits on the wall and asked who the men were. "They are my trinity of the three greatest men the world has ever produced," Jefferson said, "Sir Francis Bacon, Sir Isaac Newton, and John Locke." Hamilton thought for a moment. "The greatest man that ever lived," he finally said, "was Julius Caesar.")

Though he had promoted a convention since 1783 and had helped engineer the call for the convention at the Annapolis meeting, Hamilton had spoken little during the first few weeks in Philadelphia. This was not like him, for Hamilton was a loose cannon in the Congress, embarrassing even Madison on occasion with his bluntness, but it was just as well. His ideas were extreme. Perhaps he had been reticent in the convention because he and Madison feared that the Hamiltonian view would shock the others. Whatever the reason, his reticence ended during the debate over the New Jersey Plan.

He rose and proposed his own scheme of government, the Hamilton Plan. It walked, talked and looked to everyone like the government of Great Britain, lacking only a hereditary monarchy. To be sure, it had a lower house elected by the people. But it had a Senate and a President elected for life, and as for the states, they were all but eliminated. "They are not necessary for any of the great purposes of commerce, revenue, or agriculture," he declared. Congress would appoint their governors (as England appointed the governors of the colonies), and the governors would have veto power over all state laws (as did the governors under the British regime). The British government, he said, was "the best in the world . . . [I doubt] much whether anything short of it would do in America."

He concluded with a concession that must have upset Madison. "I confess," Hamilton said, "that this plan and that from Virginia are very remote from the idea of the people. Perhaps the Jersey plan is nearest their expectation. But the people are gradually ripening in their opinions of government—they begin to be tired of an excess of democracy—and what even is the Virginia plan, but pork still, with a little change of the sauce?"

His speech probably struck a chord. The British system was indeed admired by these men. But America was not Britain, and even Hamilton acknowledged in his speech that he might "shock public opinion."

"The gentleman from New York," as William Samuel Johnson later described it, "was praised by all, but supported by no gentleman. He goes directly to the abolition of the state governments."

Hamilton's speech smoothed the way for Madison and made him seem all the more reasonable when he took the floor on the nineteenth as the final speaker.

The object of a "proper plan" for the country, he said, should be twofold: "first, to preserve the Union; secondly, to provide a government" that would "remedy the evils felt by the states, both in their united and individual capacities," i.e., the familiar horribles—broken treaties, paper money, "insurrections in Massachusetts," "trespasses of the states" on one another. . . .

"Examine Mr. Paterson's plan, and say whether it promises satisfaction in these respects." Could the New Jersey Plan, leaving the states as uncontrolled as ever, cure these ills?

"Will it prevent those violations of the law of nations and of treaties which if not prevented must involve us in the calamities of foreign wars? . . ." The answer was no.

"Will it prevent encroachments on the federal authority? . . ." Again the answer was no.

"Will it prevent trespasses of the states on each other? . . .

"Will it secure the internal tranquility of the states themselves? The insurrections in Massachusetts admonish all the states of the danger to which they are exposed. Yet the plan of Mr. Paterson contains no provisions for supplying the defect of the Confederation on this point. . . .

"Will it secure the Union against the influence of foreign powers over its members? . . ."

He must have spoken all morning and into the afternoon. Listening to him, watching him hold the floor in defense of his dream, it must have been hard to believe that a few years ago he had sat timidly in the Virginia Assembly afraid to open his mouth. Perhaps, as Delegate Pierce wrote in his sketch of Madison in convention, the Virginian still could not be called a great orator. But he had become "a most agreeable, eloquent, and convincing speaker."

Madison made his final plea to the small states directly: "Let the Union of the states be dissolved, and one of two consequences must happen. Either the states must remain individually independent and sovereign or two or more confederacies must be formed among them. In the first event, would the small states be more secure against the ambition and power of their larger neighbors than they would be under a general government pervading with equal energy every part of the empire, and having an equal interest in protecting every part against every other part? In the second, can the smaller expect that their larger neighbors would confederate with them on the principle of the present Confederacy, which gives to each member an equal suffrage; or that they would exact less severe concessions from the smaller states than are proposed in the scheme of Mr. Randolph?"

It was time for the small states to face reality, he was saying. They were risking the convention and they would be sorry for it.

Randolph, Wilson and Madison had cut the Paterson plan to shreds and, in the process, presented the best, most coherent, most convincing and certainly most impassioned defense of the Virginia Plan the convention had yet heard.

At the end of that day, the states cast their votes. An aye vote would preserve the Virginia Plan as the basis of the new government, consigning the New Jersey Plan to oblivion.

Voting aye were Massachusetts, Pennsylvania, Virginia, North Carolina, South Carolina, Georgia and Connecticut.

Voting no were New York, New Jersey and Delaware. Maryland split, nullifying its ballot.

Seven to three. The New Jersey Plan hadn't even held the Connecticut delegation.

As a consolation prize, the convention agreed the next day to Ellsworth's request that the word "national" be dropped from the resolution calling for a "supreme national" government.

"The present Federal Government seems near its exit," Nathaniel Gorham of Massachusetts wrote to a friend that week, "and whether we shall in the Convention be able to agree upon mending it, or forming and recommending a new one, is not certain."

CHAPTER EIGHT

Ultimatums

The Paterson plan was an assault on radical change, a defense of the present and of the past. The convention had rejected it, but the vote did not guarantee smooth passage for the alternative. The small-state delegations were not about to give up.

The committee of the whole had debated and voted tentatively on the entire structure of government, resolution by resolution. The convention now had to repeat the process from top to bottom. In a way, the battle just lost could be turned to the advantage of the losers, for it had consumed much time and the convention was growing restless and impatient, and the dreaded Philadelphia summer was closing in, bringing with it a slow bake, which by the fifteenth of June brought the temperature into the midnineties.

Perhaps, by dragging it on further, they could wear down the other side. Perhaps at night, in the taverns, a vote here or there could be swayed. Perhaps the lost tribe of New Hampshire, which had yet to find its way to Philadelphia, would appear. New Hampshire's legislature had readily appointed delegates, but the state had not come up with funds for the long journey and for the stay in Philadelphia. Since New Hampshire was among the smallest of the thirteen states (population 141,885), its absence was counted as a plus for the large states. Perhaps they could chip away at Madison's majorities by sheer obstinacy and vituperation. Not everyone was as dead set against them as were Madison and Wilson, and there were already some signals, from Franklin and others, of a willingness to compromise.

The racket outside the State House, the scraping and rasping and clanking of metal-rimmed wagon wheels on cobblestone, was getting on everyone's nerves. On June 22, the Philadelphia street commissioners, at the request of the convention, sent a crew to the Fourth Street sewer project for a load of gravel to spread on the street, in hopes of at least cushioning the noise.

The delegates were beginning to think about home. "The older men grow the more uneasy they are [away] from their wives." Therefore, Oliver Ellsworth supposed, as he was two-thirds the age of Sherman and Johnson, his co-delegates from Connecticut, he would be able to survive one-third longer than they in abstinence. He would manage until "about the last of August."

Nevertheless, he teased in a letter to his wife, "I frequently stop in and take a little chat and tea sipping with good Connecticut women who are dispersed about in different parts of the City. They are all very agreeable, but as Mrs. Lockwood I think is the most like yourself, you will allow me to like her a little the best. I can add, however, if it will be any satisfaction to you, that my friend Mr. Lockwood is a home man and generally makes one of the party."

The long summer's ordeal resumed on the morning of June 20, and over the next several days the convention inched along, filling in the details concerning the nature of the lower house and the upper house; agreeing, though not without a fight, that the lower house would be popularly elected. But they were still far away from a design for the other branches of the government and had not even begun to tackle some of the explosive issues that they knew lay ahead, such as slavery. And looming ahead of them was yet another conflagration about representation in the Senate.

If there was one man in the room capable of trying men's patience even further, it was Luther Martin, delegate from Maryland. And on the twenty-seventh of June the opposition unleashed him.

Compared with Washington, Franklin, Hamilton and Madison, and lesser lights as well, Luther Martin was a nobody, not a war hero, not a great thinker, not a member of a great family and, above all, not a continentalist. He was merely a spear carrier for the political organization in Maryland headed by Samuel Chase.

Martin was the clever son of a poor New Jersey farmer who had managed to put Luther through Princeton. Afterward Martin became a lawyer and went to Virginia to practice, attempting without success to break into a closed circle of patrician lawyers—the Randolphs among them—in Williamsburg. Failing that, Martin went to Maryland's Eastern Shore, hoping that the recent death of one of the three important lawyers there might make room for another. He was successful in Maryland, where he tied his fate to Chase, the wealthy former Revolutionary leader of the state and now a major political power.

Martin probably could have gone farther in life than he had, but he had his share of personal problems. Rumors of heavy drinking and profligacy pursued him throughout his life. While studying to become a lawyer he had been a schoolmaster, and it was rumored that he lost that job because he "spent most of his time in drinking and finally left the county because his attention to a daughter of a prominent planter was very objectionable." Plus, he was constantly in debt and had a famous temper.

The accumulation of troubles must have hurt him, for though he progressed in Maryland, he was never the first choice for anything. Chase got him appointed attorney general in Maryland only after someone else turned down the job. When it came time for Maryland to choose delegates to the convention, Martin was not a second choice or a third choice, but last on a list of ten or more.

Martin favored paper money. That alone was enough to raise the eyebrows of his convention colleagues, for the one class of humanity more contemptible than the paper-money-loving mob was the class of politicians who encouraged it. The mob didn't know any better; the politicians did. Thus Martin was the odd man out even among the other partisans of the New Jersey Plan. Ellsworth, Paterson and the other Princetonians among that small group may have wondered to themselves where Martin had gone wrong, how one of "them" had gotten in there. For his part, Martin thought they, not he, had a paper-money problem. The fanatic opponents of paper money, he felt, were obsessed, haunted by the "paper money dread."

Martin probably had a chip on his shoulder even before he arrived at the convention, not only because of paper money, but because of the long-standing jealousy Marylanders harbored toward the state of Virginia, particularly its vast land claims. Maryland and Maryland's speculators—with whom Martin was close—wanted their share.

So Martin was probably looking for a fight before he left Maryland. He arrived late in Philadelphia, on June 9, and as he inspected the journal of the convention he grew angry. To him, Madison's great dream looked like a dark conspiracy: first, the doors had been shut, communications with the outside world forbidden; then, in a rapid succession of votes behind closed doors, the convention had begun constructing a system of government in which three states—Massachusetts, Pennsylvania and the commonwealth of Virginia—would hold massive sway over everything: vetoing state laws, choosing the executive, choosing the judiciary.

It was, Martin believed, a "system of slavery, which bound hand and foot ten states in the union, and placed them at the mercy of the other three, and under the most abject and servile subjection to them. . . ."

Martin began arming himself, consuming all his spare time in Philadelphia in libraries, studying. "I applied to history for what lights it could afford me, and I procured everything the most valuable I could find in Philadelphia on the subject of governments in general, and on the American revolution and governments in particular," he recalled later. On June 27, in the convention, he took the floor and launched his counterattack, regurgitating all he had learned, reading at length from Locke, Vattel, Lord Somers, Joseph Priestley and anybody else he could think of. He went on for hours, starting in the morning and continuing into the afternoon, when, pleading exhaustion, he stopped, declaring that he would continue the next day, which he did.

The next day he began anew, continuing for the better part of the twenty-eighth as well.

He made some solid points. He said that the general government "was meant merely to preserve the state governments, not to govern individuals," and that "its powers ought to be kept within narrow limits," and so on.

But he spoke too long, and the reviews, though biased, were uniformly negative. Martin spoke, said Madison, "with much diffuseness and considerable vehemence." "This gentleman possesses a good deal of information," Pierce of Georgia wrote, "but he has a very bad delivery, and is so extremely prolix, that he never speaks without tiring the patience of all who hear him." Whether Martin intended it or not, his little filibuster had the effect probably desired by the small-state men: it wore down the convention. All around the room, said Oliver Ellsworth, there were "marks of fatigue and disgust. . . ."

After Martin sat down, Madison apparently felt the need to get even. Instead of allowing everyone a rest, he stood up and delivered his own treatise on the history of the Western world, Carthage, Rome, the Heroic Age of Ancient Greece, the "existing condition of the American savages," and the "condition of the lesser states in the German Confederacy."

When it was all over, two full days had passed, and the mood of the convention was foul.

Franklin, greatly disturbed by now, decided it was time once again to intervene, before the explosion. As the convention prepared to recess, he asked for the floor and made a plea:

"The small progress we have made after four or five weeks' close attendance and continual reasonings with each other . . . is, methinks, a melancholy proof of the imperfection of the human understanding. We indeed seem to feel our own want of political wisdom, since we have been running about in search of it. We have gone back to ancient history for models of government, and examined the different forms of those republics which, having been formed with the seeds of their own dissolution, now no longer exist. And we have viewed modern states all round Europe, but find none of their constitutions suitable to our circumstances.

"In this situation of this assembly, groping, as it were, in the dark to find political truth, and scarce able to distinguish it when presented to us, how has it happened, sir, that we have not hitherto once thought of humbly applying to the Father of lights to illuminate our understandings? In the beginning of the contest with Great Britain, when we were sensible of danger, we had daily prayer in this room for the divine protection. Our prayers, sir, were heard, and they were graciously answered. All of us who were engaged in the struggle must have observed frequent instances of a superintending Providence in our favor. To that kind Providence we owe this happy opportunity of consulting in peace on the means of establishing our future national felicity. And have we now forgotten that powerful Friend? Or do we imagine that we no longer need His assistance?

"I have lived, sir, a long time, and the longer I live, the more convincing proofs I see of this truth—that God governs in the affairs of men. And if a sparrow cannot fall to the ground without His notice, is it probable that an empire can rise without His aid? We have been assured, sir, in the sacred writings, that 'except the

Lord build the House they labor in vain that build it.' I firmly
believe this; and I also believe that without His concurring aid we
shall succeed in this political building no better than the builders
of Babel. We shall be divided by our little partial local interests;
our projects will be confounded and we ourselves shall become a
reproach and byword down to future ages. And, what is worse,
mankind may hereafter, from this unfortunate instance, despair
of establishing governments by human wisdom and leave it to
chance, war and conquest."

Finally he came to the point. "I therefore beg leave to move
that, henceforth, prayers imploring the assistance of Heaven and
its blessings on our deliberations be held in this assembly every
morning before we proceed to business, and that one or more of
the clergy of this city be requested to officiate in that service."

They were in no mood for Franklin's proposal, and a good deal
of hemming and hawing ensued.

Madison, in his notes, reported the response:

> Mr. Hamilton & several others expressed their apprehensions
> that however proper such a resolution might have been at the
> beginning of the convention, it might at this late day, 1. bring on
> it some disagreeable animadversions, & 2. lead the public to be-
> lieve that the embarrassments and dissensions within the Conven-
> tion, had suggested this measure.
>
> It was answered by Dr. Franklin, Mr. Sherman & others, that
> the past omission of a duty could not justify a further omission—
> that the rejection of such a proposition would expose the Conven-
> tion to more unpleaseant animadversions than the adoption of it:
> and that the alarm out of doors that might be excited for the state
> of things within, would at least be as likely to do good as ill.
>
> Mr. Williamson observed that the true cause of the omission
> could not be mistaken. The Convention had no funds.
>
> Mr. Randolph proposed in order to give a favorable aspect to ye
> measure that a sermon be preached at the request of the conven-
> tion on the 4th of July, the anniversary of Independence; &
> thenceforward prayers be used in ye Convention every morning.

Dr. Franklin seconded this motion. After several unsuccessful attempts for silently postponing the matter by adjourning, the adjournment was at length carried, without any vote on the motion.

Over the next few days, as the convention moved through the resolutions headed for a final vote on representation in the Senate, Franklin's worst fears materialized: the delegates got more and more belligerent, the rhetoric more and more feverish.

The notes of Madison and the other delegates do not record the volume of the voices or the color of the faces, or whether the delegates were quivering with anger or steely-eyed as they spoke. But from the words spoken, coming from men ordinarily so measured, only one conclusion can be drawn: they had to have been shouting.

Ellsworth declared that if the large-state delegates did not compromise, the convention and, worse, the union of the states itself were finished. "Let a strong executive, a judiciary, and a legislative power be created, but let not too much be attempted, by which all may be lost."

Wilson shot back: "If the minority of the people of America refuse to coalesce with the majority on just and proper principles, if a separation must take place, it could never happen on better grounds. . . . If issue must be joined, it is on this point that I would choose to join it. . . ."

If the small states are fixed in their view, said Rufus King of Massachusetts, so are we. "I conceive this to be the last opportunity of providing for [America's] liberty and happiness. . . . My mind is prepared for every event, rather than to sit down under a government founded in a vicious principle of representation, and which must be as short-lived as it would be unjust."

Dayton of New Jersey responded: "When assertion is given for proof, and terror substituted for argument, I presume they would have no effect, however eloquently spoken. . . . I consider the system on the table as a novelty, an amphibious monster; . . . it would never be received by the people."

Martin: Maryland "will never confederate if it cannot be done on just principles."

Bedford of Delaware: "We have been told with a dictatorial air that this is the last moment for a fair trial in favor of a good government. It will be the last indeed if the propositions reported from the committee go forth to the people. I am under no apprehensions. The large states dare not dissolve the Confederation. If they do, the small ones will find some foreign ally of more honor and good faith, who will take them by the hand and do them justice."

King: "I cannot sit down without taking some notice of the language of the honorable gentleman from Delaware. It was not I that have uttered dictatorial language. This intemperance has marked the honorable gentleman himself. It was not I who with a vehemence unprecedented . . . declared himself ready to turn his hopes from our common country and court the protection of some foreign hand. This too was the language of the honorable member himself. I am grieved that such a thought entered into his heart. I am more grieved that such an expression dropped from his lips. The gentleman could only excuse it to himself on the score of passion. For myself, whatever might be my distress, I would never court relief from a foreign power."

It was Saturday, June 30. The convention recessed. The first item on Monday would be the vote on the motion to allow each state one vote in the Senate.

CHAPTER NINE

Deadlock

The rest of the world was not standing still during the month of June 1787, and events outside the sealed room were now to make a difference.

Congress, meeting in New York, was considering an ordinance for the partition of the Western lands north of the Ohio River and for their eventual division into states. Spurring on Congress, a company of land speculators had offered to buy five to six million acres of those lands for sale to settlers. Action on the ordinance had been delayed for weeks, in part because so many congressmen were attending the convention in Philadelphia that Congress could not achieve a quorum. As the convention dragged on, Congress tired of waiting, and put out an urgent call for the return of the members needed to fill out several congressional delegations, Georgia among them. In response, William Pierce and William Few left Philadelphia for New York. (Pierce had another reason to go to New York: one John Auldjo had insulted his good name, and Pierce had challenged him to a duel.) The departure left William Houston and Abraham Baldwin to represent Georgia in Philadelphia.

The Maryland delegation, three men up till now, had also lost a member when James McHenry left the convention to tend to an ill younger brother in Baltimore. That left in the Maryland delegation Luther Martin and Daniel of St. Thomas Jenifer, who disagreed on many of the issues and had often split the state's vote, nullifying it at crucial junctures since McHenry's departure.

Monday arrived. The motion before the convention was the proposition—defeated when last considered—to give each state one vote in the upper house.

The roll of the states was called, as always, in geographical order, from north to south.

Massachusetts: No.

Connecticut: Aye.

New York: Aye.

New Jersey: Aye.

Pennsylvania: No.

Delaware: Aye.

So far everything was as expected.

Then came Maryland, which had split its vote on the last occasion.

Jenifer was absent. No one said why, whether he had overslept, or was ill, or had simply decided to be absent. In any case, Martin alone was, for the moment, the Maryland delegation.

Maryland: Aye.

The roll call continued:

Virginia: No.

North Carolina: No.

South Carolina: No.

The vote was tied.

It was up to Georgia, which had consistently voted with Madison against equality in the Senate. Everyone expected the state to do so again, breaking the tie and settling the issue.

But when the state's name was called on the question of equality in the Senate, the delegation, now reduced to two, was divided:

Georgia: "Mr. Baldwin, aye. Mr. Houston, no."

Baldwin, who had favored proportional representation before, had changed his mind and his vote. He did not explain. Martin speculated later that the Georgian voted as he did in order to prevent the collapse of the convention. Possibly. Perhaps it was his Connecticut background (he had been born, raised and educated there and had only recently migrated to Georgia), his Yale education and his close friendship with the members of that state's delegation. Perhaps he had made a deal and expected something in return, later.

The convention was deadlocked—five states for equal representation, five states against, Georgia divided.

For the first time, the large states' majority had been broken. It was a breakthrough.

Rufus King of Massachusetts, upset by Jenifer's absence, futilely called for another vote. But it was too late.

The deadlock sobered the convention. It was understood that whether or not Madison and his allies could regain their majority by turning the votes of one or two states, a constitution wrought by such thin margins could not long survive outside the room.

And they knew that once they got over this hump—if they did —others lay ahead, that not a single important clause would be forged without some clash of interests. No one needed to be reminded of the explosiveness of the issue of slavery; and they hadn't begun to wrestle with the executive branch and its powers, or with the authority to be granted to Congress itself—sensitive matters indeed.

The war that had unified the country was four years over. Absent some new bond, how long would it hold? How long before dissolution? "As yet we retain the habits of union," Hamilton had said. ". . . Henceforward, the motives will become feebler, and the difficulties greater. It is a miracle that we are here now exercising our tranquil and free deliberations. It would be madness to trust to future miracles."

And Martin was not overstating the case when later he said that the Federal Convention of 1787 was "scarce held together by the strength of a hair. . . ." Franklin compared it to the two-headed snake he kept at home pickled in a vial. Suppose, he said, that this snake, while slithering along in search of food, confronted the stem of a bush. And suppose one head of that snake chose to go in one direction around the stem, while the other head, feeling uncooperative, took the opposite route. Imagine the consequences.

Washington had feared this all along. Why not wait, he had thought, rather than try before the time was right and fail? An abortive convention would be considered as "unequivocal evidence that the states are not likely to agree on any general measure which is to pervade the union."

Washington had said nothing throughout the convention, in keeping with his role as presiding officer. Never for a moment did he drop the confident public pose that had helped make him such a hero, as he continued his Philadelphia routine of concerts, teas and ceremonial visits to places of local note. One Sunday, he rode to Germantown to inspect the farm of a celebrated horticulturist, holding the man's grandson on his knee and taking the infant in his arms.

But he was frustrated, angry, and looking for someone to blame for the course the convention had taken. He was beginning to believe he had made a mistake after all in coming; he was beginning to be sorry he had had anything to do with it.

It was time for the supporters of proportional representation to step back and ask themselves how much they really cared about that single issue. Did Virginia, Georgia and the Carolinas want a federal army to put down the Indians, or did they want to continue struggling along on their own? Did Massachusetts want another Shays' Rebellion? "Ye flame," William Samuel Johnson had warned, "might spread." Did they or did they not want to put an end to paper money? Would all the states soon become like Rhode

Island? Where would the "leveling spirit" stop? Were they or were they not helpless, pathetically helpless, in the face of Britain's trade wars, which, in a way, were as threatening to the country's prosperity as the real war had been? Were they proud of a nation that couldn't pay its debts to its own citizens, let alone to foreign governments?

Was proportional representation worth it?

Immediately after the tie vote, that very morning, the answer came. Suddenly, delegates even from the large states began to talk of compromise. Even Gouverneur Morris, even Randolph and young Pinckney. "I am extremely anxious that something should be done," said Pinckney, "considering this as the last appeal to a regular experiment. Congress have failed in almost every effort for an amendment of the federal system. Nothing has prevented a dissolution of it but the appointment of this convention."

Charles Cotesworth Pinckney of South Carolina now came forward: he proposed that a committee be appointed to "devise and report" a compromise.

Committees had certain advantages over conventions, chief among them being smallness and informality. In a committee, "a compromise would be pursued with more coolness," said Hugh Williamson of North Carolina.

"We are now at a full stop," declared Sherman, "and nobody . . . meant that we should break up without doing something. A committee I think most likely to hit on some expedient."

"When a broad table is to be made," said Franklin of Pennsylvania, "and the edges of the planks do not fit, the artist takes a little from both, and makes a good joint. In like manner here both sides must part with some of their demands, in order that they may join in some accommodating proposition."

Madison knew what this meant. His friends were losing their nerve; they were buckling. It was *his* "broad table" that Franklin was talking about, and he, for one, wanted no part of any "good joint." Madison and Wilson fought the committee proposal—but they fought it alone. The convention established the committee, and the two of them must have watched in disgust as its members were selected:

Martin of Maryland; Bedford, the hothead from Delaware; Yates, lieutenant of the antifederal Clintonians in New York; Paterson, spokesman for the New Jersey Plan; Ellsworth of Connecticut, chosen but "indisposed," and replaced by Sherman, the architect of the plan of equal representation in the Senate; Franklin of Pennsylvania, he of the good joint.

From Virginia, the convention selected not Madison or Randolph but, of all people, George Mason. Mason, of all the Virginians, was the least agreeable to Madison. A senior statesman before Madison even entered politics, Mason, sixty-two, had always gone his own way in Virginia, often to the consternation of his friends Jefferson and Madison and Washington. He had taken his own path at the convention as well, arguing against some of the fundamental principles of the Virginia Plan, though he was ostensibly one of its sponsors.

From Massachusetts came Gerry, calling for concessions from both sides, lamenting in convention that "instead of coming here like a band of brothers, belonging to the same family, we seemed to have brought with us the spirit of political negotiators."

From Georgia came Baldwin, the man responsible for the deadlock with his change of vote.

William Davie of North Carolina and John Rutledge of South Carolina completed the group.

Davie was not in favor of equal representation. But he had found a fatal contradiction in the idea of a Senate based on proportions. One conviction shared by virtually all the delegates was that the Senate should be small, an elite corps, so as to act as a check on the larger and more democratic house. Davie had done some arithmetic to determine how small a Senate based on proportional representation could possibly be. If the smallest state were to have one senator, the largest state, he calculated, would have about sixteen, the next largest fourteen or fifteen, and so on. The senate would be too big. There would be "ninety members in the outset," Davie guessed, "and the number will increase as new states are added." It would be "impossible" for "so numerous a body" to possess the qualities of a senate, he told the convention. His projection was overstated, but the point was made. It impressed even Wilson, who conceded "embarrassment" over the dilemma.

The makeup of the committee all but assured a compromise. The surest sign of this was that the men with the most extreme positions in the convention packed up and went home. Yates and Lansing, who would have been just as happy had the convention collapsed, returned to New York. Hamilton, equally offended, albeit for different reasons, took off to tend to his law practice. With Yates and Lansing gone, and with New York's requirement that three be present in its delegation, he had lost his franchise anyway.

He wrote to Washington from New York:

I have conversed with men of information not only of this City but from different parts of the state; and they agree that there has been an astonishing revolution for the better in the minds of the people. The prevailing apprehension among thinking men is, that the convention, from a fear of shocking the popular opinion, will not go far enough. They seem to be convinced that a strong well mounted government will better suit the popular palate than one of a different complexion. . . . I am seriously and deeply distressed [about the course of the convention, and] "fear that we shall let slip the golden opportunity of rescuing the American empire from disunion, anarchy and misery. . . . I shall of necessity remain here ten or twelve days; if I have reason to believe that my attendance at Philadelphia will not be mere waste of time, I shall after that period rejoin the convention.

The convention recessed for two days, to let the committee do its work and to let the others celebrate the Fourth of July, which began with the boom of artillery shells, thirteen rounds, one for each state. A military procession marched through town to martial music and the ringing of bells. Crowds gathered for ritual Independence Day orations. This year, eleven years after the signing of the Declaration, the speeches had a different theme.

James Campbell, speaking at the Reformed Calvinist Church, addressed himself directly to the convention, knowing that some of its delegates, including Washington, were listening in the audience: "Illustrious Senate! To you your country looks with anxious expectation, on your decisions she rests, convinced that men who cut the cords of foreign legislation are competent to framing a system of government which will embrace all interests, call forth our resources, and establish our credit. But in every plan for improvement or reformation, may an attachment to the principles of our present government be the characteristic of an American, and may every proposition to add kingly power to our federal system be regarded as treason to the liberties of our country."

"The American War is over," declared Benjamin Rush on this day. "But this is far from being the case with the American Revolution. On the contrary, nothing but the first act of the great drama is closed."

Other ideas for compromise had been mentioned during the convention, but in the committee only one was taken seriously: Sherman's proposal for proportional representation in the House and equal representation in the Senate.

The more the delegates had talked about it, the more sense Sherman's reasoning made. The country was partly federal, partly national. The scheme would assure, as Sherman put it, that "there must always be a majority of states *and* a majority of people on the side of public measures." That would restore confidence in the government, and confidence would induce obedience, which was so desperately lacking in the existing Confederation. The Sherman scheme would also give the states a power of self-defense, the power to preserve as much of their sovereignty as they could.

There was one problem: the large states had already adamantly rejected the Sherman scheme in the convention. To go back to their delegations with it now would look like a capitulation, not a compromise. Some new concession—something for the small states to give up in return—was needed to go with it, to allow the large-state delegates to save face, if nothing else.

Franklin had analyzed the situation. In his opinion, the real reason for opposition to equal representation was money, fear that the populous states, most of them also wealthier, would lose control over the taxing power and pay dearly for it. The large states needed some assurance.

To provide it, the committee revived an idea previously rejected by the full convention: let the lower house, with its proportional representation, have exclusive authority to propose "money bills." Let the upper house concur or reject but not amend them. The British Parliament and many of the states employed such a device, which appealed to purists because it centered the power of the purse in the house closer to the people.

There was more. The committee decided to create districts for the lower house that would provide one representative for every forty thousand persons. But who was a "person" for this purpose? This one was perilous. Counting all persons, including slaves, the five slaveholding Southern states were roughly equal in population to the eight Northern states and would have roughly equal power. Subtract the slaves in the South, however, and suddenly these same five states represented only one third of the nation's population.

By law and tradition in the South, slaves were property, bought and sold, no different from cattle and hogs. For purposes of maximizing Southern political power in the new Congress, however, the Southerners wanted the slaves counted as persons. For purposes of minimizing Southern power, the Northern states wanted the slaves ignored. The Confederation Congress had confronted this issue before, in another context, and had arrived at a compromise: each slave would be counted as three fifths of a person.

The committee incorporated the three-fifths formula for representation in the House. Every district would get one representative for each forty thousand residents, the number to be computed by counting free persons as one and slaves as three fifths of one.

Here was Franklin's "good joint." He moved acceptance of the compromise in the committee. The deal was made: proportional representation in the House; equal representation in the Senate; all matters of money to originate in the popularly elected House.

It was a package, each element conditioned on the other. Each side would be bound only insofar as the other side made good on its concessions. Should one part fail, all bets were off.

The committee returned to the floor and presented the package on July 5.

To Madison and Wilson, the money bill provision was a meaningless sop. Unacceptable. Instead, joined by Gouverneur Morris in a last desperate attempt to hold together their crumbling coalition, they resorted to their own legalisms and vituperation. Wilson, Madison and Morris, so cavalier about form and propriety when it came to the powers of the convention, were offended about the form and propriety of what the committee had done. It had exceeded its powers, Wilson charged. A shabby performance, said Morris, feigning shock and disbelief at the very idea of such wheeling and dealing. "[I] came here as a representative of America, . . . as a representative of the whole human race. . . . If I am to believe some things which I have heard, I should suppose that we were assembled to truck and bargain for our particular states. I cannot descend to think that any gentlemen are really actuated by these views."

The convention had enough posturing. As Morris spoke, the compromise was picking up support in two critical delegations, Massachusetts and North Carolina.

On the question of state equality, the Massachusetts delegation had held solid for a month and a half, but had shown signs of wavering when Gerry signaled a willingness to compromise just before the committee had gone behind closed doors to work out the deal.

Gerry was from a large state, but he was a states'-rights man at heart, fearing centralized government with a passion that was beginning to override his large-state loyalty. Gerry didn't think the money bill provision was much of a concession, either, but it gave him an excuse to go over the edge and support the compromise.

King and Gorham of Massachusetts held fast against the deal, which left, as the swing vote in the state's delegation, one Caleb Strong.

One of the marvelous features of the convention was how much difference obscure characters were making. Strong, like Martin and Baldwin, was a dwarf among giants, a man of some note at home but none at all beyond it. In the convention, he was overshadowed by the other delegates from Massachusetts and rarely spoke up. Strong had listened quietly for six weeks. He now believed that without some accommodation the convention and the Union would fall apart. To him, the money bill restriction was a considerable concession on the part of the small states. It was time now, he had decided, for some concessions on the other side.

Strong sided with Gerry in favor of the compromise. Massachusetts was now evenly divided, 2–2.

The change in North Carolina's attitude was a tribute to Franklin's sagacity. Money was indeed on that state's mind. The "chief thing" that concerned that state's delegation was not high republican theory or the sway of the state legislatures or even slavery. It was taxation. North Carolina, while expanding in population, was poorer than the others and had been less able than other states to furnish the Confederation with money when requisition time rolled around each year. Influence over tax legislation was of crucial importance to North Carolina, and the committee, by proposing to confine revenue bills to the House, appeared to have helped relieve the state's earlier reservations about proportional representation. The state had an immediate stake in a more powerful Union as well, for it was desperate about the Indian wars it confronted on its borders and needed help.

If the money bill provision passed, it indicated, it would support the deal.

North Carolina now quietly abandoned Madison's fold.

This wasn't supposed to be happening. Madison had been certain before the convention that the states would fall neatly into line according to their size and their anticipated size. Surely, the large states, and those expecting to be large, would see what was good for them and go along. Surely, the small states would bend. How confident he had been, and how wrong.

CHAPTER TEN

Power in the House

The compromise forced a major new issue to the floor. The tension between North and South was always just beneath the surface at the convention, submerged under the large-state/small-state imbroglio. It hadn't been necessary to get into it so far—everyone knew it would come soon enough. Just as predictable was the knowledge that when it did surface, Gouverneur Morris of Pennsylvania would have something to do with it.

As the population stood then, the Northeast tier of the country would easily outvote the South in the new House of Representatives. But no one expected this to last more than a few years, a decade at most. The Northeast was saturated with people, but, it was thought, the South would grow, and, of course, the West would expand dramatically. Because people believed that so many of the people heading west were Southerners, it was expected that the South and the new states of the West would someday strike up an alliance.

Morris and others from the maritime states were deeply alarmed by the prospect. The South and the Northeast were already locked in bitter struggle over the future of the Mississippi River. The Mississippi was then under the control of the Spanish, a situation which the South and the West aimed to change, for their future commercial prosperity depended on the river. The maritime interests along the Atlantic, on the other hand, were trying to trade away permanent control of the Mississippi to Spain, in exchange for a commercial treaty which would fill Spanish bellies with New England cod and help revive New England shipping in the Atlantic.

The North was in control now, and Morris had a plan to make sure it stayed that way. It was simple: Let the first Congress be apportioned proportionately, with all equally sized districts having one representative each. But thereafter, as population increased and as new states entered the Union, let Congress dole out seats in the House as it pleased. Let it not be bound by any formula or any requirement.

The scheme would lock in the balance of power as it existed in 1787. The compromise's provisions on the makeup of the House gave Morris his opportunity.

After the "Great Compromise" proposal hit the floor, Morris got the whole question of the apportionment of the House referred to yet another committee, this one with five members: Gorham, King, Rutledge, Randolph and, of course, Morris himself.

Dominated by Northerners, it quickly endorsed Morris' idea, recommending that the Constitution first fix a suitable allocation of seats in the House: thirty-one seats for the eight Northern states (New Hampshire, Massachusetts, Rhode Island, Connecticut, New York, New Jersey, Pennsylvania and Delaware) and twenty-five for the five Southern states.

Second, and more important, it proposed leaving Congress at liberty in the future to alter the allocation or not alter it as it pleased. Rather than automatically giving seats in Congress to districts as they grew and entered the Union, it would leave the congressmen free to freeze themselves in power, doling out seats to the new states only insofar as it was safe.

Morris' intentions were badly concealed. He and Gerry first

tried an appeal to mutual dread of the mob. The people going west, they said, were the same sorts of people stirring up trouble in western Massachusetts. They would be small farmers. Agrarian troublemakers. The same men who had brought paper money to the country. The mob was bad enough. Think of it multiplied, a hundred, a thousand times over, swarming over the interior, unruly, unenlightened. They would be a lower breed, Morris said, unsuited to wield power. "They would not be able to furnish men equally enlightened, to share in the administration of our common interests. . . . The busy haunts of men, not the remote wilderness, was the proper school of political talents.

"If the Western people get the power into their hands," he declared, "they will ruin the Atlantic interests."

"They will, if they acquire power like all men, abuse it," said Gerry. "They will oppress commerce, and drain our wealth into the Western country."

Wait a minute, Sherman interjected. "We are providing for our posterity, for our children and our grandchildren, who would be as likely to be citizens of new Western states as of the old states. On this consideration alone, we ought to make no such discrimination as is proposed by the motion."

"If some of our children should remove, others will stay behind," responded Gerry, "[and it is] incumbent on us to provide for their interests. There is a rage for emigration from the Eastern states to the Western country, and I do not wish those remaining behind to be at the mercy of the emigrants. Besides, foreigners are resorting to that country, and it is uncertain what turn things may take there."

"The best course that could be taken would be to leave the interests of the people to the representatives of the people," Morris said. Trust Congress. Trust me.

The Southerners saw the proposal for what it was. Not only did the Morris plan frustrate their partnership with the West, it removed the three-fifths provision (for the counting of slaves) from the representation scheme, further diluting Southern clout.

Trust Congress? If any of the Southerners had been of a mind to trust the North in the future, or to trust to events, here was the first good lesson.

The plan threatened the security of the South. What did that mean? The Mississippi was indeed at stake. But there was more.

"The security the Southern states want," Pierce Butler of South Carolina declared as the convention warmed to the subject, "is that their Negroes may not be taken from them—which some gentlemen within or without doors have a very good mind to do."

The Southerners rose in indignation.

"From the nature of man," George Mason said, "we may be sure that those who have power in their hands will not give it up while they can retain it. On the contrary, we know they will always, when they can, rather increase it. If the Southern states therefore should have three fourths of the people of America within their limits, the Northern will hold fast the majority of representatives. One fourth will govern the three fourths. The Southern states will complain: but they may complain from generation to generation without redress. Unless some principle therefore which will do justice to them hereafter shall be inserted in the Constitution, disagreeable as the declaration is to me, I must declare that I could neither vote for the system here nor support it in my state."

The principle now put forward by Randolph and by Williamson of North Carolina was this: Let there be a regular census of the number of inhabitants in each state and let Congress readjust the representation, force Congress to readjust it, accordingly (with the slaves counting at the three-fifths rate, of course).

The Morris plan, so blatant, so patently unfair, never had a chance. Even Gorham of Massachusetts deserted it before the debate was through, and it was defeated soundly.

In its place, the convention accepted the Randolph-Williamson plan—all but the three-fifths formula, that is.

There would be a census every ten years, the results of which would determine representation in the House.

* * *

The three-fifths formula for "representation" of blacks now moved to center stage.

There was nothing sacred about the three-fifths fraction, except that everyone was familiar with it as a compromise wrought in the year 1783, when the Confederation Congress was studying a tax-ing plan for the country based on population and wealth. In 1783 the Southerners argued that the slaves should be worth nothing in the count—since counting them would increase the slaveown-ers' taxes—while Northerners pushed for a full accounting. Now, in the convention, here were the Northerners claiming that the slaves were worth nothing, while the Southerners, seeing the slaves as a political asset, fought for their greater equality. Equal-ity, in this debate, had nothing to do with freedom. Neither side actually proposed allowing the slaves to vote or to actually be represented.

In fact, agreement on three fifths was never really in doubt. Three fifths it was. Three fifths it would stay.

Madison watched all this with great interest as he prepared for a last-ditch attempt to prevail on the final vote on the Great Compromise. The convention was no longer interested in his arguments about the injustice of state equality. His large-state bloc had crumbled.

But a new fissure, North versus South, had emerged, and now, as a final stab, he would try to exploit it.

On Saturday, July 14—with the final vote expected on Monday —Madison took the floor.

After repeating all his earlier arguments about the dangers of the Senate they were about to approve, he added one he had not used before: There were five states in the South and eight in the North, he said. The South might indeed someday control the lower house, but with an equal vote for each state in the Senate the North could control it forever.

It was obvious what he was getting at, but he made it explicit anyway: "It seems now to be pretty well understood that the real difference of interests lies not between the large and small but between the Northern and Southern states. The institution of slavery and its consequences form the line of discrimination."

Point made.

"So great is the unanimity we hear that prevails in the convention upon all great federal subjects," reported *The Pennsylvania Packet*, "that it has been proposed to call the room in which they assemble Unanimity Hall." The delegates must have gotten a laugh out of that as they gathered on Monday, the sixteenth, to vote on the compromise.

The secretary called the role from north to south:

Massachusetts: Divided, Gerry and Strong voting aye, King and Gorham no.

Connecticut: Aye.

New Jersey: Aye.

Pennsylvania: No.

Delaware: Aye.

Maryland: Aye.

Virginia: No.

North Carolina: Aye.

The rest was irrelevant. With New York, New Hampshire and Rhode Island absent, the compromisers had their majority. It was over.

The role call went on:

South Carolina: No.

Georgia: No.

The next morning, Madison and some other large-state delegates caucused privately, hoping for some new inspiration. But, as Madison, deeply frustrated, wrote of the session, "The time was wasted in vague conversation on the subject, without any specific proposition or agreement."

It was an enormous disappointment to Madison, and he was

still thinking about it more than a year later when, in the Federalist Papers, he alluded to what had happened. If one looked carefully at the Constitution, he wrote, there were a number of features suggesting there had been "difficulties" in the convention. He was not at liberty to disclose what they were, but "it shews that the Convention must have been compelled to sacrifice theoretical propriety to the force of extraneous considerations."

BOOK TWO

BUILDING A GOVERNMENT

CHAPTER ELEVEN

The House and the Senate

You had to admire Madison's spirit.

His Virginia Plan was an organism, with balance and symmetry. All of its parts were interdependent. Replace one part with another that didn't quite fit, and the whole would be thrown off. That was exactly what the convention had done to it on July 16 when it voted for equal suffrage in the Senate. In Madison's plan, the choice of the executive, the choice of the judges, the exercise of vast power over the nation, had belonged to a national legislature representing *people,* according to their number. The whole point, the whole point of the convention itself, should anyone care to remember, was to create a powerful national government by removing the states as agents in it. When the convention had changed the national legislature to include representation for the states as equals, it had made the states partners, almost a fourth branch of government. The convention had defaced Madison's canvas.

You had to admire his spirit because, like Hamilton, he might have stalked away leaving word to let him know when it was over. Madison was, after all, a purist.

But he was a politician too, and he understood that complete theoretical propriety could be obtained only in a plan formed in the imagination, as he would later concede in the Federalist Papers. If he hadn't understood this at the beginning of the convention, he understood it now.

Madison would now try to restore as much balance as he could, by a readjustment of the parts. Since the character of the national legislature had been changed dramatically, so must its weight in the scale of government be reduced.

He had to work fast.

On July 19, the original Madison proposal for election of the executive by the national legislature came up again. Now, in readjustment number one, Madison abandoned it. The executive, he declared, should not be appointed by the legislature, but by the people at large through a system of electors. ". . . if it be a fundamental principle of free government that the legislative, executive and judiciary powers should be separately exercised," said he, "it is equally so that they be independently exercised."

On July 21, the question of who would appoint members of the judiciary arose. Madison's Virginia Plan had given the power of appointing judges also to the national legislature. Now, in adjustment number two, he abandoned that approach in favor of a judiciary appointed by the executive.

But after all those long and hot days of struggle, the convention finally had a chance to regain its momentum, and Madison could not stop it.

The delegates, having been sold by him on the original scheme of government, refused to cooperate in revamping it. They raced past him, consolidating all the tentative decisions about the structure they had taken over the past six weeks into one; finally beginning in earnest the process of constructing a government for the United States.

The fundamentals were familiar: All governments should be divided into three parts, legislative, executive and judicial. To the extent possible, each part should be separate and distinct, each armed with a means of self-defense to keep itself so. And each of the parts should be in a position to check the excesses of the other.

Separation of powers. Checks and balances. These were the great principles of government, stated over and over again during the convention, not as matters of debate—they were beyond debate—but as incantation, as the "Received Wisdom," the standard to which all real government must measure up, the starting point.

So familiar was the construct, that one was inclined to overlook its beauty and how well it captured America's aspirations: the aspirations for order, on the one hand, and for liberty on the other; for an energetic government, but a government under control. The tension between these goals—maintaining and containing a powerful government at once—was keenly felt, and there were plenty who felt that inevitably one would be sacrificed for the other, that the two were irreconcilable. The beauty of the three-part, separated, checked and balanced government was that it could, in fact, reconcile the irreconcilable.

That was because the characteristics that made such a system effective also made it safe. Governments were divided into three parts—legislative, executive and judicial—because each would act as a check on the power of the other. But they were also divided into three parts because that was the best way to get things done. Energetic government required the effective performance of certain functions: the making, execution and interpretation of laws. Each of those functions could best be performed by institutions with certain characteristics: Lawmaking required a numerous body, a legislature large enough and varied enough to give voice to all interests. Execution of the laws required efficiency and dispatch and thus a smaller and more smoothly functioning branch, run by a few people, or perhaps just one. Interpretation of the laws, and careful judgment as to their constitutionality, required specialized knowledge, neutrality and thoughtful contemplation, the qualities associated with handpicked judges.

It was not only dangerous to combine these functions in one

branch, giving it a monopoly over power; it was also downright stupid. The existing Congress had amply demonstrated that when it tried to administer the affairs of the country as if it were an executive branch. Thirty or forty men in a room were simply incapable of running the day-to-day affairs of a government.

It was a fine balance: Separation was required, but too strict a separation might prevent one branch from checking the other. An executive's power to veto legislation, for example, directly involved him in the legislative function. But without the veto power he would be unable to exercise any control over the legislative branch.

The fundamentals had been handed down from European and English philosophers, especially Montesquieu. In Europe and Britain, the tripartite model of government had been also designed to guarantee representation for particular classes of society: the Crown, the nobility, the people. Those distinctions, and that rationale, had broken down in America, but not the form itself.

The delegates took these theories dead seriously. "Swallow up," "usurp," "destroy," "overwhelm," "encroach," "devour"—these words were among the favorites to describe what one branch of government might, if given the chance, do to another, or what the whole would do to the states, or the states to the whole. They had learned from experience.

They saw the various parts of government as armed camps and a properly designed Constitution as one equipped with devices to guarantee that none of them would overcome the others. "It may be a reflection on human nature," Madison wrote later in Federalist No. 51, "that such devices should be necessary to controul the abuses of government. But what is government itself but the greatest of all reflections on human nature? If men were angels, no government would be necessary. If angels were to govern men, neither external nor internal controuls on government would be necessary. In framing a government which is to be administered by men over men, the great difficulty lies in this:

You must first enable the government to controul the governed; and in the next place, oblige it to controul itself."

However useful the model of government was as an abstraction, it provided only the barest outline of how to construct a real government. Its goal was a kind of equilibrium among the branches, but in order to achieve it one had to make certain judgments about the relative weight and potential danger of each branch at any particular time.

At this particular time, in this particular room, the legislative branches, especially the lower houses, elected by the people, were perceived overwhelmingly as the truly dangerous branch.

The delegates had nothing against "the people" per se. One couldn't be against the people any more than one could be against children. The people were children, unable to distinguish right from wrong, easily led astray, like blind men.

Let the people choose the executive? It "would be as unnatural to refer the choice of a proper character for chief magistrate to the people, as it would to refer a trial of colors to a blind man," said Mason.

Let the people elect the national legislature? Never, said Gerry. "The evils we experience flow from the excesses of democracy. The people do not want virtue, but are the dupes of pretended patriots. In Massachusetts, it has been fully confirmed by experience that they are daily misled into the most baneful measures and opinions by the false reports circulated by designing men, and which no one on the spot can refute."

The people? The people, said Sherman, "should have as little to do as may be about the government. They want information and are constantly liable to be misled."

"If this convention had been chosen by the people," said John Rutledge of South Carolina, ". . . it is not to be supposed that such proper characters would have been preferred." The ultimate proof.

The best evidence of the poor judgment of the people was to

be found in the low caliber of the men they were electing to the state legislatures. And this problem was compounded by the fact that in the governments of the states the legislatures held so much sway. The consequences of this dangerous lack of structural balance were to be found everywhere. In Pennsylvania, a one-house assembly ran everything, with the unrestrained freedom to enact any law it pleased. It chose and removed Supreme Court justices, fully controlled the executive council of the state and appointed and removed all state officers. The measures carried out by the men who had control of this government sickened the delegates. The "radicals" or "constitutionalists," as supporters of Pennsylvania's government were called, forced people to take oaths of loyalty to the state constitution, to God and to Jesus as a requirement for office holding and voting. They forced similar oaths on all teachers at colleges and academies in the state. And, of course, they issued paper money.

In Virginia, Jefferson had complained while serving as governor in 1781, "all the power of government, legislative, executive and judiciary, result to the legislative body. The concentrating [of] these in the same hands is precisely the definition of despotic government. It will be no alleviation that these powers will be exercised by a plurality of hands. 173 despots would surely be as oppressive as one. . . . An elective despotism was not the government we fought for."

Rhode Island was by far the worst offender. As the convention began, the delegates read with outrage about how that state's legislature had summoned before it the judges who had invalidated a state law requiring acceptance of paper money as legal tender, demanded an explanation for their ruling and then ousted them from office.

Among the delegates to the convention of 1787, there weren't enough epithets in the language for Rhode Island, nor for any legislature favoring paper money, nor, for that matter, for any state legislature at all. It was all of a piece: the "turbulence and folly" of democracy; the "democratic licentiousness," the "unrighteous projects," the "pernicious measures," "the prejudices, passions and improper views" of the state legislatures.

"Can any man be safe in his house while the legislature are sitting?" William Blount had asked.

"What led to the appointment of this convention?" Mercer of Maryland asked at one point in the debates. "The corruption and mutability of the legislative councils of the states."

"Experience in all the states," Madison declared on the floor, "has evinced a powerful tendency in the legislature to absorb all power into its vortex. This is the real source of danger to the American Constitutions."

Madison, like most of the others in the room, believed nonetheless deeply in a government based on the consent of the people, *as long as the direct involvement of the people was strictly limited.* Early in his political career he had seen the ways of popular politics, and the experience made him uncomfortable. In Madison's Virginia, men got elected to office by plying the freeholders with bumbo—in the vernacular of the day. Rum punch was preferred, accompanied by cookies and ginger cake and occasionally a barbecued bullock or a hog. For one election, in 1758, George Washington supplied 160 gallons of liquor to 391 voters—one and a half quarts per voter.

That was the way it was done. Though good enough for the likes of Washington, Jefferson, Henry, Mason and the rest, to young Madison it was a "corrupting influence," inconsistent with the "purity of moral and republican principles." During his second run for the Virginia House of Delegates, in 1777, he decided to set an example. He refused to supply the bumbo.

Madison lost that election—to a tavernkeeper.

In Madison's Virginia Plan, the lower house of the national legislature was the only concession to the people of America—the only part of the government directly chosen by the people. The popular will would be filtered upward from the House as it chose the Senate and as the legislative branch, in turn, chose the executive and the judiciary. To be sure, this was the cornerstone of his plan; principles of republicanism required the continuing consent of the governed.

The House was to be "the grand depository of the democratic principle of the government," said Mason. "It is, so to speak, to be our House of Commons. It ought to know and sympathize with every part of the community. . . ."

It was to be the base of the "federal pyramid," said Wilson. "No government could long subsist without the confidence of the people."

Without a popularly elected house, said Madison, "the people would be lost sight of altogether, and the necessary sympathy between them and their rulers and officers too little felt."

But direct elections for the House were just as important as a device to provide the new government with a base independent of the states. As long as the state governments chose delegates to the Congress, they would remain in control of that Congress and of the acts of the national government.

Madison felt that direct elections would be safe because the districts from which representatives were to be elected would be very large, large enough to minimize the parochial and petty instincts of voters. The convention voted for popular elections in the House early in the convention, though not without a valiant effort later on to make them more palatable by restricting the vote —as did many of the states—to men who held a certain amount of property or wealth.

"Give the votes to people who have no property," said Gouverneur Morris, "and they will sell them to the rich who will be able to buy them. We should not confine our attention to the present moment. The time is not distant when this country will abound with mechanics and manufacturers who will receive their bread from their employers. Will such men be the secure and faithful guardians of liberty? Will they be the impregnable barrier against aristocracy? . . . The man who does not give his vote freely is not represented. It is the man who dictates his vote [who is represented]. Children do not vote. Why? Because they want prudence, because they have no will of their own. The ignorant and the dependent can be as little trusted with the public interest."

The debate on restricting the vote came on August 7, and it was reassuring: It showed that after all they had been through, mob or no mob, some could still put aside their fears and rise to the defense of the democratic principles; there was indeed a spark left in them.

"There is no right of which the people are more jealous than suffrage," proclaimed Pierce Butler of South Carolina.

"We all feel too strongly the remains of ancient prejudices, and view things too much through a British medium," said Mason. "A freehold is the qualification in England, and hence it is imagined to be the only proper one. . . . Every man having evidence of attachment to and permanent common interest with the society ought to share in all its rights and privileges."

"It is of great consequence that we should not depress the virtue and public spirit of our common people, of which they displayed a great deal during the war, and which contributed principally to the favorable issue of it," said Franklin.

But it wasn't Franklin's speech that dissuaded the convention from imposing a property qualification. It was the inability of the delegates to come up with a standard that would fit the whole diverse nation. If they weren't careful, they might wind up disqualifying one of their own, maybe even someone sitting in the room.

A two-year term for members of the House of Representatives was a compromise. One-year terms were preferred by some of the delegates, in part because voters were accustomed to annual elections for the lower houses of the state legislatures. Others, such as Hamilton, wanted longer terms. "There ought to be neither too much nor too little dependence on popular sentiments," he said.

Madison too favored elections every three years. "Instability is one of the great vices of our republics to be remedied," he said. "Three years will be necessary, in a government so extensive, for members to form any knowledge of the various interests of the states to which they do not belong, and of which they can know little from the situation and affairs of their own. One year will be almost consumed in preparing for and traveling to and from the seat of national business."

The House members, Madison said, "would have to travel seven or eight hundred miles from the distant parts of the Union; and would probably not be allowed even a reimbursement of their expenses. Besides, none of those who wished to be reelected would remain at the seat of government."

All the members of Congress would be paid out of the national treasury, as Madison had desired. This was no small matter, since financial dependence by the members of the Confederation Congress had been an effective tool of state control over the Congress itself. When it suited them, the state legislatures could and did cut off their congressmen, forcing them to abandon the Congress and deny it a quorum. Compensation from the national treasury was a major step toward national government.

If there was to be a House, by God, there better be a Senate to watch over it. The very thought of not having a Senate was ranked among "the wildest ideas of government in the world," as Gerry put it. "The democratic licentiousness of the state legislatures proved the necessity of a firm Senate," said Randolph. "The object of this second branch is to controul the democratic branch of the national legislature." Though four states had only one house, there was to be no debate in this room on the question of whether or not to have a senate. The House was necessary, the Senate essential.

The Senate of the state of Maryland served as the model because it had ridden to the rescue against the lower house and fought paper money. The Senate of Maryland, fifteen men with five-year terms, each member required to possess at least one thousand pounds in property, and elected by an electoral college composed of only the propertied, was the envy of all.

Franklin, who preferred unicameralism, knew better than to try to go against the tide.

The love of the Senate was to some extent remnant of days gone by. Once, in England, the divisions of government had reflected the divisions of society, and the upper house was seen as the guardian of the nobility, the landed. By British standards, there were no formal orders or society in America. But there was an aristocracy of the respectable, and the convention was it. If the House was to speak for the many, said Hamilton, the Senate would be the voice of the few—an elite corps of the most distinguished character.

Throughout the debate on the Senate, one got the idea that the delegates were talking about themselves, prompting Franklin to caution them not to make the job of senator too lucrative, for "we might be chargeable with having carved out places for ourselves."

The great task in building a senate was limiting admissions to it: keeping it small, keeping the wrong people out, letting the right people in and giving it stability.

The convention made the Senate older, and presumably wiser, by setting a minimum age of thirty for admission. The minimum age for the House was to be twenty-five.

The delegates gave it stability by giving senators a long term. The proposals ranged from three years to nine to service during good behavior, or life. The idea of eight- or nine-year terms brought out the delegates' continuing concern that long, uninterrupted residence at the seat of government would divorce representatives from their real constituencies back home. It also raised the specter of aristocracy.

The convention first settled on seven-year terms. But Randolph pointed out that continuity was critical in the Senate and that it would be undermined if all the senators' terms expired at the same time. The solution: Let the terms be staggered in such a way as to guarantee a continuing "corps" of senators at all times. Let no more than one third of them go out of office at one time.

Seven years being mathematically inconvenient, the choice

came down to nine or six, and the convention settled on six, with only one third of the senators facing reelection at the same time.

The senate was to be on a par with the executive, sharing in the making of foreign policy, war and peace and, until very near the end of the convention, appointing the members of the federal judiciary. This was as Madison originally intended it.

No one proposed direct popular elections for the Senate; this was not a body with which the people could be trusted. Election of the Senate would be left to the state legislatures. Out of this decision, yet another role for the Senate emerged, one never intended by Madison: the Senate as the voice of the states.

Madison had wanted to deny the states, as states, any formal voice in the government, but the majority of the convention believed that the states were entitled to their own share of power and to their own means of self-defense.

"Whatever power may be necessary for the national government," Mason had said, "a certain portion must necessarily be left with the States. It is impossible for one power to pervade the extreme parts of the United States so as to carry equal justice to them. The state legislatures, also, ought to have some means of defending themselves against encroachments of the national government. In every other department, we have studiously endeavored to provide for its self-defense. Shall we leave the states alone unprovided with the means for this purpose? And what better means can we provide than giving them some share in, or rather to make them a constituent part of, the National Establishment?"

To the House and the Senate combined, over Madison's belated objections, the convention gave the choice of the President and of the members of the Supreme Court.

Where did the executive and the judicial branches fit into all of this? They didn't. Not yet. All energy had been focused on the Congress, while the other two branches had received only intermittent attention, as if they were afterthoughts. In the plan as it stood in mid-August, the executive and the judiciary were mere creatures of Congress. Much remained to be done.

CHAPTER TWELVE

"Slaves to the Public"

The convention had been going seven hours a day, from 10 A.M. to 4 P.M., six days a week, for more than two full months. Each day the routine was the same. New Hampshire Delegate John Langdon, who finally arrived July 23, described it in a letter to a friend: "The Great Washington, with a Dignity peculiar to himself, [takes] the Chair, the Notables are Seated, in a moment and after a short Silence, the Business of the day is opened, with great solemnity and good order." Then would follow seven hours of declarations, declamations, animadversions and resolveds; the scratching sound of quills on paper; occasionally someone raising his voice to make a point; others droning on in two- or three-hour disquisitions.

At night and in the delegates' spare hours, the business continued unabated, for often the parties they held among themselves were mere extensions of the formal sessions at the State House. What they resolved in private, how many potential clauses were washed down with the Madeira, no delegate ever chose to say, but there is evidence that this convention within the convention was used to limit the agenda, rather than expand it.

William Samuel Johnson, for example, years later recounted how at one of these nighttime gatherings he had raised the idea of introducing a provision to help the future government deal properly with the status of territories acquired from foreign nations by treaty, conquest or purchase. Should these lands become states, and if so, how? Should they be treated as colonies?

> I then thought to mention the subject in the convention, but first, as was usual in every case, committed the matter to my colleagues. I stated the question to them in this manner. Suppose G.B. should make war upon us and in the course of such war we should conquer Nova Scotia and retain it at a peace. Could this territory be admitted into the union? They both answered without hesitation that it might be held and governed as a subordinate territory. Shall we make it a question before the convention as a subject for their deliberation? They both agreed it was a matter so obvious that it was not advisable to trouble the convention with it. However I made it a subject of conversation among all the little parties of the members for some time and I believe mentioned it on several committees but in no instance did I find any gentleman who thought there would be any grounds for such an admission . . .

One can only imagine the scene: eight or nine delegates together, chewing over Johnson's idea, deep into the night, around a long table, as the china was being cleared away and the after-dinner drinks were being served.

He never raised it in convention.

Similarly, Hamilton and Madison, during an afternoon's walk, decided between themselves not to raise the question of whether or not the new government should be required to assume the outstanding debts of the states. They decided that this would be better dealt with in the new Congress, so as to avoid controversy over small details when the Constitution went public.

State delegations held their own informal meetings too, preparing their own wish lists, as when the Marylanders, meeting privately, decided that to protect the future prosperity of Maryland ports the Constitution ought to include some guarantee that Congress could not favor one state's ports over another's, a guarantee which the convention ultimately provided.

The convention—so many important men in one place—was an irresistible target for petitioners and favor seekers of every stripe: from Manasseh Cutler, the wheeling and dealing preacher from New England who was trying to put together the biggest Western-land deal in America's history, to John Fitch, who was seeking official support for the steamboat he was developing, to a Cherokee Indian chief seeking justice, to a Philadelphian named Jonas Phillips appealing to the delegates on behalf of Jews to strike from Pennsylvania's constitution the required oath to Jesus and the New Testament.

Upon returning to their lonely rooms, they wrote letters home, some of them filled with woe.

"I have twice wrote to you," Richard Dobbs Spaight of North Carolina advised his Governor,

on the subject of receiving for me and remitting to me, two months salary which the deputies have wrote to the Governor to advance to them. I shall however rely upon your friendship in this instance, and depend upon the remittance being made by you. Indeed, if you do not undertake it I know not to Whom to apply. The time which I expected to stay here is already elapsed, and as I did not provide for a longer stay, my cash is already expended. Judge then my situation should I receive no further supplies.

"Our business is yet unfinished," wrote Ellsworth to his wife.

It yet remains uncertain when I shall return home—I am sure I wish for the time, for this city has no charms for me—I mix with company without enjoying it and am perfectly tired with flattery and forms—To be very fashionable we must be very trifling and make and receive a thousand professions, which everybody knows there is no truth in. Give me a little domestick circle where affection is natural and friendship sincere and I do not care who takes the rest.

They missed their wives and their families, and they were themselves missed, some sorely missed. The wife of William Samuel Johnson of Connecticut went into deep melancholy in her husband's absence. For the Johnsons, it was a second lengthy separation of the past year, since Johnson had previously been in New York in the Congress. The next thing she knew, he was on his way to Philadelphia for another long absence.

"It is hard for our dear mamma who has experienced so many misfortunes to be ever combating against the gloominess of her mind," wrote Johnson's daughter, Elizabeth Ver Plank. "In Papa's company she can ever support her spirits. . . . I wish I could look forward to the day when he would be free from being a slave to the public. It is, I think almost time for him to live for his family. . . ."

She wrote this at the beginning of the convention, in May. Then it seemed to go on and on. In July: "I am every day more persuaded that this separation of our worthy parents must continue no longer. . . . Mamma cannot support it."

Why didn't they bring their wives with them? Some did. Others, like Gerry, brought their families, only to send them away for fear of Philadelphia's unhealthy air. Gerry sent his wife and infant to New York, where the baby and the mother promptly took ill.

"You must be a very good girl," John Dickinson wrote to his young daughter.

You must be sure to say your prayers every Morning and every Night—and mind to Say them slowly and plainly, and think what you are doing. For, when you pray, you speak to the great and good God who made you, and keeps you alive, and feeds and clothes you. So you must love him a great deal more than you love Mamma and Sister and Papa. Do everything mamma bids you. Never go into the kitchen, when they are washing. Never go into the Piazza, without somebody to go with you, for fear one of the doors should be blown upon you and hurt you very much.

In May, delegates had trickled in. As early as June and July, they began trickling out.

For some, like Paterson, who went back to New Jersey, it was as if they were characters in a play. Having come onstage, uttered their important lines, they would now exit. Others, like James McClurg of Virginia, never had any lines, or had so few they felt useless and over their heads. "If I thought my return could contribute in the smallest degree . . . ," McClurg wrote from Richmond on August 5, "nothing should keep me away." No one disabused him. He never returned.

Tragedy intervened in the life of another Virginian, George Wythe, early in the convention. He had gone home to tend to his ailing wife, who soon died. He too did not return. Still others could no longer justify staying away from their livelihoods. Court sessions had begun, and the lawyers among them had to earn their livings.

Sleep. Up again in the morning. Yet another day of convention business. Out into the heat and the congestion described by Cutler in his journal: "The crowds of people seemed like the collection at the last day, for there was of every rank and condition in life, from the highest to the lowest, male and female, of every age and every color. Several of the market women who sold fruit, I observed, had their infants in their arms and their children about them, and there seemed to be some of every nation under Heaven."

And into the State House again, for more talk of nation building, and foundations, and cornerstones of this, that and the other institution of government. " . . . there is so much to be said about foundations, cornerstones and all the rest of the stones," Baldwin wrote on July 26, "that I expect we shall not have the raising for several days."

"I was never more sick of any thing than I am of convention-
eering," Gerry wrote home.

On July 26, the convention handed twenty-three resolutions
to a committee of five delegates, with the assignment of adding detail and providing coherence. The committee members were
Rutledge, Randolph, Gorham, Ellsworth and Wilson. The convention then recessed for eleven days. Some delegates went
home. Others went sightseeing. Washington journeyed from Philadelphia to nearby Valley Forge.

All were under strict instructions to return punctually on August 6. They were—for a moment at least—free at last.

CHAPTER THIRTEEN

"Essential Principles"

Copies of the Committee of Detail report were printed and circulated to the delegates when they reconvened at the State House on August 6. It looked important. They could handle it, feel it. For the first time, everything they had done was before them in one document. It *looked* like a constitution. It had a preamble: "We the People of the States of New-Hampshire, Massachusetts, Rhode Island . . . ," it said, listing all the states, "do ordain, declare and establish the following Constitution for the Government of Ourselves and Our Posterity."

The report for the first time enumerated the powers of the new government. Dry as it sounded, the enumeration expressed a vision of what a national government *ought* to be able to do, starting with what Randolph called "the soul" of the sovereignty, the taxing power.

"The Legislature of the United States shall have the power to lay and collect taxes, duties, imposts and excises." That alone was awesome. That single sentence could do more for the independence of the new government than perhaps any other part of the Constitution.

The legislature should also have the power, said the document:

To regulate commerce with foreign nations, and among the several states.

To establish an uniform rule of naturalization throughout the United States.

To coin money.

To regulate the value of foreign coin.

To fix the standard of weights and measures.

To establish Post-offices.

To borrow money and emit bills on the credit of the United States.

To appoint a Treasurer by ballot.

To constitute tribunals inferior to the Supreme Court.

To make rules concerning captures on land and water;

To declare the law and punishment of piracies and felonies committed on the high seas, and the punishment of counterfeiting the coin of the United States, and of offenses against the law of nations.

To subdue a rebellion in any State, on the application of its legislature.

To make war.

To raise armies.

To build and equip fleets.

To call forth the aid of the militia, in order to execute the laws of the Union, enforce treaties, suppress insurrections, and repel invasions.

And to make all laws that shall be necessary and proper for carrying into execution the foregoing powers, and all other powers vested, by this Constitution, in the government of the United States, or in any department or officer thereof.

The "necessary and proper" clause was potentially a blank check. Any law not otherwise prohibited was permissible if necessary to carry out any of the enumerated powers.

Some of the enumerated powers came straight out of the Articles of Confederation or from bills that had failed in the Confederation Congress. Some came from state constitutions, and some came from English law. Five of them had something to do with money; seven had to do with war and insurrection. The rest, and the totality, were concerned with uniformity and cooperation among the states.

Enumeration. To some, perhaps, it was reassuring, safer certainly than the previous vague and unlimited grant of authority the convention had been contemplating.

To many, enumeration meant that by listing some powers the committee foreclosed others; that authority ungranted was authority not possessed. It meant that the Congress should have these powers and no others.

On the other hand, it has also been interpreted to mean that the Congress alone should have these powers, and that no one else, not the other branches of government and not the states, should have them. It has been seen as a reinforcement of separation of powers.

The executive power as well was outlined for the first time in the report. That branch—as yet undeveloped by the convention —had possessed only the veto power over laws of Congress when it went into the committee. It came out considerably stronger: "He shall, from time to time, give information to the Legislature, of the state of the Union: he may recommend to their consideration such measures as he shall judge necessary, and expedient . . . ; he shall take care that the laws of the United States be duly and faithfully executed. . . . He shall be commander in chief of the Army and Navy of the United States. . . ." The wording was adapted from the constitution of the state of New York, which had the strongest chief executive in the country.

"The Executive Power of the United States shall be vested in a single person," the report went on. "His stile [sic] shall be, 'The President of the United States of America;' and his title shall be, 'His Excellency.' He shall be elected by ballot by the Legislature. He shall hold his office during the term of seven years; but shall not be elected a second time."

The Committee of Detail had done something extraordinarily important: it had divided the powers of government among the two branches with particularity.

The report was drafted with a certain vision of how a constitution should be interpreted. The committee had allowed in "essential principles only," in Randolph's words, "lest the operations of government should be clogged by rendering those provisions permanent and unalterable, which ought to be accommodated to times and events. . . ."

It took thirty-seven paragraphs of reading to get to the document's crowning commandment, the supremacy clause:

> The Acts of the Legislature of the United States made in pursuance of this Constitution, and all treaties made under authority of the United States shall be the supreme law of the several states, and of their citizens and inhabitants; and the judges in the several states shall be bound thereby in their decisions; anything in the Constitutions or laws of the several states to the contrary notwithstanding.

CHAPTER FOURTEEN

"National Sins"

In the summer of 1787 another convention took place in Philadelphia, the convention of the Pennsylvania Society for Promoting the Abolition of Slavery. The society, composed largely of
Quakers and headed now by Franklin, believed that the slave
trade, not paper money or the federal debt or the excesses of
democracy, was America's great weakness, for it exposed the nation to charges of hypocrisy: the words "all men are created
equal," crafted solemnly in this city just eleven years past, rang
hollow in the face of slavery. The abolitionists also believed that
slavery was the nation's greatest peril, for they foresaw a judgment
day, a great and awful day of retribution, when the country would
pay, and pay heavily, for this sin.

The presence of abolitionists in Philadelphia was one of the
things, along with the horseflies, that made Southern slaveholders
uncomfortable about coming there with their servants. Slaveholders complained that abolitionists enticed slaves away or absconded
with them. Slaves themselves, it was known, sometimes just got
the urge to run once they were in the City of Independence.

The papers offered rewards for their return, along with the notices for lost watches and clothing and white indentured servants.

> Forty Dollars Reward. Ran Away from the subscriber . . . a Negro fellow, named Tom, about 25 years of age, a well set fellow . . . much addicted to lying and can invent the most plausible account of himself. . . .
> Twenty Dollars Reward. Ran away from the subscriber . . . a Mulatto wench, named Chloe. . . . She is a stout, well-featured wench, nearly 22 years of age . . . a plausible, cunning hussy. . . .

Both ads appeared while the convention was in town. Invariably the return of a slave fetched a larger reward, two or three times larger, than the reward for a returned indentured servant. A slave was an investment for life.

Knowing that the other convention was assembling in the same city, the abolitionist decided in June to deliver to it their prophecy and their plea against the slave trade:

> To the revival of this trade The Society ascribe part of the Obloquy with which foreign Nations have branded our infant states. In vain will be their Pretentions to a love of liberty or regard for national Character, while they share in the profits of a Commerce that can only be conducted upon Rivers of human tears and Blood.
> By all the Attributes, therefore, of the Deity which are offended by this inhuman traffic—by the Union of our whole species in a common Ancestor and by all the Obligations which result from it —by the apprehensions and terror of the righteous Vengeance of God in national Judgements—by the certainty of the great and awful day of retribution—by the efficacy of the Prayers of good Men, which would only insult the majesty of Heaven, if offered up in behalf of our Country while the Inequity we deplore continues among us—by the santctity of the Christian name—by the Pleasures of domestic Connections and the pangs which attend their Dissolution—by the Captivity and Sufferings of our *American*

bretheren [sic] in Algiers which seem to be intended by divine
Providence to awaken us to a sense of the Injustice and Cruelty of
dooming our African Bretheren to perpetual Slavery and Misery—
by a regard to the Consistency of principles and Conduct which
should mark the Citizens of Republics—by the magnitude and
intensity of our desires to promote the happiness of those millions
of intelligent beings who will probably cover this immense Continent with national life—and by every other consideration that
religion Reason Policy and Humanity can suggest—The Society
implores the present Convention to make the Suppression of the
African trade in the United States, a part of their important deliberations.

The abolitionists' petition was supposed to be given to Franklin
for presentation to the convention. While a number of the delegates were indeed nominally abolitionists themselves, and others
had conscientiously pushed their own states into doing the right
thing with regard to the slave traffic, no one who understood
politics in 1787 seriously believed that the convention would, or
could, contemplate "the suppression of the African trade in the
United States."

Plus, of the fifty-five convention delegates, at least twenty-five
themselves owned slaves.

The abolitionist society didn't care. The members drew up their
petition and gave it to the society's secretary, Tench Coxe. He,
on the other hand, was apparently more the realist. Coxe gave
the petition to Franklin, all right, but in such a way as to make
sure it would never see the light of day again. Coxe later described
the event: "A very strong paper was drawn & put into my hands
to procure the signature of Dr. Franklin to be presented to the
federal convention. I enclosed to the Dr. with my opinion that it
would be a very improper season & place to hazard the Application considering it was an over zealous act of honest men."

Franklin must have agreed with him, for he said not a word in
the convention about the petition or about the "suppression of
the African trade."

The convention never considered it.

* * *

It did make the subject of slavery a part of its deliberations, but not in quite the form the society had hoped.

Just before the Committee of Detail retired to begin its work, Charles Cotesworth Pinckney of South Carolina had bluntly told the convention that if the committee should fail to insert some "security to the Southern states" with regard to slavery, he "should be bound by duty" to his state to vote against the report.

The Committee of Detail, in response, had brought back a special clause for the Deep South. The last eight words of the clause were the crucial ones: "No tax or duty shall be laid by the legislature on articles exported from any state; nor on the migration or importation of such persons as the several states shall think proper to admit; *nor shall such migration or importation be prohibited.*"

The provision would make the slave trade untouchable by the national government. Slavery would be purely the business of each state.

It brought home a truth about the convention, one already taught by the small states. The states wanted union, all right, but their support was always conditional.

Each would exact a price.

Ships entering Charleston harbor could see the mansion from the water, looming over the smaller shops and homes, as if to remind everyone who had clout in Charleston, should they not already know. A high flight of stone steps led to gleaming white columns, and into a paved entry hall. As described by one historian of Charleston, "the whole house was wainscotted in the heaviest panelling, the windows and doors with deep projecting pediments and mouldings in the style of Chamberlayne. The mantel pieces were very high and narrow, with fronts carved in processions of shepherds and shepherdesses, cupids, etc., and had square frames in the panelling above, to be filled with pictures."

The Pinckney mansion. The Home of Brigadier General

Charles Cotesworth Pinckney and a generation of Pinckneys before him; a monument to a handful of families—the Rutledges, the Middletons, the Butlers, the Pinckneys—who ruled South Carolina as an oligarchy.

Charleston, its dynasties, and the mansion itself had seen better days. The British had occupied the town and had ravaged it and the Pinckney mansion, which they used as a headquarters.

The period had been traumatic for everyone, especially for the Pinckneys: Charles Cotesworth and his cousin had been taken prisoner. Brother Thomas had been grievously wounded. The patriarch of the family, Charles Pinckney the elder, had made a deal with the British occupiers to save his own skin; vengeful state officials then slapped a punitive tax on the father to get even. Charles Cotesworth lost a son to smallpox, and the British would not allow him to attend the funeral; then his wife died of tuberculosis, leaving him with three daughters.

The state was rebuilding, and a union of the states could be helpful, opening up new markets for rice and indigo, providing defense not only from future invasions but from possible slave rebellions. Thus South Carolina's establishment had been ready and willing to attend the convention

There was another reason for this too, one shared with so many of the other states. The oligarchy of Charleston faced a threat from the men of the up-country, seeking a share of the power.

Much could be gained from a new republic, but much also could be lost. The state depended for its economic prosperity on slaves and the slave trade—its population of 140,000 whites used the labor of more than 100,000 blacks.

For its delegation, South Carolina's legislature chose men who it knew would understand this: Charles Cotesworth Pinckney; Charles Pinckney, twenty-nine, the cousin once removed of the General; Pierce Butler, a former British officer who had fought on the British side at Bunker Hill, then defected and married into a prominent Charleston family; and John Rutledge, so powerful in Revolutionary South Carolina he had been called the dictator of the state. They knew what would be acceptable back home and they knew what would not.

All the states had slaves at one point or another. But eight of them—the eight to the north—had so few in 1787 that slaves played a negligible role in their economies. Massachusetts and Pennsylvania had already taken steps toward emancipation.

In Maryland, Virginia, the two Carolinas and Georgia, slavery thrived: their populations were two-thirds free and one-third slave. But Maryland and Virginia were already overstocked with slaves and no longer needed the slave traffic.

Thus the clause protecting the slave trade would benefit only the deepest South.

The debate began late in the afternoon of Tuesday, August 21.

Luther Martin (who himself had a slave servant) rose. He had three points to make, and this time he did so succinctly.

The convention, he said, had previously approved the three-fifths formula, giving the South representation in the Congress for its slave population. Thus the South would have an incentive to continue the slave trade to enhance its political power.

Point two: Slavery, while confined to the South, was a burden on the entire country. Why? "Because slaves weaken one part of the Union which the other parts are bound to protect." He wasn't explicit, but everyone understood what he referred to: the prospect of slave insurrection, to which the armed forces of the entire Union would have to respond under the new Constitution.

The point was important. The Southerners claimed that slavery was a local matter. Not so, Martin was saying; it was a national concern.

Point three: "It is inconsistent with the principles of the Revolution and dishonorable to the American character to have such a feature in the Constitution."

Martin moved to allow either a tax on the importation of slaves, as a disincentive to the traffic, or outright prohibition of the trade.

It is difficult from written words alone to gauge the tone of the debate that followed on that day. But it leaves the impression of having been cold and hard and impersonal rather than heated and emotional. The South had known that this was coming. Its delegates were used to all the preaching about slavery.

Rutledge responded to Martin point by point.

First: "I do not see how the importation of slaves could be encouraged by this section."

Second: "I am not apprehensive of insurrections and would readily exempt the other states from the obligation to protect" the South against them.

Third: "Religion and humanity have nothing to do with this question. Interest alone is the governing principle with nations. The true question at present is whether the Southern states shall or shall not be parties to the Union. If the Northern states consult their interest, they will not oppose the increase of slaves. . . ." It would benefit the North too, he said, for it would enhance the agricultural output of the South, and the Northern shipping industry would become the carriers of those crops.

Ellsworth of Connecticut was next. Connecticut owed one to Georgia, or at least to Baldwin, who had split Georgia's vote and produced the deadlock on representation in the Senate. Connecticut's position on slavery might indeed have been a payback; but it was also consistent with the limited role the state's delegation saw for a national government.

"Let every state import what it pleases," said Ellsworth. "The morality and wisdom of slavery are considerations belonging to the states themselves. What enriches a part enriches the whole, and the states are the best judges of their particular interest. The old Confederation has not meddled with this point, and I do not see any greater necessity for bringing it within the policy of the new one."

Charles Pinckney: "South Carolina can never receive the plan if it prohibits the slave trade. In every proposed extension of the powers of Congress, that state has expressly and watchfully excepted that of meddling with the importation of Negroes. If the states be all left at liberty on this subject, South Carolina may perhaps by degrees do of herself what is wished [end the slave traffic], as Virginia and Maryland already have done."

It was late in the day. The convention recessed. The position of the Deep South was now on the table. It had three layers.

We all benefit from slavery, the South Carolinians were saying.

If you don't accept that, try this: It's a local matter, reserved for the states, none of anyone else's business.

If you don't accept either argument, here's the bottom line: Give us what we want or else.

The next day, Wednesday, August 27, Roger Sherman rose in support of Ellsworth. Of course, Sherman hastened to say, he disapproved of the slave trade. "Yet as the states are now possessed of the right to import slaves, as the public good does not require it to be taken from them, and as it is expedient to have as few objections as possible to the proposed scheme of government, I think it best to leave the matter as we find it. . . . The abolition of slavery seems to be going on in the United States, and . . . the good sense of the several states will probably by degrees complete it." Let the convention get done with this business, he said.

Virginia had been silent. For Washington, Madison, Mason and the others (including Jefferson, had he been there) this was a difficult moment, personally and politically. Slavery was the chink in their moral armor, the institution that made their crusade for individual liberty sound like hypocrisy. "Hypocrisy" was the wrong word. They actually believed what they said about slavery. They simply did not or could not act on it. Many of them had talked for years about manumitting their own slaves. It didn't happen. Here was a chance for a modest statement. What would it cost Virginia to oppose the clause? What would it cost Virginia if the slave traffic were prohibited? Very little.

Mason felt the dilemma deeply. His claim to fame was the Virginia Declaration of Rights and the words "All men are naturally equal." Yet he was among the largest, if not *the* largest, slaveholder in the room. His lavish estate on the Potomac, Gunston Hill, with its famous gardens, teemed with slaves: Bess, Nell, Hannah, Venus, Mima, Ann, Nell, Jenny, Vicky, Sarah, Rachel, Penny, Priss, Nan, Alice, Bob, Dunk, Dick, Bob, Peter, Judy, Lucy, Dick, Tom, Milly, Sampson, Cato, Sally, Joe, Cupid, Harry, Peg, Kack, Daphne and the rest. And Liberty.

Mason owned five thousand acres protected by a fence long enough to enclose virtually the entire city limits of Philadelphia. The estate included a spacious deer park studded with trees, an extensive lawn, a fabulous garden, a pasture, the mansion, a fine schoolhouse, stables, a boat landing, an orchard of fruit trees, a horse farm, a "little village" for the slaves, and four plantations. About five hundred people lived and worked at Gunston Hall, and it was totally self-sufficient.

On the morning of August 22, Mason broke Virginia's silence.

His opening words were the same old Virginia song: Blame it on the British. "This infernal traffic originated in the avarice of British merchants. The British government constantly checked the attempts of Virginia to put a stop to it."

Then his tone changed. Slavery was not simply a local matter, he declared. It concerned the whole Union. Slave insurrections had taken place in Greece and Sicily. So why not here? And contrary to what the South Carolinians were telling them, the trade would not go away of its own accord. "The Western people are already calling out for slaves for their new lands and will fill that country with slaves if they can be got through South Carolina and Georgia."

Here was Mason, a Southerner to his bones, taking on the South and its most cherished institution. "Slavery discourages arts and manufactures. The poor despise labor when performed by slaves. They prevent the immigration of whites, who really enrich and strengthen a country."

George Mason was a proud and imperious man, and what he said next, whether he planned to say it or whether it just came out, had to be painful. "Slaves produce the most pernicious effect on manners. Every master of slaves is born a petty tyrant. They bring the judgment of heaven on a country. As nations cannot be rewarded or punished in the next world, they must be in this. By an inevitable chain of causes and effects Providence punishes national sins by national calamities." It was time to give it up.

Mason's speech, part confession, part prophecy, was an irresistible target. It was one thing to hear it from Luther Martin; wholly another to hear a lecture on the morality of slavery from the largest slaveholder in the room.

Oliver Ellsworth had heard just about enough. "As I have never owned a slave," he replied to Mason, "I cannot judge of the effects of slavery on character. However, if it was to be considered in a moral light, we ought to go farther and free those already in the country."

Virginia and Maryland could afford to moralize, he went on. "Slaves multiply so fast in Virginia and Maryland that it is cheaper to raise than import them, whilst in the sickly rice swamps foreign supplies are necessary." If we strike the clause, Ellsworth said, "we shall be unjust towards South Carolina and Georgia. Let us not intermeddle. As population increases, poor laborers will be so plenty as to render slaves useless. Slavery in time will not be a speck in our country."

Mason's speech may or may not have pricked the consciences of other Northerners. It was always hard at the convention to determine motivation, to decide whether conscience or politics, both or neither, was at work at any particular time.

But one by one, as other delegates spoke, Mason's position picked up strength. They were beginning to understand that the slavery provisions could be seen as a blot on the Constitution.

Gerry: "We have nothing to do with the conduct of the states as to slaves, but ought to be careful not to give any sanction to it."

Dickinson: It is "inadmissible on every principle of honor and safety that the importation of slaves should be authorized to the states by the Constitution. The true question is whether the national happiness would be promoted or impeded by the importation, and this question ought to be left to the national government, not to the states particularly interested."

John Langdon of New Hampshire: "I could not with a good conscience leave it with the states, who could then go on with the traffic without being restrained by the opinions here given that they will themselves cease to import slaves."

Rutledge delivered the South's response. Only one thing mattered and it was this: "If the convention thinks that North Carolina, South Carolina and Georgia will ever agree to the plan, unless their right to import slaves be untouched, the expectation is in vain. The people of those states will never be such fools as to give up so important an interest."

Had a vote been taken at this point, it might have been close. On the other hand, how much, really, did the slave traffic matter to the Northern maritime states? As a matter of morality, maybe it did matter. As a matter of reality, probably not. What, after all, did Massachusetts or Connecticut have to lose by allowing the slave trade to continue? Was it worth risking the Constitution itself?

In that Committee of Detail report, however, there sat a clause that the maritime states truly loathed. It said: "No navigation act shall be passed without the assent of two thirds of the members present in each house." Navigation acts—laws requiring that all commodities be transported in ships belonging to a particular nation—were used by Britain to force Americans to ship their goods exclusively in British vessels. Americans hated navigation acts when applied to them. But when the acts were used by them, the potential gain for Northern shippers made New Englanders salivate.

For the same reason the shippers liked navigation acts, Southerners feared them, for they would allow the shippers to charge however much they pleased. In the Confederation Congress, "special majorities" of two thirds had been required for action on anything that really mattered. This mattered, and the committee had inserted the two-thirds requirement on behalf of the South.

The maritime states had other nits to pick with the committee report. All imports were to be taxable except one, the importation of slaves. This "inequality," said Rufus King, "could not fail to strike the commercial sagacity of the Northern and middle states."

Enter Gouverneur Morris. He had studied the Committee of Detail report carefully. The slave traffic. Import duties. Navigation acts. They were all on the floor now. Perhaps this could be settled with a deal. Let all of these provisions be referred to a committee, he suggested. "These things may form a bargain among the Northern and Southern states."

It was late August. Three long months had gone by. The delegates were exhausted, anxious to get it over with. There was so much yet to be done. The convention went along with the committee idea.

The members appointed were John Langdon of New Hampshire, Rufus King of Massachusetts, William Samuel Johnson of Connecticut, William Livingston of New Jersey, George Clymer of Pennsylvania, John Dickinson of Delaware, Luther Martin of Maryland, James Madison of Virginia, Hugh Williamson of North Carolina, Charles Cotesworth Pinckney of South Carolina and Abraham Baldwin of Georgia.

It was done in less than a day. Martin later described what happened in the committee.

> I found the eastern States, notwithstanding their aversion to slavery, were very willing to indulge the southern states, at least with a temporary liberty to prosecute the slave-trade, provided the southern States would, in their turn, gratify them, by laying no restriction on navigation acts; and after a very little time the committee, by a great majority, agreed on a report, by which the general government was to be prohibited from preventing the importation of slaves for a limited time [until 1800] and the restrictive clause relative to navigation acts was to be omitted.

The Southerners also quickly agreed that a duty could be levied on the slave traffic—provided it wasn't too high.

On Saturday, August 25, the convention considered the deal. Unlike the bargain which led to the Great Compromise, no grand conflict followed.

On every element, seven states—New Hampshire, Massachusetts, Connecticut, Maryland, North Carolina, South Carolina and Georgia—voted as one. For good measure, the year 1800 was changed to 1808, making it an even two decades before Congress could tamper with the slave trade.

There were a few protests.

Sherman and Madison objected to the duty to be allowed on slaves, as if they were a commodity. It would acknowledge in the Constitution of the United States of America that human beings were property.

This was the "price" of the rest of the deal, said King and Langdon.

On August 29, the younger Pinckney, feeling obstreperous, attempted to restore the special majority requirement for navigation acts, only to get a lecture from his elder cousin, the General, about the art of compromise.

Yes, said General Pinckney, it was true that it was in the interest of the Southern states to have no regulation of commerce. "But considering the loss brought on the commerce of the Eastern states by the revolution, their liberal conduct towards the views of South Carolina, and the interest the weak Southern states had in being united with the strong Eastern states, I think it proper that no fetters should be imposed on the power of making commercial regulations; and my constituents, though prejudiced against the Eastern states, will be reconciled to this liberality. I had myself prejudices against the Eastern states before I came here, but would acknowledge that I have found them as liberal and candid as any men whatever."

Pierce Butler agreed with the General. "I consider the interests of these [the Southern states] of the Eastern states to be as different as the interests of Russia and Turkey. Being, notwithstanding, desirous of conciliating the affections of the Eastern states, I would vote against requiring two thirds instead of a majority" for navigation acts.

On August 29, the special majority provision was stricken, without dissent.

Butler had one other motion on his mind: "If any person bound to service or labor in any of the United States shall escape into another State, he or she shall not be discharged from such service or labor, in consequence of any regulations subsisting in the state to which they escape, but shall be delivered up to the person justly claiming their service or labor."

This was the "fugitive-slave clause." It was an exact replica of a clause inserted into the recently enacted congressional ordinance which had provided for the opening of the West. It would eliminate "free" states as sanctuary, as refuge for runaway slaves, for men seeking their freedom.

It passed, without dissent.

Then the second part of the deal, removing slavery from the realm of national power, was agreed to, unanimously.

The business was done.

CHAPTER FIFTEEN

The Judiciary: A Quest
for "Purity"

In the Convention of 1787 there were dozens of imaginative phrases to describe the ghastly consequences of a legislative branch run wild or an executive branch turned despotic. But a search of the debates for comparable words about the third branch of government will be in vain, for the notion that judges could become dangerous seems not to have occurred to the delegates. The judiciary enjoyed a special dispensation.

This may explain why the judicial branch of the United States government emerged with so much authority, and with that authority so unchecked.

What had judges done to deserve all this respect? The better question was: What had the other branches done to lose it? Executives had been tarnished by the conduct of the royal governors in colonial days and by the specter of monarchy. Elected assemblies, once the great hope of America, were, in the eyes of many of the delegates, at that very moment betraying their trust.

The judges, on the other hand, were increasingly standing up to those legislatures, striking down laws for the first time in American history, as they did in Rhode Island and elsewhere. In Great Britain, said James Wilson, "the security of private rights is owing entirely to the purity of her tribunals of justice."

It happened with little debate and no drama. The convention spent week after week considering ways to control the other two branches; but the time consumed by the intermittent debates on the judiciary would fit into a single afternoon, and the quest was most often not for ways to control the judges, but for ways to protect them. It was a quest, as Wilson said, for purity.

The Supreme Court in Madison's Virginia Plan, while novel, was little more than a glorified referee for disputes among the states that involved "the national peace and harmony," controversies over federal taxation and cases implicating America's foreign relations—such as captures from enemies on the high seas and piracy.

In fact, the seed of the United States Supreme Court was planted on the high seas during the war. One day in 1777, the British sloop *Active*, bound for New York from Jamaica, appeared off Cape Charles carrying a cargo of rum, coffee and four captured American sailors, including Gideon Olmstead. In a stunning act of courage, the captured Americans seized control of the *Active*, driving the crew and its passengers below deck. Just then two ships appeared on the scene: the warship *Convention*, commissioned by the state of Pennsylvania, and the privateer *Gerard*. The *Convention* captured the *Active* while the *Gerard* stood guard.

The *Active* was hauled into Philadelphia to be sold. And that was when the real fighting began. Olmstead, the *Gerard* and the *Convention* became embroiled in the Admiralty Court of Pennsylvania in a battle over how the booty would be split. Ultimately, Olmstead lost. But he appealed to a special committee Congress had established to deal with the disposal of enemy vessels, which overturned the decision of the Pennsylvania court and awarded a larger share to Olmstead.

The reaction of the Pennsylvania court was predictable: It ignored the congressional ruling. In response, Congress created a new court, a Court of Appeals for Capture, the first United States court in history. Madison's Supreme Court was an extension of this early court of appeals, and, in its simplest form, it was approved and entrenched a few weeks into the convention.

His Virginia Plan idea for the lower federal courts was not so well received.

In the Virginia Plan, federal judges were to be Madison's army of national power, scattered throughout the land, guarding the Constitution and the laws against encroachments from the states. As there was no provision for a federal police force or a federal bureaucracy, the lower-court judges were to be the only agents of federal authority "dispersed throughout the Republic," as Madison put it, away from the seat of government.

The idea was shouted down. A Supreme Court was one thing; the notion of a phalanx of meddling federal judges was another, too much, especially for the Southerners.

"The people will not bear such innovations," said Pierce Butler of South Carolina. "The states will revolt at such an encroachment."

Too expensive, said Sherman.

On June 5, Madison's proposition creating the lower federal courts was laid to rest. Madison came forward with an alternative: rather than mandating the lower courts in the Constitution, he proposed a clause authorizing Congress to create them if it pleased. Safe enough, the compromise passed easily.

Nowhere in the Virginia Plan was the Supreme Court or a lower court granted authority to rule on the constitutionality of state or national law. Nowhere was there to be found a power of judicial review. The basis of that sweeping authority—authority that would make the Supreme Court the most powerful tribunal ever created—was constructed later in the convention, or, rather, it evolved, with a few strokes of the quill.

One of the fathers of the clause reinforcing the federal judiciary's power to strike down state laws—though he later pleaded ignorance about what he was doing—was none other than Luther Martin, the states'-rights booster.

Madison originally proposed a congressional veto over state laws that contravened the Constitution, an idea he had dreamed up back in the mountains of Virginia as a way to stop the states from riding roughshod over national policy and individual rights. Once the delegates realized the provision's implications, however, they buried it.

Even Gouverneur Morris objected. It "would disgust all the states," he said. Besides that, Madison's proposal was frightfully inefficient: How could the states function if implementation of their laws had to be delayed while they wended their way to the national seat of government to await the word of Congress?

Yet the delegates agreed that somebody had to enforce the Constitution against the states.

Enter Luther Martin. In July, Martin came up with a clever way to crush the supremacy movement once and for all, while making it appear that he was doing just the opposite. He would offer an alternative to Madison's proposal—but one so worded as to be harmless to the states. Martin's vehicle was the supremacy clause he had first written for inclusion in the Paterson plan. In July, he dusted it off and moved that the laws of Congress be made superior to all state laws. Missing once again was any wording making the state constitutions inferior to national law. A state could easily get around Martin's supremacy clause by amending its constitution. The loophole was big enough to drive a paper-money bill through.

The convention approved Martin's motion unanimously, and it was sent along with all the other resolutions to the Committee of Detail.

The Committee of Detail was full of lawyers, one of whom (it is not known just who) spotted the omission immediately and corrected it. When Martin's supremacy clause came out of the committee, a phrase specifying state constitutions was written in.

Federal law would be superior to "anything in the Constitutions or laws of the several states."

On August 23, the full convention approved the new wording without debate. Martin must have been out of the room or asleep, for there is no record of any protest from him. (He had had a rough month: he had been in and out of the convention attending to business and had been spotted by Gerry at one point dismounting from a horse in a state of near-collapse on account of the heat.)

After the convention, Martin took some abuse over the supremacy clause and became defensive about it. He explained that at the time the clause passed, he had assumed that it would be wielded primarily by state judges, and that the Constitution would be, from his viewpoint, safe in their hands. Martin's excuse—though it overlooked the Supreme Court—was plausible: the convention had indeed refused to create a lower federal judiciary.

The effect of the supremacy clause was to transfer the review of state laws from the Congress, where Madison had wanted it, to the judiciary.

The convention completed the power on August 27. The Committee of Detail had gone part of the way when it gave the Supreme Court jurisdiction to rule on "all cases arising under the laws" of the United States. It said nothing, however, about cases arising under the Constitution.

On the twenty-seventh, William Samuel Johnson of Connecticut—a lawyer who had served briefly as a judge—noticed the gap. Johnson moved the addition of three words. Instead of just saying that "the jurisdiction of the Supreme Court shall extend to all cases arising under the laws," Johnson proposed saying that it extended to "all cases arising under this Constitution and the laws."

These words resolved any doubt about who would ultimately enforce the supremacy clause against the states: the Supreme Court.

* * *

Those same words had even more powerful implications, and it is a wonder that they were approved with no debate whatsoever. If the Supreme Court was charged with reviewing "all cases arising" under the Constitution, that meant that it could review constitutional challenges to acts of Congress as well as acts of the state legislatures. And if the Court could review those acts, that meant it could invalidate them—exercising the power of judicial review.

Though some would challenge this power in years to come, long after John Marshall's 1803 opinion in Marbury v. Madison, there was no debate about it in the convention, for it was understood throughout that a primary role of the Supreme Court would be to keep the legislative branch within the boundaries of the Constitution. The delegates had discussed the subject earlier, when debating the Virginia Plan's proposal to combine the judges of the Supreme Court with the executive in a special Council of Revision to review the constitutionality of congressional acts. The convention defeated that proposal after several delegates pointed out that involving judges in such a review would prejudice them when the same laws came before them for judicial review. "As to the constitutionality of laws," Luther Martin had said during this debate, "that point will come before the judges in their proper official character. In this character they have a negative on the laws. Join them with the executive in the revision and they will have a double negative."

"A law violating a constitution established by the people themselves would be considered by the judges as null and void," Madison had declared on July 23.

No delegate challenged those words.

Judicial review was a novel concept in eighteenth-century America—only a few state courts had struck down legislative acts —but it was familiar to the delegates and was generally praised. Three of the delegates who were judges had endorsed the idea in state court opinions, the most eloquent of which was written by

Virginia Delegate George Wythe in a 1782 ruling voiding a Virginia law: "If the whole legislature . . . should attempt to overleap the bounds prescribed to them by the people, I, in administering the public justice of the country, will meet the united powers at my seat in this tribunal; and, pointing to the Constitution, will say to them, here is the limit of your authority, and hither shall you go, but no further."

The convention's allocation of authority to the Court was not only noncontroversial; it was taken for granted. The alternative would have been to leave the elected branches free to interpret the Constitution as they pleased, and among men so distressed by the excesses of democracy, by legislative attacks on property rights in particular, that would have been unthinkable.

As they debated the Constitution in Philadelphia, the delegates' convictions were being reinforced by what they were reading in the newspapers.

In September 1786, a cabinetmaker in Rhode Island named John Trevett went to John Weeden's butcher shop in Newport and handed him a wad of Rhode Island paper money in payment for meat. The currency, though issued only that spring, was already worth less than a third of its face value, and Weeden, who wanted real money, refused to take it. Trevett, invoking a state law requiring merchants to accept the money or be punished, took Weeden to court.

The judges, however, refused to enforce the law, declaring it invalid because it denied the accused the right to a jury trial. The Rhode Island legislature summoned the judges to "render their reasons for adjudging an Act of the General Assembly unconstitutional and so void." The following spring, as the Constitutional Convention began, the legislature punished the offending judges by declining to reappoint them.

The news traveled fast. To most of the delegates in the convention, there was no doubt about the propriety of what the Rhode Island judges had done. The state's legislature, on the other hand, was seen as "a full illustration of . . . the length to which a public body may carry wickedness and cabal," as Nathaniel Gorham said on the floor of the convention.

The Convention of 1787 was bound and determined to prevent such a travesty from taking place in the government it was designing.

The combination of the supremacy clause and the clause on jurisdiction meant that every line in the Constitution was subject to enforcement by the federal judiciary. Every word constituted an instruction to the Supreme Court, and the more instructions there were, the more formidable became the Court's arsenal and its responsibilities.

All the restrictions on the states devised by the convention thus became mandates to the Court. Among them: no state was to enter into treaties, alliances or confederations; no state was to pass any law "impairing the obligation of contracts"; no state, without the consent of Congress, was to lay duties on imports or exports, keep troops or warships or engage in war.

These things, the convention was saying, were the province of the national government. No longer might the states be nations.

And not to be forgotten was paper money. The convention decided with pleasure that the states should simply be barred from issuing it. Period. No state was to emit bills of credit or make anything but gold and silver coin a tender in payment of debts. Not only that, the convention removed from the draft constitution the authority of the national government to issue paper money.

Everyone got into this act.

"This is a favorable moment to shut and bar the door against paper money," said Ellsworth. "The mischiefs of the various experiments which have been made are now fresh in the public mind and have excited the disgust of all the respectable part of America. By withholding the power from the new government more friends of influence will be gained to it than by almost anything else."

"I think the words, if not struck out, would be as alarming as the mark of the Beast in Revelations," George Read piped up.

"I would rather reject the whole plan than retain the three words 'and emit bills,' " declared Langdon of New Hampshire.

"It will have a most salutary influence on the credit of the United States to remove the possibility of paper money," said Wilson. "This expedient can never succeed whilst its mischiefs are remembered. . . ."

Thus the power of the federal judiciary expanded, until by late August it had become the ultimate guardian of national power and of the Constitution, the only branch that no other branch could overrule.

The Court's authority was not unlimited. It was not to involve itself in policy-making, but was to confine itself to cases or controversies of a "judicial nature," as Madison put it. Nor was the judiciary endowed with a means of enforcing its decisions—an army or a police force. And while neither the executive nor the judicial branch could overrule the Supreme Court's constitutional decisions, the people—by amending the Constitution—could.

The convention was acutely aware that it was not enough to grant authority to judges. If judges were to be free to make decisions contrary to popular opinion, it would be necessary to insulate them from popular passion. Eighteenth-century judges had been whipped for their rulings by the Regulators in Georgia and beaten and terrorized by the Shaysites in Massachusetts. More gentle methods had been used in Pennsylvania, where legislators displeased with judges had cut their salaries to the bone, and in Rhode Island and elsewhere, where judges had simply been fired.

To protect federal judges and Supreme Court justices from political retribution, the delegates decided they should hold their offices during "good behavior," subject only to impeachment for high crimes and misdemeanors. And to protect them from financial retribution, the convention barred Congress from cutting the pay of sitting judges.

By the end of August, only one significant question about the judiciary remained unanswered: Who would appoint the judges?

Delegates said over and over again that this branch in particular should consist of the very best men. For that reason alone, no one thought judges should be elected. The choice came down to appointment by the executive or the Senate, and through the beginning of September the Senate it was.

CHAPTER SIXTEEN

" . . . we never once thought of a king."

Much speculation about what the delegates were up to appeared in the press throughout the convention, and it fell into several categories:

Wishful Thinking:

> We are informed that the Federal Convention, among other things, has resolved that Rhode Island should be considered as having virtually withdrawn herself from the Union. . . . It is proposed in the first case that for the proportion of the federal debt now due from Rhode Island, she shall be held, and if gentler means will not avail she shall be compelled to be responsible but upon no account shall she be restored to her station in the Union. [*Pennsylvania Herald*, June 8, 1787]

Covering All the Bases:

> We hear with great satisfaction that the convention for revising the confederation is now assembled and doing business at Philadel-

phia. Among the many important matters to be taken under consideration by that august body the following are said to be the
principal ones: 1st. That the Thirteen states be divided into three
distinct Republics, who ought to stick together for their common
defense as so many separate governments independent of each
other; 2ndly. If the Thirteen states remain as they are confeder-
ated, to lessen their sovereignty by abolishing their State Legislatures and leaving the whole laws to be made by the national
congress, assembly, or parliament; 3rdly. The Thirteen states to
remain as they are, except that their laws be revised by Congress
so as to make the whole act in conformity as of one, and the
executive powers of Congress enlarged. It is much to be wished
that the latter may be adopted. [*Georgia State Gazette*, July 21]

Understatement:

Nothing as yet has transpired. All that we know is that a committee is appointed to collect materials and to form a report for the
discussion of this respectable body. [*Pennsylvania Packet*, June 23]

The Truth:

Whatever measure may be recommended by the federal convention . . . it will in effect be a revolution in government, accomplished by reasoning and deliberation; an event that has never
occurred since the formation of society and which will be strongly
characteristic of the philosophic and tolerant spirit of the age.
[*Pennsylvania Herald*, June 20]

The delegates made no comment on any of these reports, in
keeping with their vow of secrecy. But they felt compelled to deny
one story, for they were anxious that it not be taken seriously.
On August 15, 1787, the delegates awoke to see hints in the
Philadelphia press that they were preparing to install a monarchy
and a monarch—Frederick, Duke of York and Albany, the second
son of George III of England. Frederick was the secular Prince-

Bishop of Osnabrück, a noble of little consequence in England and of even less in America.

One can only imagine them reading about it over breakfast, turning to one another and gasping. Was this someone's idea of a joke? Of all the impressions the convention was anxious to discourage, it was the idea that they were about to establish a monarchy for America.

The man most aroused by the story was Alexander Hamilton, who perhaps felt self-conscious about that speech he had given back in June suggesting a President for life. Hamilton launched an investigation and discovered that the rumor had been first circulated in Connecticut, whence it spread. As to the motive, the theories were various. Some said it was "fabricated to excite jealousy against the convention," to stir up opposition to its recommendations. Others said it was supposed to generate support for the convention, on the premise that whatever constitution emerged would look mild by contrast with the Osnabrück rumor. Yet another theory held that the story was a trial balloon floated by loyalist-monarchists, who had long talked of drafting Frederick for the American throne.

The British took it all quite seriously. "The report of an intention on the part of America to apply for a sovereign of the house of Hanover has been circulated here," said a confidential communiqué circulated at Whitehall, "and should an application of that nature be made, it will require a very nice consideration in what manner so important a subject should be treated."

In response to the spreading story, the convention on August 22 issued its first public statement about its proceedings. It appeared in *The Pennsylvania Journal:*

> We are informed, that many letters have been written to the members of the foederal convention from different quarters, respecting the reports idly circulating, that it is intended to establish a monarchical government, to send for the bishop of Osnaburgh, &c., &c.—to which it has been uniformly answered, tho' we

cannot affirmatively tell you what we are doing, we can, nega-
tively, tell you what we are not doing—we never once thought of
a king.

Talk of monarchy was indeed no laughing matter, not in 1787.

One day in the convention, James McHenry, a delegate from
Maryland, happened to glance over and notice that fellow Marylander John Francis Mercer was making out a little list. On it were
the names of all the delegates, with the words "for" or "against"
written after each one.

For and against what? McHenry asked him.

Those marked with a "for" were for a king, Mercer replied,
laughing.

McHenry asked how he knew they were for a king.

"No matter," said Mercer. "The thing is so."

McHenry copied down the list and promptly informed Luther
Martin that a considerable number of the delegates who would
never say so in public were secretly in favor of a monarchical
system of government. Martin also copied down the list. It later
became the subject of considerable controversy, with Mercer vehemently denying the story. There was a list, all right, he
claimed, but it had nothing to do with who was for or against
monarchy, but rather who was for or against national government.

CHAPTER SEVENTEEN

The Executive:
The Convention Confounded

It was true that at the time the Osnabrück story appeared, the convention had not decided on a king. But it hadn't come up with the alternative either. For months, it had been tied in knots over the executive.

Every delegate, it seemed, had a scheme to propose:

Three executives, each from a different part of the country.
An executive joined with a council.
A single executive with a life term.
A President, without a life term, chosen by the people.
A single executive, chosen by the Congress and eligible for reelection.
A single executive chosen by the Congress and ineligible for reelection.
An executive chosen by the governors of the states.
A President chosen by members of the Congress, to be drawn by lot, or chosen by the Congress the first time and by electors the second time, or chosen by electors all the time. Electors chosen by the state legislatures. Electors chosen by the people.

* * *

The debate on the length of the term sounded like bidding at an auction: three years; four years; six years; eleven years, eight years. Fifteen years.

"Twenty years," cracked Rufus King. "This is the medium life of princes."

And the delegates flipflopped half a dozen times on whether or not the executive should be eligible for a second term.

The presidency was confounding the convention. The subject was "in truth the most difficult of all we have had to decide," said James Wilson.

The convention was caught in two powerful and opposite currents.

The office it was to create could look nothing like a monarchy; the mere idea of a single executive officer was in some minds too close a resemblance. The executive could not remind Americans of the hated royal governors of the colonial era, in reaction to whom most of the states had reduced their governors to functionaries chosen and controlled by the state legislatures.

On the other hand, the delegates were equally disgusted by the behavior of the state legislatures and desperately felt the need for a counterweight.

One man in the convention, James Wilson, knew for certain what he wanted. The country could no longer be run by committees or anything resembling committees, and certainly not by a legislature or anyone controlled by a legislature, Wilson believed. It needed good management. There were laws to be executed, financial needs to be met, treaties to be negotiated, armies to be commanded, and officers to be appointed to do all of the above. Legislatures or multiple executives were simply unfit to do these things, for they required, as Wilson said, "energy, dispatch and responsibility." Only a single executive could meet these requirements.

And that single executive must be made strong and independent enough to stand up to the legislative branch. Let the legislature choose the executive, as so many desired, said Wilson, and "there would be a constant intrigue kept up for the appointment. The legislature and the candidates would bargain and play into one another's hands, votes would be given by the former under promises or expectations from the latter, of recompensing them by services to members of the legislature or to their friends."

The executive must be chosen by the people—directly or indirectly. For this would provide him with his own base of strength, and only then could he *"stand the mediator between the intrigues and sinister views of the representatives and the general liberties and interests of the people."*

Some men in the convention thought it was dangerous, the "foetus of monarchy," as Randolph said. Some thought it was unnecessary. Sherman said that he "considered the executive magistracy as nothing more than an institution for carrying the will of the legislature into effect," and that "the person or persons ought to be appointed by and accountable to the legislature only, which was the depositary of the supreme will of society."

Some, like Mason, thought Wilson's idea mobbish because it involved the people in the choice.

Wilson was ready with an answer to each.

Dangerous? Not if the President was given a short term, say three years. Not if he was impeachable. Not if his powers were limited. The only powers Wilson conceived to be "strictly executive were those of executing the laws, and appointing officers. . . ." Other powers, like the power of making war and peace, should be shared with the legislative branch. "Unity in the executive instead of being the fetus of monarchy would be the best *safeguard against tyranny,*" he declared.

Was it mobbish? Wilson did not insist on *direct* election of the President by the people. Instead, the people would choose "electors" who would, in turn, choose the President. The districts would be so large as to screen out the worst people, avoiding the dangers of the state legislatures, whose members were elected from

small districts. Because it was a national election, the choices of
candidates would be confined to "persons whose merits have general notoriety."

Wilson's views grew out of his experience. He had been inti-
mately involved in the congressional system of government by
committee. He had seen decisions held up or not made at all
because of petty personal quarrels; he had seen appointments to
offices embroiled in endless intrigue. Having worked side by side
with Robert Morris, who, as wartime financier, had been the
closest thing the Congress had ever had to a real executive, Wilson understood how effective the leadership of one skillful man
could be.

As Maryland was the model for the Senate, New York was
Wilson's model for the presidency. Wilson and his crowd didn't
much like New York's Governor Clinton, an archenemy of nationalism. But Clinton was powerful, and they respected that.
They attributed his power, in part, to the fact that he had a base
independent of the legislature—he was popularly elected to a
three-year term.

The problem was that few in the convention *fully* shared Wilson's views. Throughout most of the convention, the majority
favored an executive elected by the legislative branch—the
method with which they were most familiar. But with a tenacity
that rivaled Madison's, Wilson began pursuing his scheme in early
June, pounded away at it through July, and still clung to it firmly
in late August.

Throughout the debates, perhaps the best thing going for Wilson was the presence of Washington. Whether or not Washington thought that the job was meant for him as he listened to this
vision of the presidency, there is no doubt that others in the room
were thinking it. He was the only man in America who fit the
bill; the only man to whom the delegates would contemplate
entrusting such responsibility. The powers of the President
emerged "full great, greater than I was disposed to make them,"
Delegate Pierce Butler complained after the convention. "Nor,

Entre Nous, do I believe they would have been so great had not many of the members cast their eyes towards General Washington as President; and shaped their ideas of the powers to be given to a president, by their opinions of his virtue."

The most important break for Wilson came with the Great Compromise, which, ironically, he had opposed. For nearly two months, the large-state delegations had gone along content with a powerhouse Congress—a Congress that appointed the President, all ambassadors, the officers of government and the Supreme Court itself. When control of the Senate passed into the hands of the states voting equally, however, they began to see things differently, with Madison helping them along.

"It is essential," Madison declared, " . . . that the appointment of the executive should either be drawn from some source, or held by some tenure, that will give him a free agency with regard to the legislature."

Ideally, he said, he would prefer that "the people at large" choose the President. But he was concerned that if the people elected the President directly, by popular vote, the South would have too little influence in the election, since a vast proportion of the Southern population—slaves—couldn't vote.

The creation of an electoral college corresponding in numerical representation with the Congress itself would solve the problem, for it would incorporate into the presidential-selection process the three-fifths formula for counting slaves and thereby give the South more weight. Let each state choose as many electors as it had representatives and senators in the Congress, and let those electors choose the President.

A second factor playing into Wilson's hands was the long-running controversy over whether the President should be eligible for reelection. There were powerful arguments on both sides. Many feared that a President who was allowed a second or third term would spend all his time wheeling and dealing with the Congress in order to guarantee reelection. On the other hand, there was equal concern that a President who was confined to a single term would be unresponsive and have little incentive to do a good job. Worse, said Morris, it could tempt a man to continue in power by the sword.

Wilson delighted in the dilemma. There was a way to make both sides happy, he said. If the obstacle to allowing reelection was the potential for constant presidential intrigue with Congress, then simply remove Congress from the equation. "I perceive with pleasure that the idea is gaining ground of an election, mediately or immediately by the people," he said as he observed the confusion.

The third favorable event was not of Wilson's doing. It is not even clear that he immediately sensed the opportunity. On so many issues of the convention the small states had provided the decisive swing vote. On the presidency, they had swung consistently in favor of an executive chosen by the national legislature. But on August 24 something happened which changed some of their minds.

The convention on that date took up the mechanics of a congressional election for the presidency. How would it be done? If the Congress treated the election of the President as it was to treat legislation, each house would have a veto over the choice; the Senate and the House, voting separately, would have to agree on the same candidate. But if the President were chosen by a joint ballot, the combined voting strengths of each state's House and Senate delegations would determine the outcome, and the Senate, bastion of the states, would lose its veto power.

Between the two options, there was no doubt where the small states stood in the convention.

On August 24, Rutledge of South Carolina moved to have the President elected by a joint ballot of both houses. A chorus of protest from small-state delegates greeted the proposal, but the large states rammed it through. As a result, Connecticut and New Jersey defected from the ranks of those supporting election of the President by the Congress. Their move wasn't enough to sink the idea, but it broke its momentum. The presidency was in stale-mate.

Seven days later, Sherman moved to refer the presidency, and all other unfinished parts of the Constitution, to a committee, the Committee on Unfinished Business. The members were Gilman, Morris, Madison, Dickinson, King, Sherman, Brearley, Carroll, Williamson, Butler and Baldwin.

The committee met behind closed doors in the upstairs library of the State House, but one of its members, John Dickinson of Delaware, left his account of what happened.

Dickinson had missed the committee's early meetings and came in one morning after it had completed much of its work on the executive branch. When he entered, the members were on their feet preparing to present their recommendation to the full convention: election of the President by the Congress. Dickinson had opposed this all along. Having served as chief executive of both Pennsylvania and Delaware, he knew too well how dependent an executive could become on the legislative branch.

Dickinson asked to be heard. ". . . The powers which we had agreed to vest in the president are so many and so great," he said, "that I do not think the people would be willing to deposit them with him unless they themselves would be more immediately concerned in his election. If this single article should be rejected . . . , the whole would be lost, and the states would have the work to go over again under vast disadvantages. . . . The only true and safe principle on which these powers could be committed to an individual is that he should be in a strict sense of the expression *the man of the people.*"

Morris, according to Dickinson's recollection, needed no further prodding. "Come, gentlemen," Dickinson quotes him as saying, "let us sit down again and converse further on this subject."

They all sat down. After some discussion, Dickinson recalled, "James Madison took a pen and paper; and sketched out a mode for electing the president."

* * *

As a member of the Congress, Madison had become skilled in
the art of "baiting" legislation. Bait was what you inserted in an
otherwise unpalatable bill to make it palatable. Something that
would make Massachusetts or Virginia or the Carolinas bite where
otherwise it wouldn't.

The bait for the presidency:

For those in the convention anxious for the President to be
allowed reelection, the committee made him eligible without
limit.

For those worried about excessive dependence of the President
on the national legislature, the committee determined that electors chosen as each state saw fit would cast ballots for the presidency.

For the large states and the South, the committee decided that
the number of these electors would be proportioned according to
each state's combined representation in the House and the Senate, thus incorporating into the formula the three-fifths provision
so cherished by the Southerners and at the same time assuring the
large states the weight due them.

For the small states, the committee determined that when no
candidate won a majority of electoral votes, the Senate would
choose the President from among the leading contenders.

For those worried that the electors might form yet another
power-hungry, intrigue-ridden branch of government, the committee recommended that the electors from the different states
never be allowed to meet together in one place.

For those, like Wilson and now Madison, who believed that
the President should appoint judges and officers of the government, the committee took away the appointment power from the
Congress and gave it to the President—with the advice and consent of the Senate.

On September 4, the Committee on Unfinished Business presented the presidency to the convention. Most of the delegates
were satisfied, except for one small item: the provision allowing

the Senate the final word on who would be President. Many believed that the Senate was already too privileged; any greater role in the government than it already had would smack of aristocracy. The problem was easily resolved, for what mattered to the small states was not which house did the choosing, but how the votes would be counted.

On September 6, 1787, in its last important vote on the presidency, the convention agreed to let the House of Representatives pick the President from among the leading candidates submitted by the Electoral College—but with *each state having only one vote.*

The presidency was complete.

Why, it is fair to ask, did the small states finally agree? They and virtually everyone else in the convention assumed that once Washington was elected, the Electoral College would never again give a majority to one man sufficient to elect him President. They thus believed that Congress, with each state voting as an equal, would effectively decide the presidency.

Their prediction was flawed: Only twice in American history (in 1801 and 1825) has the presidency been decided in the Congress.

The whole affair was a stunning triumph for Madison.

On August 31, the legislative branch had gone into committee as the unquestioned powerhouse of the United States government, with exclusive authority to appoint the President, all his officers and ambassadors, and the Supreme Court. In six days' time, all those legislative prerogatives were gone.

Madison's plan was back in balance.

CHAPTER EIGHTEEN

The Disaffected

Those who knew Elbridge Gerry of Massachusetts probably could have predicted that he would sour on the convention, for he had a remarkable propensity to conjure up the worst and most extreme possibility in any idea.

Consider, for example, the clauses approved by the convention allowing the government to purchase and control land for forts and for a seat of government. To most in the convention, this was a necessity (all recalled Pennsylvania's refusal to protect the Congress in 1783) and a harmless one at that. To Gerry, these provisions would allow the government to go around buying up states and enslaving them. He opposed them vehemently.

On the other hand, some of his other worries were not so farfetched. The draft constitution provided that Congress could make any law it considered "necessary and proper" to carry out its responsibilities—any law it "pleased" to call necessary and proper, he said sarcastically. He understood its elasticity, and he disliked it. Gerry also wanted a ban on a standing army in peacetime, and the convention rejected that proposal as well.

Gerry had a deep aversion to big government—an aversion he shared with the average eighteenth-century American. But these men were not average Americans—and what he was beginning to realize as this government took shape was that it would be bigger than anything that had come before it in America.

By mid-August Gerry was alienated, and began spilling out his unhappiness in letters to his young wife.

[August 17] . . . Entre nous, I do not expect to give my voice to the measures.

[August 26] I am exceedingly distressed at the proceedings of the Convention being apprehensive and almost sure that they will if not altered materially lay the foundation of a civil war. This entre nous . . . had I known what would have happened, nothing would have induced me to come here.

[August 29] . . . I have been a spectator for some time; for I am very different in political principles from my colleagues. I am very well but sick of being here . . .

[September 1] I would not remain here two hours was I not under a necessity of staying to prevent my colleagues from saying that I broke up the representationn, and that they were averse to an arbitrary system of government; for such it is at present and such they must give their voice to unless it meets with considerable alterations.

[September, no date] I am pretty well myself, altho a little fatigued with a view of our present state. . . . I am determined to leave no stone unturned to prevent measures which if adopted will probably produce the most fatal consequences.

Fueling his anger was his belief that someone was opening his mail.

. . . There are a set of beings here capable of any kind of villainy to answer their purposes [he wrote to his wife]. . . . I think they need not open this letter, to know my opinion of them: but if that measure is necessary, they have my permission. I think they have intercepted some before and that a person who is a notorious turn-coat knows the contents. If he should open this he will know who I mean, by his interrogating me whether I had heard from a particular friend. I will seal with my Cypher in future.

In late August, Elbridge Gerry began to look for allies in his campaign "to leave no stone unturned."

Among those he approached was Luther Martin of Maryland, who by this time, according to McHenry, was going around outside the convention saying things like "I'll be hanged if ever the people of Maryland agree to it."

One day Martin said that to Jenifer, his fellow Marylander.

"I advise you," McHenry quotes Jenifer as replying, "to stay in Philadelphia lest you should be hanged."

George Mason also signed on.

Mason was one of the country's elder statesmen. Yet in the convention he had gotten little respect. His emotional speech about slavery had been dismissed as irrelevant and hypocritical. His beloved restriction on the origination of money bills had been twisting precariously for months, put in, taken out, dangled about as bait. And he was still burning about the Morris-engineered bargain that gave a simple majority in Congress the power to pass navigation acts, which, as a large tobacco grower and a Virginian, he loathed. This clause, he said, would deliver the South "bound hand and foot" to the "Eastern states."

For Mason, the presidency was the last straw. He wanted to create a six-member executive council, appointed by the Congress, to share executive power with the President. Many of the states, including Virginia, had such councils, which were like little senates. What the convention had now created, he said, was "an experiment on which the most despotic Governments had never ventured."

"I will bury my bones" in Philadelphia rather than go home without a constitution, Mason had declared early in the convention. Now, as September began, he declared to the delegates: "I would sooner chop off my right hand than put it to the Constitution as it now stands."

Then he joined Gerry and Martin's group. So did some others, though it is not certain who they were. Martin reported in a series of newspaper broadsides after the convention that delegates from New Jersey, Connecticut, Delaware, South Carolina and Georgia were among the little group of dissidents. All "considered the system, as then under consideration and likely to be adopted, extremely exceptionable and of a tendency to destroy the rights and liberties of the united states." They met together in the evenings as the end of the convention approached.

A dilemma remained for convention strategists: how best to breathe life into the Constitution; how best to have it ratified.

They knew there would be howls and they thought they knew where the howls would come from: the paper-money boys; state officers who would lose power; Patrick Henry in Virginia; Clinton in New York, who was already attacking it even before he knew what the Constitution would say.

Article XIII of the Articles of Confederation said explicitly that any amendment had to be approved by Congress and by each and every state: ". . . The articles of this confederation shall be inviolably observed by every state, and the union shall be perpetual; *nor shall any alteration at any time hereafter be made in any of them; unless such alterations be agreed to in a congress of the united states, and be afterwards confirmed by the legislatures of every state.*" The resolution of Congress calling for the convention in Philadelphia also said that any alteration must have the approval of Congress, as did the instructions of nine of the twelve states that sent delegates.

But the question was not what was strictly legal, but what would work.

Were they to seek approval by Congress and all the state legislatures, the chances were good they would lose. No one was so naive as to think that the state legislatures would happily surrender a large measure of their sovereignty, as the new Constitution required. Even if some did hand it over, even if a majority did, the odds against getting all of the legislatures to do so were slim. Rhode Island could wreck the entire Constitution. Besides, the delegates considered it essential that the Constitution be ratified by the people, by which they meant not a plebiscite but state ratifying conventions of delegates elected by the people. Any lesser sanction would leave it subordinate to the state constitutions, most of which *were* approved by the popularly elected conventions.

As the convention voted on a procedure for ratification, the charade that it was somehow just revising the Articles of Confederation formally ended.

Over the objections of Martin, and of a few others who wanted unanimous approval of the states, the delegates decided that ratification by conventions in nine states would be adequate to give effect to the Constitution. Nine was a familiar number: in the Confederation Congress, nine states were required to approve major acts.

They then decided that the document would only be "laid before" Congress, not actually voted up or down there.

The strategy: *Present* the document to Congress with an explanatory letter. Move it quickly, as quickly as possible, to the states, with a mandate that the legislatures organize elections for delegates to ratifying conventions. Get the Constitution's supporters home from Philadelphia. Fill the newspapers with pro-Constitution letters. Mobilize public opinion. The longer the process took, the greater the danger from the opposition.

At this point, in mid-September, the Gerry-Martin-Mason group began its last-ditch campaign, picking up allies where it could find them.

They demanded congressional approval of the document. What's more, some of them wanted to give the states an opportunity to offer up amendments to it before it took effect. And some of them wanted, God forbid, a second constitutional convention at which these amendments would be considered.

The battle began September 10. The convention had voted
once to bypass Congress; Gerry now moved to reconsider that
decision, saying he "objected to proceeding to change the government without the approbation of Congress, as being improper and
giving just umbrage to that body."

Then came a surprise.

Alexander Hamilton, the archnationalist, who had swept down
from New York for the grand finale after missing much of the
convention, stood up and said he "concurred with Mr. Gerry, as
to the indecorum of not requiring the approbation of Congress,"
adding, "I consider this a necessary ingredient in the transaction."

Hamilton had made no secret of his dislike for the plan. It
simply wasn't "high-toned" enough for him. But he had also said
grudgingly that he would support it. Surely he understood the
risks of sending the Constitution to Congress for its approval.
Perhaps he secretly hoped that the constitution would fail, the
crisis would intensify and the country would then see things more
his way.

Wilson sputtered. "It is necessary now to speak freely," he said.
If the Constitution went to Congress, it could die there. "After
spending four or five months in the laborious and arduous task of
forming a government for our country, we are ourselves at the
close throwing insuperable obstacles in the way of its success."

Wilson won this one: The dangerous Hamilton-Gerry idea was
defeated.

But then came another volley and another surprise.

Edmund Randolph, the man who had presented the Virginia
Plan, the very first delegate to address the convention in May,
took the floor. One by one, he ticked off his objections to the
system. The House of Representatives was too small; the "necessary and proper" clause was too general; there was no guard against
standing armies, no restraint on navigation acts; the Constitution
needed more definite boundaries between the national and state
legislatures, between the federal and state judiciaries. And more.

"With these difficulties in my mind, what course am I to pursue? Am I to promote the establishment of a plan which I verily believe will end in tyranny?"

The only way he would be satisfied, Randolph concluded, would be if the Constitution was submitted to Congress, then to the state legislatures, then to state conventions, for the approval of all; finally, the process must close with "another general convention with full power to adopt or reject the alterations proposed by the state conventions and to establish finally the government." He so moved.

First Hamilton. Now Randolph. Who next?

What was going through Madison's mind is unknown. His note-taking was becoming less and less complete. Perhaps, with the end so near, he was finally exhausted. Perhaps he was listening too hard to bother.

The convention waited to see who would second Randolph's motion. The voice that was heard was none other than Franklin's.

This was hard to explain. Most likely, it was Franklin's way of acting the conciliator. The one goal Franklin had worked for most diligently throughout the convention was consensus. Perhaps he hoped to force the convention into amendments which would placate Randolph and Mason and the others. Franklin himself offered no explanation, but immediately after he seconded Randolph, Mason, as if on cue, moved that the motion lie on the table "to see what steps might be taken with regard to the parts of the system objected to by Mr. Randolph."

No one expected the proposal for a second convention to pass, but its very emergence, and the sources from which it came, suggested that the Constitution might go forth to the world as the product of a divided convention. It would be hard to get the document ratified as it was. With such prominent men in opposition the danger loomed still larger.

A wholly new and remarkable phase of the convention now began. In an effort to appease the doubters, the convention reopened debate on virtually every article and, in the course of ten days, ranged across the entire Constitution, rehashing dozens of issues that had been thought settled or nearly settled. It became a free-for-all in which everyone who had any complaint joined.

The convention had decided earlier that a three-fourths vote of the Congress would be necessary to override a presidential veto. Randolph, Gerry, Mason and Pinckney, among others, objected on the grounds that this fraction was too large. The President would make deals with a few members of Congress and no veto would ever be overriden. Morris, Hamilton and Madison (and in one of his few recorded votes, Washington) opposed reducing the fraction, but the convention agreed to lower the figure to two thirds.

The provision concerning impeachment of the President, as it stood, allowed removal only for treason or bribery. That was not sufficient, said Mason. "Treason . . . will not reach many great and dangerous offenses. . . . Attempts to subvert the Constitution may not be treason. . . ." He suggested allowing impeachment for "maladministration," but after being convinced that that was too vague he substituted language permitting impeachment for treason, bribery and "other high crimes and misdemeanors." It passed.

The pardon power, as it stood, gave the President authority to pardon anyone for any offense against the United States. Randolph thought that too broad. The President, he said, should not have the authority to pardon people convicted of treason. "The President may himself be guilty. The traitors may be his own instruments." Mason supported Randolph's motion to narrow the pardon power, but the convention defeated it.

The provisions concerning amendments to the Constitution had been little discussed, but they were critically important because a single amendment could radically alter the form of government or wipe out any provision of state law. The clause was vague: "On the application of the Legislatures of two-thirds of the States in the Union, for an amendment of the Constitution, the Legislature of the United States shall call a convention for that purpose." It didn't say what would happen then. What sort of convention would it be?

Gerry complained bitterly. The clause, without more, permitted a majority of the states meeting in convention to gang up and "subvert" any state constitution.

Hamilton had a different objection. The provision allowed *only* the states to initiate the amendment process. Would they not use it to enhance their own power against the national government? Shouldn't Congress be involved?

Madison too was concerned. How was a convention to be formed? he asked. What would be its rules?

Madison proposed allowing two routes for amendment: Let two thirds of both houses of Congress offer amendments; *or* let two thirds of the legislatures of the states apply to Congress for amendments. In either case, the amendments would be ratified by three fourths of the state legislatures or by conventions in three fourths of the states, the choice being left to Congress. Madison's substitute passed.

Mason was dissatisfied. Nothing in Madison's proposal forced Congress to respond to the application of the states for an amendment. Where the provision had originally given too much authority to the states, now it gave sole discretion to Congress. Suppose, he said, that the government "should become oppressive, as I verily believe will be the case. . . . No amendments of the proper kind" could ever be obtained by the people on their own.

In response, Gerry and Morris, on September 15, proposed that on the application of two thirds of the states Congress be *required* to call a convention to amend the Constitution.

Madison, though uneasy about amending conventions ("Difficulties might arise," he said) agreed, and the Gerry-Morris provision passed:

> The Congress, whenever two-thirds of both Houses shall deem it necessary, shall propose Amendments to this Constitution, or, on the Application of the Legislatures of two-thirds of the several

States, shall call a convention for proposing amendments, which, in either case, shall be valid . . . when ratified by the Legislatures of three-fourths of the several States, or by Conventions in three-fourths thereof, as the one or the other Mode of Ratification may be proposed by the Congress. . . .

The debate over the amendment process gave the jitters to the Southerners and the small-state delegates, for it reminded them that their hard-fought victories in the convention could be wiped out by constitutional amendments. At their urging, the convention added two qualifying provisions to the Constitution:

No state, without its consent, could be deprived of equal suffrage in the Senate.

No amendment prior to 1808 could change the slavery clauses of the Constitution.

Of all the proposals that failed during this period, one stood out above all the others.

Seven of the states had bills of rights protecting fundamental liberties from government infringement: declarations guaranteeing the right to a trial by jury and to freedom of speech, of the press, of religion. Bills of rights were often breached, sometimes in the same documents in which they were proclaimed, but they stood nonetheless as powerful symbols.

The convention had already included some of these protections in the document:

The privilege of the Writ of Habeas Corpus shall not be suspended, unless when in Cases of Rebellion or Invasion the public Safety may require it.

No Bill of Attainder or ex post facto Law shall be passed. . . .

No State shall . . . pass any . . . Law impairing the Obligation of Contracts. . . .

The trial of all Crimes, except in Cases of Impeachment, shall be by jury. . . ."

. . . no religious Test shall ever be required as a Qualification to any Office or public Trust under the United States.

But the provisions fell far short of some of the state declarations, and Mason, Gerry and Charles Pinckney wanted to go further.

On September 12, Mason rose. "I wish that the plan had been prefaced with a bill of rights, and would second a motion if made for the purpose. It would give great quiet to the people, and with the aid of the state declarations, a bill might be prepared in a few hours."

Gerry moved that a committee be appointed to draft a bill of rights, and Mason seconded it.

The debate was brief.

Sherman declared that since the state declarations of rights were not repealed by the Constitution, they would protect the people. The Congress, he said, perhaps with a side glance at Mason, "may be safely trusted."

When the roll of the states was called, not a single state voted to have a bill of rights.

Two days later, Gerry and Pinckney proposed adding to the Constitution a declaration "that the liberty of the press should be inviolably preserved." If they couldn't get a bill of rights, they would settle for one right.

Sherman again answered. "It is unnecessary. The power of Congress does not extend to the press."

On the roll call, only one state voted aye: Maryland.

Madison, Hamilton, Wilson and others later defended the convention's refusal to incorporate a bill of rights in the Constitution. It was indeed unnecessary, they said, because without the explicit authority to meddle with people's rights Congress was already restrained from doing so.

It didn't wash with Jefferson. When he heard that the convention had failed to include a bill of rights, he was furious. He wrote to Madison from Paris: ". . . A bill of rights is what the people are entitled to against every government on earth, general or particular, and what no just government should refuse or rest on inference."

CHAPTER NINETEEN

"We the People"

On September 9 the convention appointed a committee to start arranging the twenty-three articles of the Constitution in a coherent form, to give it style and grace. The five members were William Samuel Johnson, Alexander Hamilton, Gouverneur Morris, James Madison and Rufus King, among the most gifted writers in the convention. All were lawyers as well, and experienced legislative draftsmen with an appreciation for the significance of a well-placed comma or semicolon.

Hamilton's election to this committee, considering his long absences from the convention, was testimony to the respect the delegates had for him. The choice of Morris, who did most of the actual writing in the committee, was an act of reckless faith.

The delegates were confident that they would catch any sleight of hand, and when the committee finished, on September 12, the convention went over the rewritten constitution line by line. Except for one semicolon that had found its way into a strategic location, everything looked fine.

The committee distilled the twenty-three articles to seven,

197

each more or less covering a different subject: Article I, the Congress and its powers; Article II, the executive and its powers; Article III, the judiciary; Article IV, provisions assuring tranquility in relations among the states; Article V, the amendment process; Article VI, miscellaneous, including the supremacy clause; and Article VII, the provisions on ratification, which were still up in the air at this late date.

Some slight changes in wording gave parts of the Constitution a new grandeur and force:

The supremacy clause went into the committee flat: the Constitution and acts of Congress "shall be the supreme law of the several States, and of their citizens and inhabitants." When it came out, it said that the Constitution and the laws "shall be the supreme Law of the Land."

The beginning of Article II, concerning the presidency, went in like this: "The executive power of the United States shall be vested in a single person. His stile [sic] shall be, 'The President of the United States of America;' and his title shall be, 'His Excellency.' " It came out this way: "The executive Power shall be vested in a President of the United States of America." The committee dropped "His Excellency" entirely.

Article I, as rewritten, finally gave Congress the name "the Congress." Throughout the convention, perhaps because of an understandable desire to forget about the Confederation Congress, the usage had been "the national legislature." The phrase "the legislative power shall be vested in a Congress" became "All legislative Powers herein granted shall be vested in a Congress of the United States." "All legislative powers" emphasized the separation of powers, a no-trespass sign in the Constitution.

The committee struck out what was, in effect, a ban on women serving in the Congress which had survived most of the convention unnoticed. As it went into the style committee, the clause read like this: "The legislative power shall be vested in a Congress to consist of two separate and distinct bodies of men, a House of Representatives and a Senate." It came out: "All legislative powers herein granted shall be vested in a Congress of the United States, which shall consist of a Senate and a House of Representatives." There is no evidence that the delegates had suddenly become concerned about the rights of women. It was still taken for granted that women were out.

Had Morris not tried at least one trick, he wouldn't have been Morris. The style committee inserted a semicolon that, had it remained, would have made a difference. The sentence went into the committee this way: "They [Congress] shall have the power . . . to lay and collect taxes duties imposts and excises, to pay the debts and provide for the common defence & general welfare, of the United States." It meant that the taxes collected were to be *for the purpose of* paying the debts and providing for the common defense and general welfare. The semicolon found its home between the words "excises" and "to pay." It came out this way: "The Congress shall have Power To lay and collect Taxes, Duties, Imposts and Excises; to pay the Debts and provide for the common Defence and general Welfare of the United States. . . ." Now it looked like yet another power being granted, the power to provide for the general welfare—a nice catch-all for Morris and Hamilton, perhaps sufficient to justify a government bank.

Somebody (reportedly Sherman) caught this one, and had the semicolon removed.

The preamble was changed, too. It went into the style committee declaring: "WE . . . the People of the States of New-Hampshire, Massachusetts, Rhode-Island and Providence Plantations, Connecticut, New-York, New Jersey, Pennsylvania, Delaware, Maryland, Virginia, North-Carolina, South-Carolina, and Georgia, do ordain and declare and establish the following Constitution for the Government of Ourselves and our Posterity."

It came out gloriously:

WE THE PEOPLE OF THE UNITED STATES, in Order to form a more perfect Union, establish Justice, insure domestic Tranquility, provide for the common defence, promote the general Welfare, and secure the Blessings of Liberty to ourselves and our Posterity, do ordain and establish this CONSTITUTION for the United States of America.

On September 15, at 6 P.M., the question before the convention, finally, was "to agree to the entire Constitution," all of it. Madison recorded the result in his notes: "All the states ay."

Accompanying the Constitution, and presented to the delegates along with it by the style committee, was a five-paragraph letter for the Congress. You couldn't just drop something like this on it. The delegates had been so long isolated from the world that some explanation was necessary, as if to say, "Are you sitting down? Before you go any further, let us explain what happened." The letter said:

We have now the honor to submit to the consideration of the United States in Congress assembled, that Constitution which has appeared to us the most adviseable.

The friends of our country have long seen and desired, that the power of making war, peace and treaties, that of levying money and regulating commerce, and the correspondent executive and judicial authorities should be fully and effectually vested in the general government of the Union; but the impropriety of delegating such extensive trust to one body of men is evident—Hence results the necessity of a different organization.

It is obviously impracticable in the foederal [sic] government of these States to secure all rights of independent sovereignty to each, and yet provide for the interest and safety of all—Individuals entering into society must give up a share of liberty to preserve the rest. The magnitude of the sacrifice must depend as well on situation and circumstance, as on the object to be obtained. It is at all times difficult to draw with precision the line between those rights which must be surrendered, and those which may be reserved; and on the present occasion this difficulty was increased by a difference among the several States as to their situation, extent, habits, and particular interests.

In all our deliberations on this subject we kept steadily in our view, that which appears to us the greatest interest of every true American, the consolidation of our Union, in which is involved our prosperity, felicity, safety, perhaps our national existence. This important consideration, seriously and deeply impressed on our minds, led each State in the Convention to be less rigid on points of inferior magnitude, than might have been otherwise expected; and thus the Constitution, which we now present, is the result of a spirit of amity, and of that mutual deference and concession which the peculiarity of our political situation rendered indispensible.

That it will meet the full and entire approbation of every State is not perhaps to be expected; but each will doubtless consider, that had her interest alone been consulted, the consequences might have been particularly disagreeable or injurious to others; that it is liable to as few exceptions as could reasonably have been expected, we hope and believe; that it may promote the lasting welfare of that country so dear to us all, and secure her freedom and happiness, is our most ardent wish.

The convention had one more problem. Gerry, Randolph and Mason would not endorse the Constitution. Others, like William Blount of North Carolina, maybe even Franklin and Hamilton, had reservations. If signing the document meant fully endorsing it, many simply could not sign.

A Constitution sent forth into the world from a divided convention would handicap it from the beginning. Some device was necessary that would make the convention appear unanimous, even though it wasn't.

Morris came up with the idea. Ask no one to actually endorse the document by his signature. Rather, have the delegates sign a carefully worded statement attesting to the undeniable fact that the *states present* were unanimous in their final consent to the Constitution. This would allow delegates to sign even though they personally might disapprove of the Constitution or some provisions of it. It would merely be a statement of fact. Let them be witnesses to unanimity.

Morris prepared the statement: "Done in Convention by the Unanimous Consent of the States present the Seventeenth Day of September in the Year of our Lord one thousand seven hundred and Eighty seven and of the Independence of the United States of America the Twelfth. In Witness whereof We have hereunto subscribed our Names."

Each person would then be asked to sign.

This deliberately ambiguous form lacked the majesty of the Declaration of Independence. In that, the delegates had signed a statement pledging their lives, their fortunes and their sacred honor in support of independence.

No matter.

To make the Morris proposal more acceptable, Franklin, rather than Morris, would suggest it on the floor.

Monday morning. September 17, 1787. It was as cold and overcast as it had been in May, when it all began.

Wilson read Franklin's speech for him:

"Mr. President:

"I confess that there are several parts of this Constitution which I do not at present approve, but I am not sure I shall never approve them: For having lived long, I have experienced many instances of being obliged by better information, or fuller consideration, to change opinions even on important subjects, which I once thought right, but found to be otherwise. It is therefore that the older I grow, the more apt I am to doubt my own judgement, and to pay more respect to the judgement of others. Most men indeed as well as most sects in Religion, think themselves in possession of all truth, and that wherever others differ from them it is so far error. Steele a Protestant in a Dedication tells the Pope that the only difference between our Churches in their opinions of the certainty of their doctrines is, the Church of Rome is infallible and the Church of England is never in the wrong. But though many private persons think almost as highly of their own infallibility as that of their sect, few express it so naturally as a certain French lady, who in a dispute with her sister, said 'I don't know how it happens, Sister, but I meet with no body but myself that's always in the right—Il n'y a que moi qui a toujours raison.'

"In these sentiments, Sir, I agree to this Constitution with all its faults, if they are such; because I think a general Government necessary for us, and there is no form of Government but what may be a blessing to the people if well administered, and believe farther that this is likely to be well administered for a course of years, and can only end in Despotism, as other forms have done before it, when the people shall become as corrupted as to need despotic Government, being incapable of any other. I doubt too whether any other Convention we can obtain, may be able to make a better Constitution. For when you assemble a number of men to have the advantage of their joint wisdom, you inevitably assemble with those men, all their prejudices, their passions, their errors of opinion, their local interests, and their selfish views. From such an assembly can a perfect production be expected? It therefore astonishes me, Sir, to find this system approaching so near to perfection as it does; and I think it will astonish our enemies, who are waiting with confidence to hear that our councils are confounded like those of the Builders of Babel; and that our States are on the point of separation, only to meet hereafter for the purpose of cutting one another's throats. Thus I consent, Sir, to this Constitution because I expect no better, and because I am not sure that it is not the best. The opinions I have had of its errors, I sacrifice to the public good. I have never whispered a syllable of them abroad. Within these walls they were born, and here they shall die. If every one of us in returning to our Constituents were to report the objections he has had to it, and endeavor to gain partisans in support of them, we might prevent its being generally received, and thereby lose all the salutary effects and great advantages resulting naturally in our favor among foreign Nations as well as among ourselves, from our real or apparent unanimity. Much of the strength & efficiency of any Government in procuring and securing happiness to the people, depends on opinion, on the general opinion of the goodness of the Government, as well as of the wisdom and integrity of its Governors. I hope therefore that for our own sakes as a part of the people, and for the sake of posterity, we shall act heartily and unanimously in recommending this Constitution wherever our influence may extend, and turn our future thoughts & endeavors to the means of having it well administered.

"On the whole, Sir, I can not help expressing a wish that every member of the Convention who may still have objections to it, would with me, on this occasion doubt a little of his own infallibility, and, *to make manifest our unanimity*, put his name to this instrument." [Italics added.]

The speech was plainly aimed at the dissidents. Please sign, Franklin was saying. And whether you like the Constitution or not, for God's sake don't go home and work against it. Above all, do not reveal what went on in this room.

The next unexpected bit of business also appeared aimed at the dissidents. A number of delegates had complained about the small size of the future House of Representatives, due to the ratio that would provide one representative for every forty thousand people.

Before anyone could respond to Franklin's speech, Gorham said he had yet another amendment—a final amendment—to the body of the Constitution itself, an amendment which might conciliate dissidents and convince them to sign. If it was not too late, Gorham said, he would propose, "for the purpose of lessening objections to the Constitution," that the ratio of representation in the House of Representatives be changed to make the body larger. Would the convention change it from one representative for every forty thousand people to one for every thirty thousand?

King and Carroll seconded the idea.

Then, for the first time in the convention, George Washington rose to speak.

"My situation," he said, "has hitherto restrained me from offering my sentiments on questions depending in the house, and, it might be thought, ought now to impose silence on me. Yet I cannot forbear expressing my wish that the alteration proposed might take place. It is much to be desired that the objections to the plan recommended might be made as few as possible. The smallness of the proportion of representatives has been considered by many members of the convention an insufficient security for the rights and interests of the people."

Without debate, the change was agreed to unanimously. The Constitution was complete.

Franklin's speech, the form of the signing, the final amendment, Washington's endorsement of it, all were aimed at winning over the signatures of the waverers.

Randolph took the floor. He understood what Dr. Franklin was saying, Randolph said. But he, Randolph, could not sign. "I do not mean by this refusal to decide that I should oppose the Constitution without doors. I mean only to keep myself free to be governed by my duty as it should be prescribed by my future judgment."

In short, Randolph wanted to keep his options open.

"I too have objections," said Gouverneur Morris, "but considering the present plan as the best that was to be attained, I will take it with all its faults. . . . The moment this plan goes forth all other considerations will be laid aside, and the great question will be, shall there be a national government or not? And this must take place or a general anarchy will be the alternative."

Besides, said Morris, signing in the form proposed related only to the fact that the *states* present were unanimous.

Hamilton was next. "Every member should sign. A few characters of consequence, by opposing or even refusing to sign the Constitution, might do infinite mischief by kindling the latent sparks which lurk under an enthusiasm in favor of the convention, which may soon subside. No man's ideas are more remote from the plan than mine are known to be; but is it possible to deliberate between anarchy and convulsion on one side and the chance of good to be expected from the plan on the other?"

Blount was convinced. He would offer himself up as an example to the others. "I have declared that I would not sign, so as to pledge myself in support of the plan, but I am relieved by the form proposed and will, without committing myself, attest the fact that the plan was the unanimous act of the states in convention."

The Morris-Franklin approach had won a signature.

Franklin decided to make one final plea to Randolph. "I have a high sense of obligation to Mr. Randolph for having brought forward the plan in the first instance, and for the assistance he had given in its progress, and I hope he will yet lay aside his objections and, by concurring with his brethren, prevent the great mischief which the refusal of his name might produce."

Franklin had the gentlest way of turning a screw. This whole thing was your idea, he was saying to Randolph. You got us into this in the first place. You pleaded with us to go along. We did. And now you have the temerity to withhold your name?

The pressure was on Randolph.

"I cannot but regard the signing in the proposed form as the same with signing the Constitution," he said. The "change of form therefore could make no difference with me. In refusing to sign the Constitution, I take a step which might be the most awful of my life, but it is dictated by my conscience, and it is not possible for me to hesitate, much less to change."

Randolph was holding out. So was Gerry. Despite this, the convention agreed to the signing in the form proposed by Franklin and Morris, and those who would sign prepared now to do so.

One by one, thirty-eight members walked to the front of the room to sign the Constitution. Washington put his name at the top, as President. Then, in geographical order, starting with New Hampshire, all those willing to sign did so.

Gerry, Randolph and Mason were the only ones present who withheld their signatures.

While they were signing, Franklin made an observation to a few delegates sitting near him regarding the President's chair, which had a sun painted in gilt on the headrest. How difficult painters found it in their work to properly render the distinction between a rising and a setting sun, he said. "I have often and often in the course of the session, and the vicissitudes of my hopes and fears as to its issue, looked at that behind the president without being able to tell whether it was rising or setting. But now at length I have the happiness to know that it is a rising and not a setting sun."

"Well, Doctor, what have we got? A republic or a monarchy?" someone asked Franklin in the summer of 1787.

Franklin responded, "A republic, if you can keep it."

CHAPTER TWENTY

Ratification and the Bill of Rights: "The Happiest Turn"

The unveiling of the Constitution set off history's greatest popular debate on government.

From America's largest cities to her smallest backwaters, exuberant election campaigns began for seats in the ratifying conventions. Thousands of people got involved, this time farmers, innkeepers and artisans as well as lawyers and merchants and politicians. A new pseudonymous army took over the nation's newspapers, filling them with arguments pro and con ranging in length from a few terse paragraphs to forty- and fifty-part treatises on government. Agrippa, Brutus, Centinel, Cato, the Landholder, the Plain Dealer and Publius became household names. Luther Martin's bitter tract against the convention ran for two full months in *The Maryland Gazette*.

The most eloquent of the written defenses was the series of essays now known as *The Federalist,* by Hamilton, Madison and John Jay, which ran in New York newspapers from October 1787 to May 1788. The most brilliant spoken words in defense of the Constitution came from James Wilson, who held forth day after day in the Pennsylvania ratifying convention, responding to every challenge in a masterful lawyerly style.

George Mason and Patrick Henry in Virginia, Elbridge Gerry in Massachusetts, George Clinton and Robert Lansing in New York, Abraham Clark in New Jersey, all were among the opponents of the Constitution. Edmund Randolph, after months of wavering, ultimately gave his support.

There were numerous criticisms: the executive was too powerful; the Congress, too weak; the "necessary and proper" clause was too broad; the Senate, too aristocratic; the slavery clauses were immoral; the scheme itself was a consolidation, rather than a federalization; the convention itself, improper and illegal.

The omission of a bill of rights sparked the loudest protest of all, and was the single greatest asset of the Constitution's opponents. In February 1788, Thomas Jefferson wrote that if he were in America, rather than in France, he would do something about it. "I would advocate it [the Constitution] warmly till nine [states] should have adopted, & then as warmly take the other side to convince the remaining four that they ought not to come into it till the declaration of rights is annexed to it. By this means we should secure all the good of it, & procure so respectable an opposition as would induce the accepting states to offer a bill of rights. This would be the happiest turn the thing could take."

Six state conventions ratified the Constitution swiftly, within five months of the adjournment of the convention. They were:

Delaware: December 7, 1787; 30 votes for, none against.
Pennsylvania: December 12, 1787; 46–23.
New Jersey: December 18, 1787; 39–0.
Georgia: January 2, 1788; 26–0.
Connecticut: January 9, 1788; 128–40.
Massachusetts: February 16, 1788; 187–168.

After February, Jefferson's views circulated widely and lent support to a movement already under way to make the addition of a bill of rights a condition of ratification. In early 1788, with seven of the states yet to ratify, state conventions began proposing actual amendments to protect the rights and liberties of the people. The pressure mounting, Madison and other influential Federalists agreed to make the addition of a bill of rights one of the first orders of business in the new Congress.

Nevertheless, the remaining ratifications came painfully slowly. On June 21, when New Hampshire put the total over the top by becoming the ninth ratifying state, the tension only mounted, for Virginia and New York had not held their conventions and no government could begin without them.

The Virginia convention was the most spirited, with Madison, Mason, Henry, Richard Henry Lee, John Marshall and others replaying all the debates of the Constitutional Convention itself —without the presence of Washington, who waited at Mount Vernon for the result. The battle lasted from June 4 to June 25, when the Constitution was ratified by a vote of 89 to 79.

New York's convention had hung in the balance until news of the Virginia vote reached it. Realizing that the state could not now remain out of the Union, the convention ratified the Constitution on July 26 by a vote of 30–27.

Two states, North Carolina and Rhode Island, had not ratified the Constitution when the first United States Congress was organized in April 1789. North Carolina's first ratifying convention, in August 1788, had rejected the Constitution by a vote of 193–75, largely because of agrarian discontent with the provisions banning paper money and because of unhappiness with the absence of a bill of rights. A second convention was held after the Bill of Rights was passed by Congress, and on November 21, 1789, North Carolina formally entered the Union.

In Rhode Island, the people voted overwhelmingly in March 1788 not to hold a ratifying convention at all. In March 1790, long after the United States government was in place, the state finally held a convention—and rejected the Constitution. Not until May 1790 did a second Rhode Island convention approve it, bringing all the states into the Union.

* * *

Benjamin Franklin died at his home in Philadelphia on April 17, 1790. He was eighty-four.

George Washington was elected the first President of the United States and served two terms in office. He died on December 14, 1799, at Mount Vernon.

Alexander Hamilton became Secretary of the Treasury in the first Washington administration and the focus of enormous intrigue and controversy before his resignation from the Cabinet in 1795. By that time, Jefferson and Madison hated him. Hamilton died on July 12, 1804, from wounds suffered in a duel with Aaron Burr the day before.

James Madison was elected to the first U.S. House of Representatives after an unsuccessful run for the Senate. In the House, he steered to final passage the first ten amendments to the Constitution—the Bill of Rights. In 1794, at age forty-three, he married Dolley Payne Todd, a twenty-six-year-old widow. When Jefferson was elected President in 1801, Madison joined his Cabinet as Secretary of State. In 1809, Madison became the fourth President of the United States, later leading America through the disastrous War of 1812 and serving two terms before retiring to Montpelier. He died there at the age of eighty-five on June 28, 1836.

Gouverneur Morris served as Washington's minister to France, where he participated in an aborted scheme to rescue King Louis XVI from the guillotine, and in a torrid love affair with a famous countess. He returned to America, served as a United States senator from Pennsylvania from 1800 to 1803, and was at Hamilton's bedside when his lifelong friend died. At age fifty-seven Morris settled down and married Anne Carey Randolph of Virginia. In 1816 he took ill from a stricture of his urinary passage and died, on November 6, after attempting to solve his problem with a sharp whalebone. He was sixty-four.

James Wilson served as an associate justice of the United States Supreme Court from 1789 to 1798. He put all his money into land speculation, and when the bubble burst he went broke and fled Pennsylvania to avoid creditors. He died a poor and mentally ravaged man in Edenton, North Carolina, on August 21, 1798, at the age of fifty-six.

Edmund Randolph became the first Attorney General of the United States. After Jefferson's resignation, Washington appointed him Secretary of State, a job from which he resigned in bitterness after Washington read an intercepted dispatch suggesting that Randolph had solicited funds from the French minister to the United States during the 1795 controversy over the Jay Treaty. During his retirement, the government won a suit against him to recover unjustified expenditures he had made while Secretary of State. He died destitute on September 12, 1813.

Robert Morris, Wilson's closest friend, served in the United States Senate from Pennsylvania from 1789 to 1795. His financial empire then collapsed, and he was jailed for debt from 1798 to 1801. Morris died in Philadelphia on May 8, 1806.

Roger Sherman served in the House of Representatives from 1789 to 1791 and in the Senate from 1791 to 1793. He died on July 23, 1793, at the age of seventy-two.

William Paterson served as United States senator from New Jersey from 1789 to 1790, as governor of New Jersey from 1790 to 1793 and as an associate justice of the Supreme Court from 1793 to 1806. He died on September 9, 1806, following a carriage accident.

Luther Martin continued as attorney general of Maryland until 1805, becoming known as the "Federal Bulldog" for his strong Federalist leanings. In 1804 he defended Supreme Court Justice Samuel Chase in a Senate impeachment trial, and later Aaron Burr in his treason trial. In 1819 he gained notoriety for a two-and-a-half-day argument before the U.S. Supreme Court in the famous case of McCulloch v. Maryland. All this time, Martin's alcoholism was sapping his strength and his spirit. He died a derelict on July 10, 1826, at the New York home of Aaron Burr, who had taken pity on him.

The full story of the Federal Convention remained a closely guarded secret for more than fifty years. Despite much pressure to publish his extensive notes from the convention, Madison vowed not to do so until the death of the last delegate. He spent the last years of his life laboriously preparing and editing the notes, dictating to an aide when his fingers became too arthritic to write. As it turned out, Madison lived longer than any other delegate. His widow, Dolley, sold his "Notes of Debates" to the government in 1840.

In his will, Madison had this to say:

> Considering the peculiarity and magnitude of the occasion which produced the convention at Philadelphia in 1787, the Characters who composed it, the Constitution which resulted from their deliberation, its effects during a trial of so many years on the prosperity of the people living under it, and the interest it has inspired among the friends of free Government, it is not an unreasonable inference that a careful and extended report of the proceedings and discussions of that body, which were with closed doors, by a member who was constant in his attendance, will be particularly gratifying to the People of the United States, and to all who take an interest in the progress of political science and the cause of true liberty.

APPENDIX

THE CONSTITUTION

OF THE
UNITED STATES OF AMERICA

(The original text of the Constitution and the amendments, as reprinted by the U.S. Government Printing office, Washington, D.C., in 1974. Brackets indicate provisions that have been amended or superseded.)

We the People of the United States, in Order to form a more perfect Union, establish Justice, insure domestic Tranquility, provide for the common defence, promote the general Welfare, and secure the Blessings of Liberty to ourselves and our Posterity, do ordain and establish this Constitution for the United States of America.

ARTICLE I.

SECTION 1. All legislative Powers herein granted shall be vested in a Congress of the United States, which shall consist of a Senate and House of Representatives.

SECTION 2. The House of Representatives shall be composed of Members chosen every second Year by the People of the several States, and the Electors in each State shall have the Qualifications requisite for Electors of the most numerous Branch of the State Legislature.

No Person shall be a Representative who shall not have attained to the Age of twenty-five Years, and been seven Years a

Citizen of the United States, and who shall not, when elected, be an Inhabitant of that State in which he shall be chosen.

[Representatives and direct Taxes shall be apportioned among the several States which may be included within this Union, according to their respective Numbers, which shall be determined by adding to the whole Number of free Persons, including those bound to Service for a Term of Years, and excluding Indians not taxed, three fifths of all other Persons.] * The actual Enumeration shall be made within three Years after the first Meeting of the Congress of the United States, and within every subsequent Term of ten Years, in such Manner as they shall by Law direct. The Number of Representatives shall not exceed one for every thirty Thousand, but each State shall have at Least one Representative; and until such enumeration shall be made, the State of New Hampshire shall be entitled to chuse three, Massachusetts eight, Rhode-Island and Providence Plantations one, Connecticut five, New-York six, New Jersey four, Pennsylvania eight, Delaware one, Maryland six, Virginia ten, North Carolina five, South Carolina five, and Georgia three.

When vacancies happen in the Representation from any State, the Executive Authority thereof shall issue Writs of Election to fill such Vacancies.

The House of Representatives shall chuse their Speaker and other Officers; and shall have the sole Power of Impeachment.

SECTION 3. The Senate of the United States shall be composed of two Senators from each State, [chosen by the Legislature thereof,] † for six Years; and each Senator shall have one Vote.

Immediately after they shall be assembled in Consequence of the first Election, they shall be divided as equally as may be into three Classes. The Seats of the Senators of the first Class shall be vacated at the Expiration of the second Year, of the second Class at the Expiration of the fourth Year, and of the third Class at the

* Changed by Section 2 of the Fourteenth Amendment.
† Changed by Section 1 of the Seventeenth Amendment.

Expiration of the sixth Year, so that one-third may be chosen every second Year; [and if Vacancies happen by Resignation, or otherwise, during the Recess of the Legislature of any State, the Executive thereof may make temporary Appointments until the next Meeting of the Legislature, which shall then fill such Vacancies.] *

No Person shall be a Senator who shall not have attained to the Age of thirty Years, and been nine Years a Citizen of the United States, and who shall not, when elected, be an Inhabitant of that State for which he shall be chosen.

The Vice President of the United States shall be President of the Senate, but shall have no Vote, unless they be equally divided.

The Senate shall chuse their other Officers, and also a President pro tempore, in the absence of the Vice President, or when he shall exercise the Office of President of the United States.

The Senate shall have the sole Power to try all Impeachments. When sitting for that Purpose, they shall be on Oath or Affirmation. When the President of the United States is tried, the Chief Justice shall preside: And no Person shall be convicted without the Concurrence of two thirds of the Members present.

Judgment in Cases of Impeachment shall not extend further than to removal from Office, and disqualification to hold and enjoy any Office of honor, Trust or Profit under the United States: but the Party convicted shall nevertheless be liable and subject to Indictment, Trial, Judgment and Punishment, according to Law.

SECTION 4. The Times, Places and Manner of holding Elections for Senators and Representatives, shall be prescribed in each State by the Legislature thereof; but the Congress may at any time by Law make or alter such Regulations, except as to the Place of Chusing Senators.

The Congress shall assemble at least once in every Year, and

* Changed by Paragraph 2 of the Seventeenth Amendment.

such Meeting shall [be on the first Monday in December,] * unless they shall by Law appoint a different Day.

SECTION 5. Each House shall be the Judge of the Elections, Returns and Qualifications of its own Members, and a Majority of each shall constitute a Quorum to do Business; but a smaller number may adjourn from day to day, and may be authorized to compel the Attendance of absent Members, in such Manner, and under such Penalties as each House may provide.

Each House may determine the Rules of its Proceedings, punish its Members for disorderly Behavior, and, with the Concurrence of two thirds, expel a Member.

Each House shall keep a Journal of its Proceedings, and from time to time publish the same, excepting such Parts as may in their Judgment require Secrecy; and the Yeas and Nays of the Members of either House on any question shall, at the Desire of one fifth of those Present, be entered on the Journal.

Neither House, during the Session of Congress, shall, without the Consent of the other, adjourn for more than three days, nor to any other Place than that in which the two Houses shall be sitting.

SECTION 6. The Senators and Representatives shall receive a Compensation for their Services to be ascertained by Law, and paid out of the Treasury of the United States. They shall in all Cases, except Treason, Felony and Breach of the Peace, be privileged from Arrest during their Attendance at the Session of their respective Houses, and in going to and returning from the same; and for any Speech or Debate in either House, they shall not be questioned in any other Place.

No Senator or Representative shall, during the Time for which he was elected, be appointed to any civil Office under the Authority of the United States, which shall have been created, or the Emoluments whereof shall have been encreased during such time; and no Person holding any office under the United States,

* Changed by Section 2 of the Twentieth Amendment.

shall be a Member of either House during his Continuance in Office.

SECTION 7. All Bills for raising Revenue shall originate in the House of Representatives; but the Senate may propose or concur with Amendments as on other Bills.

Every Bill which shall have passed the House of Representatives and the Senate, shall, before it become a Law, be presented to the President of the United States; If he approve he shall sign it, but if not he shall return it, with his Objections to that House in which it shall have originated, who shall enter the Objections at large on their Journal, and proceed to reconsider it. If after such Reconsideration two thirds of that House shall agree to pass the Bill, it shall be sent, together with the Objections, to the other House, by which it shall likewise be reconsidered, and if approved by two thirds of that House, it shall become a Law. But in all such Cases the Votes of both Houses shall be determined by Yeas and Nays, and the Names of the Persons voting for and against the Bill shall be entered on the Journal of each House respectively. If any Bill shall not be returned by the President within ten Days (Sundays excepted) after it shall have been presented to him, the Same shall be a Law, in like Manner as if he had signed it, unless the Congress by their Adjournment prevent its Return, in which Case it shall not be a Law.

Every Order, Resolution, or Vote to which the Concurrence of the Senate and House of Representatives may be necessary (except on a question of Adjournment) shall be presented to the President of the United States; and before the Same shall take Effect, shall be approved by him, or being disapproved by him, shall be repassed by two thirds of the Senate and House of Representatives, according to the Rules and Limitations prescribed in the Case of a Bill.

SECTION 8. The Congress shall have Power To lay and collect Taxes, Duties, Imposts and Excises, to pay the Debts and provide for the common Defence and general Welfare of the United

States; but all Duties, Imposts and Excises shall be uniform throughout the United States;

To borrow money on the credit of the United States;

To regulate Commerce with foreign Nations, and among the several States, and with the Indian Tribes;

To establish a uniform Rule of Naturalization, and uniform Laws on the subject of Bankruptcies throughout the United States;

To coin Money, regulate the Value thereof, and of foreign Coin, and fix the Standard of Weights and Measures;

To provide for the Punishment of counterfeiting the Securities and current Coin of the United States;

To establish Post Offices and post Roads;

To promote the Progress of Science and useful Arts, by securing for limited Times to Authors and Inventors the exclusive Right to their respective Writings and Discoveries;

To constitute Tribunals inferior to the supreme Court;

To define and punish Piracies and Felonies committed on the high Seas, and Offenses against the Law of Nations;

To declare War, grant Letters of Marque and Reprisal, and make Rules concerning Captures on Land and Water;

To raise and support Armies, but no Appropriation of Money to that Use shall be for a longer Term than two Years;

To provide and maintain a Navy;

To make Rules for the Government and Regulation of the land and naval Forces;

To provide for calling forth the Militia to execute the Laws of the Union, suppress Insurrections and repel Invasions;

To provide for organizing, arming, and disciplining the Militia, and for governing such Part of them as may be employed in the Service of the United States, reserving to the States respectively, the Appointment of the Officers, and the Authority of training the Militia according to the discipline prescribed by Congress;

To exercise exclusive Legislation in all Cases whatsoever, over such District (not exceeding ten Miles square) as may, by Cession of particular States, and the acceptance of Congress, become the Seat of the Government of the United States, and to exercise like Authority over all Places purchased by the Consent of the Legislature of the State in which the Same shall be, for the Erection of Forts, Magazines, Arsenals, dock-Yards, and other needful Buildings;—And

To make all Laws which shall be necessary and proper for carrying into Execution the foregoing Powers, and all other Powers vested by this Constitution in the Government of the United States, or in any Department or Officer thereof.

SECTION 9. The Migration or Importation of such Persons as any of the States now existing shall think proper to admit, shall not be prohibited by the Congress prior to the Year one thousand eight hundred and eight, but a tax or duty may be imposed on such Importation, not exceeding ten dollars for each Person.

The privilege of the Writ of Habeas Corpus shall not be suspended, unless when in Cases of Rebellion or Invasion the Public Safety may require it.

No Bill of Attainder or ex post facto Law shall be passed.

No capitation, or other direct, Tax shall be laid, unless in Proportion to the Census or Enumeration herein before directed to be taken. *

No Tax or Duty shall be laid on Articles exported from any State.

No Preference shall be given by any Regulation of Commerce or Revenue to the Ports of one State over those of another: nor shall Vessels bound to, or from, one State, be obliged to enter, clear, or pay Duties in another.

No Money shall be drawn from the Treasury, but in Consequence of Appropriations made by Law; and a regular Statement and Account of the Receipts and Expenditures of all public Money shall be published from time to time.

No Title of Nobility shall be granted by the United States: And

* But see the Sixteenth Amendment.

no Person holding any Office of Profit or Trust under them, shall, without the Consent of the Congress, accept of any present, Emolument, Office, or Title, of any kind whatever, from any King, Prince, or foreign State.

Section 10. No State shall enter into any Treaty, Alliance, or Confederation; grant Letters of Marque and Reprisal; coin Money; emit Bills of Credit; make any Thing but gold and silver Coin a Tender in Payment of Debts; pass any Bill of Attainder, ex post facto Law, or Law impairing the Obligation of Contracts, or grant any Title of Nobility.

No State shall, without the Consent of the Congress, lay any Imposts or Duties on Imports or Exports, except what may be absolutely necessary for executing its inspection Laws: and the net Produce of all Duties and Imposts, laid by any State on Imports or Exports, shall be for the Use of the Treasury of the United States; and all such Laws shall be subject to the Revision and Controul of the Congress.

No State shall, without the Consent of Congress, lay any duty of Tonnage, keep Troops, or Ships of War in time of Peace, enter into any Agreement or Compact with another State, or with a foreign Power, or engage in War, unless actually invaded, or in such imminent Danger as will not admit of delay.

Article II.

Section 1. The executive Power shall be vested in a President of the United States of America. He shall hold his Office during the Term of four Years, and, together with the Vice-President, chosen for the same Term, be elected, as follows.

Each State shall appoint, in such Manner as the Legislature thereof may direct, a Number of Electors, equal to the whole Number of Senators and Representatives to which the State may be entitled in the Congress: but no Senator or Representative, or Person holding an Office of Trust or Profit under the United States, shall be appointed an Elector.

[The Electors shall meet in their respective States, and vote by

Ballot for two persons, of whom one at least shall not be an Inhabitant of the same State with themselves. And they shall make a List of all the Persons voted for, and of the Number of Votes for each; which List they shall sign and certify, and transmit sealed to the Seat of the Government of the United States, directed to the President of the Senate. The President of the Senate shall, in the Presence of the Senate and House of Representatives, open all the Certificates, and the Votes shall then be counted. The Person having the greatest Number of Votes shall be the President, if such Number be a Majority of the whole Number of Electors appointed; and if there be more than one who have such Majority, and have an equal Number of Votes, then the House of Representatives shall immediately chuse by Ballot one of them for President; and if no Person have a Majority, then from the five highest on the List the said House shall in like Manner chuse the President. But in chusing the President, the Votes shall be taken by States, the Representation from each State having one Vote; a quorum for this Purpose shall consist of a Member or Members from two thirds of the States, and a Majority of all the States shall be necessary to a Choice. In every Case, after the Choice of the President, the Person having the greatest Number of Votes of the Electors shall be the Vice President. But if there should remain two or more who have equal Votes, the Senate shall chuse from them by Ballot the Vice-President.]*

The Congress may determine the Time of chusing the Electors, and the Day on which they shall give their Votes; which Day shall be the same throughout the United States.

No person except a natural born Citizen, or a Citizen of the United States, at the time of the Adoption of this Constitution, shall be eligible to the Office of President; neither shall any Person be eligible to that Office who shall not have attained to the Age of thirty-five Years, and been fourteen Years a Resident within the United States.

* Superseded by the Twelfth Amendment.

[In Case of the Removal of the President from Office, or of his Death, Resignation, or Inability to discharge the Powers and Duties of the said Office, the same shall devolve on the Vice President, and the Congress may by Law, provide for the Case of Removal, Death, Resignation or Inability, both of the President and Vice President, declaring what Officer shall then act as President, and such Officer shall act accordingly, until the Disability be removed, or a President shall be elected.]*

The President shall, at stated Times, receive for his Services, a Compensation, which shall neither be encreased nor diminished during the Period for which he shall have been elected, and he shall not receive within that Period any other Emolument from the United States, or any of them.

Before he enter on the Execution of his Office, he shall take the following Oath or Affirmation:—"I do solemnly swear (or affirm) that I will faithfully execute the Office of President of the United States, and will to the best of my Ability, preserve, protect and defend the Constitution of the United States."

SECTION 2. The President shall be Commander in Chief of the Army and Navy of the United States, and of the Militia of the several States, when called into the actual Service of the United States; he may require the Opinion in writing, of the principal Officer in each of the executive Departments, upon any subject relating to the Duties of their respective Offices, and he shall have Power to Grant Reprieves and Pardons for Offenses against the United States, except in Cases of Impeachment.

He shall have Power, by and with the Advice and Consent of the Senate, to make Treaties, provided two-thirds of the Senators present concur; and he shall nominate, and by and with the Advice and Consent of the Senate, shall appoint Ambassadors, other public Ministers and Consuls, Judges of the supreme Court, and all other Officers of the United States, whose Appointments are not herein otherwise provided for, and which shall be estab-

* This clause has been affected by the Twenty-fifth Amendment.

lished by Law: but the Congress may by Law vest the Appointment of such inferior Officers, as they think proper, in the President alone, in the Courts of Law, or in the Heads of Departments.

The President shall have Power to fill up all Vacancies that may happen during the Recess of the Senate, by granting Commissions which shall expire at the End of their next Session.

Section 3. He shall from time to time give to the Congress Information of the State of the Union, and recommend to their Consideration such Measures as he shall judge necessary and expedient; he may, on extraordinary Occasions, convene both Houses, or either of them, and in Case of Disagreement between them, with Respect to the Time of Adjournment, he may adjourn them to such Time as he shall think proper; he shall receive Ambassadors and other public Ministers; he shall take Care that the Laws be faithfully executed, and shall Commission all the Officers of the United States.

Section 4. The President, Vice President and all civil Officers of the United States, shall be removed from Office on Impeachment for, and Conviction of, Treason, Bribery, or other high Crimes and Misdemeanors.

ARTICLE III.

Section 1. The judicial Power of the United States, shall be vested in one supreme Court, and in such inferior Courts as the Congress may from time to time ordain and establish. The Judges, both of the supreme and inferior Courts, shall hold their Offices during good Behaviour, and shall, at stated Times, receive for their Services, a Compensation, which shall not be diminished during their Continuance in Office.

Section 2. The judicial Power shall extend to all Cases, in Law and Equity, arising under this Constitution, the Laws of the United States, and Treaties made, or which shall be made, under their Authority;—to all Cases affecting Ambassadors, other public Ministers and Consuls;—to all Cases of admiralty and maritime Jurisdiction;—to Controversies to which the United States shall be a Party;—to Controversies between two or more States; —between a State and Citizens of another State;—between Citizens of different States;—between Citizens of the same State claiming Lands under Grants of different States, and between a State, or the Citizens thereof, and foreign States, Citizens or Subjects.

In all Cases affecting Ambassadors, other public Ministers and Consuls, and those in which a State shall be Party, the supreme Court shall have original Jurisdiction. In all the other Cases before mentioned, the supreme Court shall have appellate Jurisdiction, both as to Law and Fact, with such Exceptions, and under such Regulations as the Congress shall make.

The trial of all Crimes, except in Cases of Impeachment, shall be by Jury; and such Trial shall be held in the State where the said Crimes shall have been committed; but when not committed within any State, the Trial shall be at such Place or Places as the Congress may by Law have directed.

Section 3. Treason against the United States, shall consist only in levying War against them, or in adhering to their Enemies, giving them Aid and Comfort. No Person shall be convicted of Treason unless on the Testimony of two Witnesses to the same overt Act, or on Confession in open Court.

The Congress shall have Power to declare the Punishment of Treason, but no Attainder of Treason shall work Corruption of Blood, or Forfeiture except during the Life of the Person attainted.

ARTICLE IV.

Section 1. Full Faith and Credit shall be given in each State to the public Acts, Records, and judicial Proceedings of every other State. And the Congress may by general Laws prescribe the Manner in which such Acts, Records and Proceedings shall be proved, and the Effect thereof.

Section 2. The Citizens of each State shall be entitled to all Privileges and Immunities of Citizens in the several States.

A Person charged in any State with Treason, Felony, or other Crime, who shall flee from Justice, and be found in another State, shall on demand of the executive Authority of the State from which he fled, be delivered up, to be removed to the State having Jurisdiction of the Crime.

[No Person held to Service or Labour in one State, under the Laws thereof, escaping into another, shall, in Consequence of any Law or Regulation therein, be discharged from such Service or Labour, but shall be delivered up on Claim of the Party to whom such Service or Labour may be due.]*

SECTION 3. New States may be admitted by the Congress into this Union; but no new State shall be formed or erected within the Jurisdiction of any other State; nor any State be formed by the Junction of two or more States, or parts of States, without the Consent of the Legislatures of the States concerned as well as of the Congress.

The Congress shall have Power to dispose of and make all needful Rules and Regulations respecting the Territory or other Property belonging to the United States; and nothing in this Constitution shall be so construed as to Prejudice any Claims of the United States, or of any particular State.

SECTION 4. The United States shall guarantee to every State in this Union a Republican Form of Government, and shall protect each of them against Invasion; and on Application of the Legislature, or of the Executive (when the Legislature cannot be convened) against domestic Violence.

ARTICLE V.

The Congress, whenever two-thirds of both Houses shall deem it necessary, shall propose Amendments to this Constitution, or, on the Application of the Legislatures of two-thirds of the several States, shall call a Convention for proposing Amendments, which, in either Case, shall be valid to all Intents and Purposes, as part of this Constitution, when ratified by the Legislatures of

* Superseded by the Thirteenth Amendment.

three-fourths of the several States, or by Conventions in three-fourths thereof, as the one or the other Mode of Ratification may be proposed by the Congress: Provided that no Amendment which may be made prior to the Year One thousand eight hundred and eight shall in any Manner affect the first and fourth Clauses in the Ninth Section of the first Article; and that no State, without its Consent, shall be deprived of its equal Suffrage in the Senate.

ARTICLE VI.

All Debts contracted and Engagements entered into, before the Adoption of this Constitution, shall be as valid against the United States under this Constitution, as under the Confederation.

This Constitution, and the Laws of the United States which shall be made in Pursuance thereof; and all Treaties made, or which shall be made, under the Authority of the United States, shall be the supreme Law of the Land; and the Judges in every State shall be bound thereby, any Thing in the Constitution or Laws of any State to the Contrary notwithstanding.

The Senators and Representatives before mentioned, and the Members of the several State Legislatures, and all executive and judicial Officers, both of the United States and of the several States, shall be bound by Oath or Affirmation, to support this Constitution; but no religious Test shall ever be required as a Qualification to any Office or public Trust under the United States.

ARTICLE VII.

The Ratification of the Conventions of nine States shall be sufficient for the Establishment of this Constitution between the States so ratifying the Same.

Done in Convention by the Unanimous Consent of the States present the Seventeenth Day of September in the Year of our Lord one thousand seven hundred and Eighty seven and of the Independence of the United States of America the Twelfth.

In Witness whereof We have hereunto subscribed our Names.

Go *WASHINGTON*
Presidt and deputy from Virginia

New Hampshire.

JOHN LANGDON
NICHOLAS GILMAN

Massachusetts.

NATHANIEL GORHAM
RUFUS KING

New Jersey.

WIL: LIVINGSTON
DAVID BREARLEY.
WM PATERSON.
·JONA: DAYTON

Pennsylvania.

B FRANKLIN
ROBT. MORRIS
THOS. FITZSIMONS
JAMES WILSON
THOMAS MIFFLIN
GEO. CLYMER
JARED INGERSOLL
GOUV MORRIS

Delaware.

GEO: READ
JOHN DICKINSON
JACO: BROOM
GUNNING BEDFORD JUN
RICHARD BASSETT

Connecticut.

WM SAML JOHNSON
ROGER SHERMAN

New York.

ALEXANDER HAMILTON

Maryland.

JAMES MCHENRY
DANL CARROL
DAN: OF ST THOS JENIFER

Virginia.

JOHN BLAIR
JAMES MADISON JR.

North Carolina.

WM BLOUNT
HU WILLIAMSON
RICHD DOBBS SPAIGHT.

South Carolina.	*Georgia.*

J. RUTLEDGE   WILLIAM FEW
CHARLES PINCKNEY   ABR BALDWIN
CHARLES COTESWORTH
    PINCKNEY
PIERCE BUTLER

Attest:

WILLIAM JACKSON, *Secretary.*

ARTICLES IN ADDITION TO, AND AMENDMENT OF, THE CONSTI-
TUTION OF THE UNITED STATES OF AMERICA, PROPOSED BY CON-
GRESS, AND RATIFIED BY THE LEGISLATURES OF THE SEVERAL
STATES, PURSUANT TO THE FIFTH ARTICLE OF THE ORIGINAL
CONSTITUTION. *

*(The first 10 Amendments were ratified December 15, 1791, and form
what is known as the Bill of Rights)*

AMENDMENT I

Congress shall make no law respecting an establishment of religion, or prohibiting the free exercise thereof; or abridging the
freedom of speech, or of the press; or the right of the people
peaceably to assemble, and to petition the Government for a
redress of grievances.

AMENDMENT II

A well regulated Militia, being necessary to the security of a
free State, the right of the people to keep and bear Arms, shall
not be infringed.

AMENDMENT III

No Soldier shall, in time of peace be quartered in any house,
without the consent of the Owner, nor in time of war, but in a
manner to be prescribed by law.

---

* Amendment XXI was not ratified by state legislatures, but by state conventions
summoned by Congress.

AMENDMENT IV

The right of the people to be secure in their persons, houses, papers, and effects, against unreasonable searches and seizures, shall not be violated, and no Warrants shall issue, but upon probable cause, supported by Oath or affirmation, and particularly describing the place to be searched, and the persons or things to be seized.

AMENDMENT V

No person shall be held to answer for a capital, or otherwise infamous crime, unless on a presentment or indictment of a Grand Jury, except in cases arising in the land or naval forces, or in the Militia, when in actual service in time of War or public danger; nor shall any person be subject for the same offence to be twice put in jeopardy of life or limb; nor shall be compelled in any criminal case to be a witness against himself, nor be deprived of life, liberty, or property, without due process of law; nor shall private property be taken for public use, without just compensation.

AMENDMENT VI

In all criminal prosecutions, the accused shall enjoy the right to a speedy and public trial, by an impartial jury of the State and district wherein the crime shall have been committed, which district shall have been previously ascertained by law, and to be informed of the nature and cause of the accusation; to be confronted with the witnesses against him; to have compulsory process for obtaining witnesses in his favor, and to have the Assistance of Counsel for his defence.

AMENDMENT VII

In suits at common law, where the value in controversy shall exceed twenty dollars, the right of trial by jury shall be preserved, and no fact tried by a jury, shall be otherwise reexamined in any Court of the United States, than according to the rules of the common law.

Amendment VIII

Excessive bail shall not be required, nor excessive fines imposed, nor cruel and unusual punishments inflicted.

Amendment IX

The enumeration in the Constitution, of certain rights, shall not be construed to deny or disparage others retained by the people.

Amendment X

The powers not delegated to the United States by the Constitution, nor prohibited by it to the States, are reserved to the States respectively, or to the people.

Amendment XI
(Ratified February 7, 1795)

The Judicial power of the United States shall not be construed to extend to any suit in law or equity, commenced or prosecuted against one of the United States by Citizens of another State, or by Citizens or Subjects of any Foreign State.

Amendment XII
(Ratified June 15, 1804)

The Electors shall meet in their respective states and vote by ballot for President and Vice-President, one of whom, at least, shall not be an inhabitant of the same state with themselves; they shall name in their ballots the person voted for as President, and in distinct ballots the person voted for as Vice-President, and they shall make distinct lists of all persons voted for as President, and of all persons voted for as Vice-President, and of the number of votes for each, which lists they shall sign and certify, and transmit sealed to the seat of the government of the United States, directed to the President of the Senate;—The President of the Senate shall, in presence of the Senate and House of Representatives,

open all the certificates and the votes shall then be counted;—
The person having the greatest number of votes for President,
shall be the President, if such number be a majority of the whole
number of Electors appointed; and if no person have such majority, then from the persons having the highest numbers not exceeding three on the list of those voted for as President, the House
of Representatives shall choose immediately, by ballot, the President. But in choosing the President, the votes shall be taken by
states, the representation from each state having one vote; a quorum for this purpose shall consist of a member or members from
two-thirds of the states, and a majority of all the states shall be
necessary to a choice. [And if the House of Representatives shall
not choose a President whenever the right of choice shall devolve
upon them, before the fourth day of March next following, then
the Vice-President shall act as President, as in the case of the
death or other constitutional disability of the President.—] * The
person having the greatest number of votes as Vice-President,
shall be the Vice-President, if such number be a majority of the
whole number of Electors appointed, and if no person have a
majority, then from the two highest numbers on the list, the
Senate shall choose the Vice-President; a quorum for the purpose
shall consist of two-thirds of the whole number of Senators,
and a majority of the whole number shall be necessary to a
choice. But no person constitutionally ineligible to the office of
President shall be eligible to that of Vice-President of the United
States.

AMENDMENT XIII
(Ratified December 6, 1865)

SECTION 1. Neither slavery nor involuntary servitude, except
as a punishment for crime whereof the party shall have been duly
convicted, shall exist within the United States, or any place subject to their jurisdiction.

---

* Superseded by Section 3 of the Twentieth Amendment.

SECTION 2. Congress shall have power to enforce this article by appropriate legislation.

AMENDMENT XIV
(Ratified July 9, 1868)

SECTION 1. All persons born or naturalized in the United States, and subject to the jurisdiction thereof, are citizens of the United States and of the State wherein they reside. No State shall make or enforce any law which shall abridge the privileges or immunities of citizens of the United States; nor shall any State deprive any person of life, liberty, or property, without due process of law; nor deny to any person within its jurisdiction the equal protection of the laws.

SECTION 2. Representatives shall be apportioned among the several States according to their respective numbers, counting the whole number of persons in each State, excluding Indians not taxed. But when the right to vote at any election for the choice of electors for President and Vice-President of the United States, Representatives in Congress, the Executive and Judicial officers of a State, or the members of the Legislature thereof, is denied to any of the [male inhabitants of such State, being twenty-one years of age,]* and citizens of the United States, or in any way abridged, except for participation in rebellion, or other crime, the basis of representation therein shall be reduced in the proportion which the number of such male citizens shall bear to the whole number of male citizens twenty-one years of age in such State.

SECTION 3. No person shall be a Senator or Representative in Congress, or elector of President and Vice-President, or hold any office, civil or military, under the United States, or under any State, who, having previously taken an oath, as a member of Congress, or as an officer of the United States, or as a member of any State legislature, or as an executive or judicial officer of any State, to support the Constitution of the United States, shall

* Changed by the Nineteenth Amendment and Section 1 of the Twenty-sixth.

have engaged in insurrection or rebellion against the same, or given aid or comfort to the enemies thereof. But Congress may by a vote of two-thirds of each House, remove such disability.

SECTION 4. The validity of the public debt of the United States, authorized by law, including debts incurred for payment of pensions and bounties for services in suppressing insurrection or rebellion, shall not be questioned. But neither the United States nor any State shall assume or pay any debt or obligation incurred in aid of insurrection or rebellion against the United States, or any claim for the loss or emancipation of any slave; but all such debts, obligations and claims shall be held illegal and void.

SECTION 5. The Congress shall have power to enforce, by appropriate legislation, the provisions of this article.

AMENDMENT XV
(Ratified February 3, 1870)

SECTION 1. The right of citizens of the United States to vote shall not be denied or abridged by the United States or by any State on account of race, color, or previous condition of servitude—

SECTION 2. The Congress shall have power to enforce this article by appropriate legislation.

AMENDMENT XVI
(Ratified February 3, 1913)

The Congress shall have power to lay and collect taxes on incomes, from whatever source derived, without apportionment among the several States, and without regard to any census or enumeration.

AMENDMENT XVII
(Ratified April 8, 1913)

The Senate of the United States shall be composed of two Senators from each State, elected by the people thereof, for six years; and each Senator shall have one vote. The electors in each

State shall have the qualifications requisite for electors of the most numerous branch of the State legislatures.

When vacancies happen in the representation of any State in the Senate, the executive authority of such State shall issue writs of election to fill such vacancies: *Provided,* That the legislature of any State may empower the executive thereof to make temporary appointments until the people fill the vacancies by election as the legislature may direct.

This amendment shall not be so construed as to affect the election or term of any Senator chosen before it becomes valid as part of the Constitution.

AMENDMENT XVIII
(Ratified January 16, 1919)

[SECTION 1. After one year from the ratification of this article the manufacture, sale, or transportation of intoxicating liquors within, the importation thereof into, or the exportation thereof from the United States and all territory subject to the jurisdiction thereof for beverage purposes is hereby prohibited.

[SECTION 2. The Congress and the several States shall have concurrent power to enforce this article by appropriate legislation.

[SECTION 3. This article shall be inoperative unless it shall have been ratified as an amendment to the Constitution by the legislatures of the several States as provided in the Constitution, within seven years from the date of the submission hereof to the States by the Congress.] *

AMENDMENT XIX
(Ratified August 18, 1920)

The right of citizens of the United States to vote shall not be denied or abridged by the United States or by any State on account of sex.

Congress shall have power to enforce this article by appropriate legislation.

* Repealed by Section 1 of the Twenty-first Amendment.

AMENDMENT XX
(Ratified January 23, 1933)

SECTION 1. The terms of the President and Vice President shall end at noon on the 20th day of January, and the terms of Senators and Representatives at noon on the 3d day of January, of the years in which such terms would have ended if this article had not been ratified; and the terms of the successors shall then begin.

SECTION 2. The Congress shall assemble at least once in every year, and such meeting shall begin at noon on the 3d day of January, unless they shall by law appoint a different day.

SECTION 3. If, at the time fixed for the beginning of the term of the President, the President elect shall have died, the Vice President elect shall become President. If a President shall not have been chosen before the time fixed for the beginning of his term, or if the President elect shall have failed to qualify, then the Vice President elect shall act as President until a President shall have qualified; and the Congress may by law provide for the case wherein neither a President elect nor a Vice President elect shall have qualified, declaring who shall then act as President, or the manner in which one who is to act shall be selected, and such person shall act accordingly until a President or Vice President shall have qualified.

SECTION 4. The Congress may by law provide for the case of the death of any of the persons from whom the House of Representatives may choose a President whenever the right of choice shall have devolved upon them, and for the case of the death of any of the persons from whom the Senate may choose a Vice President whenever the right of choice shall have devolved upon them.

SECTION 5. Sections 1 and 2 shall take effect on the 15th day of October following the ratification of this article.

SECTION 6. This article shall be inoperative unless it shall have been ratified as an amendment to the Constitution by the legislatures of three-fourths of the several States within seven years from the date of its submission.

AMENDMENT XXI
(Ratified December 5, 1933)

SECTION 1. The eighteenth article of amendment to the Constitution of the United States is hereby repealed.

SECTION 2. The transportation or importation into any State, Territory, or possession of the United States for delivery or use therein of intoxicating liquors, in violation of the laws thereof, is hereby prohibited.

SECTION 3. This article shall be inoperative unless it shall have been ratified in an amendment to the Constitution by conventions in the several States, as provided in the Constitution, within seven years from the date of the submission hereof to the States by the Congress.

AMENDMENT XXII
(Ratified February 27, 1951)

SECTION 1. No person shall be elected to the office of the President more than twice, and no person who has held the office of President, or acted as President, for more than two years of a term to which some other person was elected President shall be elected to the office of the President more than once. But this Article shall not apply to any person holding the office of President when this Article was proposed by the Congress, and shall not prevent any person who may be holding the office of President, or acting as President, during the term within which this Article becomes operative from holding the office of President or acting as President during the remainder of such term.

SECTION 2. This article shall be inoperative unless it shall have been ratified as an amendment to the Constitution by the legislatures of three-fourths of the several States within seven years from the date of its submission to the States by the Congress.

AMENDMENT XXIII
(Ratified March 29, 1961)

SECTION 1. The District constituting the seat of Government of the United States shall appoint in such manner as the Congress may direct:

A number of electors of President and Vice President equal to the whole number of Senators and Representatives in Congress to which the District would be entitled if it were a State, but in no event more than the least populous State; they shall be in addition to those appointed by the States, but they shall be considered, for the purposes of the election of President and Vice President, to be electors appointed by a State; and they shall meet in the District and perform such duties as provided by the twelfth article of amendment.

SECTION 2. The Congress shall have power to enforce this article by appropriate legislation.

AMENDMENT XXIV
(Ratified January 23, 1964)

SECTION 1. The right of citizens of the United States to vote in any primary or other election for President or Vice President, for electors for President or Vice President, or for Senator or Representative in Congress, shall not be denied or abridged by the United States or any State by reason of failure to pay any poll tax or other tax.

SECTION 2. The Congress shall have power to enforce this article by appropriate legislation.

AMENDMENT XXV
(Ratified February 10, 1967)

SECTION 1. In case of the removal of the President from office or of his death or resignation, the Vice President shall become President.

SECTION 2. Whenever there is a vacancy in the office of the

Vice President, the President shall nominate a Vice President who shall take office upon confirmation by a majority vote of both Houses of Congress.

Section 3. Whenever the President transmits to the President pro tempore of the Senate and the Speaker of the House of Representatives his written declaration that he is unable to discharge the powers and duties of his office, and until he transmits to them a written declaration to the contrary, such powers and duties shall be discharged by the Vice President as Acting President.

Section 4. Whenever the Vice President and a majority of either the principal officers of the executive departments or of such other body as Congress may by law provide, transmit to the President pro tempore of the Senate and the Speaker of the House of Representatives their written declaration that the President is unable to discharge the powers and duties of his office, the Vice President shall immediately assume the powers and duties of the office as Acting President.

Thereafter, when the President transmits to the President pro tempore of the Senate and the Speaker of the House of Representatives his written declaration that no inability exists, he shall resume the powers and duties of his office unless the Vice President and a majority of either the principal officers of the executive department or of such other body as Congress may by law provide, transmit within four days to the President pro tempore of the Senate and the Speaker of the House of Representatives their written declaration that the President is unable to discharge the powers and duties of his office. Thereupon Congress shall decide the issue, assembling within forty-eight hours for that purpose if not in session. If the Congress, within twenty-one days after receipt of the latter written declaration, or, if Congress is not in session, within twenty-one days after Congress is required to assemble, determines by two-thirds vote of both Houses that the President is unable to discharge the powers and duties of his office, the Vice President shall continue to discharge the same as Acting

President; otherwise, the President shall resume the powers and duties of his office.

Amendment XXVI
(Ratified July 1, 1971)

Section 1. The right of citizens of the United States, who are eighteen years of age or older, to vote shall not be denied or abridged by the United States or by any State on account of age.

Section 2. The Congress shall have power to enforce this article by appropriate legislation.

SOURCES

CHAPTER ONE

21 "There is a Critical . . .": Madison, *Papers* 1:9.

22 Madison and the others: Madison to Washington, 8 Nov. 1786, 7 Dec. 1786, 21 Feb. 1787, Madison, *Papers* 9:166–67, 199–200, 285–86.

22 "Those who may lean . . .": Madison to Washington, 21 Feb. 1787, ibid., p. 286.

22 "You talk, my good Sir . . .": Washington to Henry Lee, 31 Oct. 1786, Washington, *Writings* 29:34.

23 "A thought . . .": Washington to Henry Knox, 8 March 1787, ibid., pp. 71–72.

23 "As my friends . . .": Washington to Edmund Randolph, 28 March 1787, ibid., pp. 186–87.

23 "it is my purpose . . .": Edmund Randolph to Washington, 2 April 1787, Madison, *Papers* 9:304.

23 "The nearer the crisis . . .": Madison to Edmund Pendleton, 22 April 1787, ibid., p. 383.

23 "It ought not . . .": Madison to Edmund Randolph, 15 April 1787, ibid., p. 9.

24 Washington's journey is described in Washington, *Diaries* 5:152–55.

25 "The American Fabius . . .": Kaminski and Saladino, *Documentary History* 1:77–78.

25 "Yesterday . . .": *Pennsylvania Packet,* 14 May 1787.

26 Madison's mood described in Madison to Jefferson, 15 May 1787, Farrand, *Records* 3:20.

27 "His countenance . . .": from "Gouverneur Morris' Funeral Oration on the death of Washington," Dec. 31, 1799, quoted in Warren, *The Making,* p. 106.

27 "Not more than . . .": Washington to Arthur Lee, 20 May 1787, Farrand, *Records* 3:22.

27 For description of meetings of Virginia delegation see George Mason to George Mason, Jr., 20 May 1787, ibid., pp. 22–23.

27 For description of Franklin during this period, see Lopez and Herbert, *The Private Franklin,* and Van Doren, *Benjamin Franklin.*

27 "I seem to have intruded . . .": quoted in Lopez and Herbert, *The Private Franklin,* p. 289.

28 "They engrossed the prime . . .": Franklin, *Writings,* p. 663.

28 "I am mortified": Rufus King to Jeremiah Wadsworth, 24 May 1787, Farrand, *Records* 3:26.

29 "Much is expected . . .": Washington to Jefferson, 30 May 1787, ibid., p. 31.

CHAPTER TWO

Among the most useful books on the period between the end of the Revolutionary War and the Convention are Jensen, *The New Nation;* Rakove, *The Beginnings of National Politics;* Wood, *The Creation;* Nevins, *The American States.* The best guide to understanding Madison during the period are his own letters and two biographies, Brant, *Madison,* Vol. 2., and Ketcham, *James Madison.*

31 "I am mortified": Washington to Henry Lee, 31 Oct. 1786, Washington, *Writings* 29:34.

PAGE

32   For description of Congress' flight from Philadelphia in 1783 see Collins, *The Continental Congress at Princeton*, and Burnett, *Letters* 7:198–300.

32   ". . . the cries of an oysterman": Charles Pettit to Jeremiah Wadsworth, 27 May 1786, Burnett, *Letters* 8:368–70.

32   On politics and government in the states, and the increasing level of participation, see Hall, *Politics Without Parties*; Main, "Government by the People: the American Revolution and the Democratization of the Legislatures"; Main, *The Anti-Federalists*; Brunhouse, *The Counter-Revolution in Pennsylvania, 1776–1790*.

34   On disputes over land, see Billington, *Westward Expansion*.

35   On trade and the economy see Nettels, *The Emergence of a National Economy, 1775–1815*, Vol. 2.

35   On slavery see Davis, *The Problem of Slavery*, Jordan, *White Over Black*.

36   "chain of debt": Szatmary, *Shays' Rebellion*, p. 19.

36   On the conflict over paper money, see Nettels, *The Emergence*.

36   "My countrymen . . .": Webster, "Diseases of the Body Politic," in *The Annals of America* 3:67.

37   "far too much . . .": Stephen Higginson to Nathan Dane, 3 March 1787, Higginson, "Letters," p. 752.

37   "When the pot boils . . .": quoted in O'Connor, *William Paterson*, p. 89.

37   "The mob begin . . .": quoted in Mintz, *Gouverneur Morris*, p. 44.

38   On Shays' Rebellion see Szatmary, *Shays' Rebellion*.

38   "The present . . .": Barlow, "The Unfinished Revolution," *Annals* 3:92.

38   "The flames . . .": quoted in Szatmary, *Shays' Rebellion*, p. 130.

38   "All respect . . .": Jefferson to Elbridge Gerry, quoted in Peterson, *Thomas Jefferson*, p. 300.

38   For report of the Annapolis Convention see Tansill, *Documents*, pp. 39–43.

39   "had no hope": Bancroft, *History* 2:399–401.

39   For resolution of Congress of Feb. 21, 1787, see Tansill, *Documents*, pp. 44–46.

40   "It appeared . . .": Hill, *Journals of the Continental Congress* 33:723–24.

CHAPTER THREE

Rossiter's *1787: The Grand Convention* includes an excellent portrait of all the delegates. *The Dictionary of American Biography* contains capsules on many of them. See Bibliography for full biographies of many of the delegates.

PAGE

41   "In general . . .": Madison to Edmund Pendleton, 27 May 1787, Madison, *Papers* 10:11–12.

41   On the Pennsylvania delegation, see Brunhouse, *The Counter-Revolution*, p. 200.

41   On the Massachusetts delegation, see Hall, *Politics Without Parties*, p. 257.

42   On the South Carolina delegation see Zahniser, *Charles Cotesworth Pinckney*, p. 87.

42   "Permit me, Sir . . .": James Varnum to George Washington, 18 June 1787, Farrand, *Records* 3:47–48.

43   The ages are as of May 14, 1787. Some dates of birth are uncertain.

PAGE

48 "immediately after hearing . . .": Rush, *Medical Inquiries and Observations*, p. 132.

48 "Having now finished the work . . .": Address to Congress, Annapolis, 23 Dec. 1783, Washington, *Papers* 27:285.

48 On the life of Gouverneur Morris, see Mintz, *Gouverneur Morris and the American Revolution*.

49 Jay's comments on Morris quoted in Swiggett, *The Extraordinary Mr. Morris*, p. 80.

49 "With respect . . .": Sparks, *The Life of Gouverneur Morris*, p. 266.

49 There are numerous biographies of Hamilton. I have drawn from Mitchell, *Alexander Hamilton*, and McDonald, *Alexander Hamilton: A Biography*, and from Hamilton, *Papers*, ed. Syrett and Cooke.

49 "Let us both erect . . .": Hamilton to Gouverneur Morris, 21 Feb. 1784, Hamilton, *Papers* 3: 513–14.

49 On Wilson, see Smith, *James Wilson, Founding Father, 1742–1798*.

50 On Robert Morris, see Oberholtzer, *Robert Morris, Patriot and Financier*.

50 The approach of the Morrises is mentioned in a Madison footnote in Madison, *Notes*, p. 25.

51 "I am in possession . . .": Read to John Dickinson, 21 May 1787, Farrand, *Records* 3:24–25. The plan Read had seen is said to be that of Charles Pinckney, which was introduced but never discussed at the convention.

CHAPTER FOUR

Descriptions of what was said and done in convention throughout the book are taken from Madison, *Notes of Debates in the Federal Convention of 1787, reported by James Madison*, with an introduction by Adrienne Koch (Ohio University Press, 1966), except where indicated. Dates of speeches are cited where not indicated in the text. Descriptions of weather are taken primarily from the readings of Peter Legaux, a farmer residing about 13 miles from Philadelphia, as reported in *The Columbian Magazine* in 1787.

PAGE

54 "Gentlemen. I am sorry . . .,": Anecdote, Farrand, *Records* 3:86–87.

54 "In furnishing you . . .": Madison to Jefferson, 6 June 1787, Farrand, *Records* 3:35–36.

55 "grafted on": Randolph to Madison, 27 March 1787, Madison, *Papers* 9:335.

55 "I think with you . . .": Madison to Randolph, 8 April 1787, Madison, *Papers* 9:369–70.

55 On Randolph's background and his mood see Reardon, *Edmund Randolph: A Biography*.

55 Randolph's speech is in Madison, *Notes*, pp. 29–30.

58 "to abolish": Charles Pinckney speech of May 30, Madison, *Notes*, p. 34. Charles Cotesworth Pinckney's speech of May 30, ibid., p. 35.

58 Morris comments and Randolph reaction of May 30, ibid., pp. 34–35.

59 Madison's theory set forth in "Vices of Political System," April 1787, Madison, *Papers* 9:348–357; and in *The Federalist Papers*, No. 10.

60 "The smaller the society . . .": *The Federalist Papers*, pp. 48–49.

CHAPTER FIVE

PAGE

63 Franklin and Rutledge comments of June 1, Madison, *Notes*, p. 45.

64 Butler's doodles reproduced in Hutson, "Pierce Butler's Record of the Federal Constitutional Convention," *Quarterly Journal of the Library of Congress*, Winter 1980, and are available in U.S. Constitution Collection, Library of Congress.

64 On Gorham's letter to Prince Henry, see Dunbar, *"Monarchical" Tendencies*, p. 60.

65 "will soon finish . . .": Benjamin Rush to Richard Price, 2 June 1787, Farrand, *Records* 3:33.

65 The tabulation is contained in the notes of Delegate John Lansing, Jr., reprinted in Strayer, *The Delegate from New York*.

67 "If a majority . . .": Madison to Jefferson, 19 March 1787, Madison, *Papers* 9:319.

67 " . . . the prospect of . . .": Randolph to Beverley Randolph, 6 June 1787, Farrand, *Records* 3:36.

68 "We have been . . .": David Brearley to Jonathan Dayton, 9 June 1787, ibid. 3:37.

68 "By the date . . .": "North Carolina Delegates to Governor Caswell," 14 June 1787, ibid. 3:46–47.

68 Brearley's speech of June 9, Madison, *Notes*, pp. 94–95.

69 Paterson's notes for his speech are contained in Tansill, *Documents*, p. 887. Paterson's speech of June 9, Madison, *Notes*, pp. 95–97.

70 Wilson speech of June 9, Madison, *Notes*, p. 97.

70 On the chill felt by Philadelphians, see William Shippen to Thomas Lee Shippen, 19 June 1787, Shippen Family Papers, Library of Congress.

CHAPTER SIX

PAGE

71 Adams' comments quoted in Boardman, *Roger Sherman: Signer and Statesman*, p. 123.

71 "Mr. Sherman exhibits . . .": "Notes of Major William Pierce in the Federal Convention of 1787" in Tansill, *Documents*, p. 98.

72 "If you attack . . .": Jeremiah Wadsworth to Rufus King, 3 June 1787, Farrand, *Records* 3:33–34

72 On Connecticut's agenda see Gerlach, "Toward 'a More Perfect Union,' " pp. 65–78.

74 Franklin's speech of June 11, Madison, *Notes*, p. 103.

76 Description of the Indian Queen quoted from Cutler's *Life, Journals and Correspondence*, 1:253–54.

76 "The Gentlemen . . .": "Invitation to McKean," 1 July 1787, Independence National Historical Park Collection.

76 The best evidence of such discussions is in an undated letter concerning Louisiana's admission into the Union written years later by William Samuel Johnson and contained in the U.S. Constitution Collection, Library of Congress.

76 On Morris' parties see James Brown to Wm. Magee, 8 June 1787, in Independence National Historical Park Collection.

PAGE

77 "At an interview . . .": Anecdote from James Parton's *Life of Thomas Jefferson* quoted in Farrand, *Records* 3:95.

78 "My curiosity . . .": Oliver Ellsworth to Mrs. Ellsworth, 21 July 1787, Independence National Historical Park Collection.

78 "A few days ago . . .": *Pennsylvania Mercury*, 18 May 1787.

79 "Such circumspection . . .": *Pennsylvania Herald*, 2 June 1787, in Kaminski and Saladino, *Documentary History* 1:122.

79 "I enclose . . .": William Shippen to Thomas Lee Shippen, 30 May 1787, Shippen Family Papers, Library of Congress.

79 For a detailed description of the work of this group and for background on Paterson, see O'Connor, *William Paterson: Lawyer and Statesman*, pp. 146–49.

80 On the New York agenda, see Young, *The Democratic Republicans of New York*, pp. 67–82.

CHAPTER SEVEN

PAGE

85 "You see the consequence . . .": Madison, *Notes*, p. 118.

86 "the key to his success . . .": Lettieri, *Oliver Ellsworth*, p. 1.

88 "They are my trinity . . .": Quoted in Brodie, *Thomas Jefferson*, p. 349.

89 "I confess . . .": Yates's notes in Tansill, *Documents*, p. 783.

89 "The gentleman from New York . . .": Rufus King's notes, ibid., p. 862.

91 "The present Federal . . .": Nathaniel Gorham to Theophilius Parsons, 18 June 1787, in Warren, *The Making*, p. 230.

CHAPTER EIGHT

PAGE

94 The June 22 action recorded in "Philadelphia Street Commissioners Minute Book," December 1786–August 1787, Independence National Historical Park Collection.

94 "The older men grow . . .": Oliver Ellsworth to Mrs. Ellsworth, 21 July 1787, Independence National Historical Park Collection.

95 For background on Martin see Clarkson and Jett, *Luther Martin of Maryland*.

95 "spent most of his time . . .": Ibid., p. 24.

96 "paper money dread": See Martin's "Genuine Information," Farrand, *Records* 3:214.

97 On Martin's activities and attitudes see ibid., p. 283.

97 Madison's reaction in *Notes*, p. 204, Pierce's in "Characters," Tansill, *Documents*, p. 103, and Ellsworth's in "The Landholder," Farrand, *Records* 3:273.

98 Franklin's speech of June 28, Madison, *Notes*, pp. 209–10.

100 Ellsworth speech of June 29, ibid., pp. 218–19; Wilson speech of June 30, pp. 220–21; King speech of June 30, pp. 227–28; Dayton speech of June 30, p. 228; Bedford speech of June 30, pp. 229–30; King speech of June 30, pp. 230–31.

CHAPTER NINE

PAGE

105 For Martin's speculation see Martin's "Genuine Information," Farrand, *Records* 3:188.

105 "As yet we retain . . .": Hamilton speech of June 29, Madison, *Notes*, p. 216.

106 "scarce held together . . .": Martin, "Genuine Information," Farrand, *Records* 3:190.

106 Franklin's analogy described in Cutler, *Life, Journals*, 1:253–71, quoted in Farrand, *Records* 3:58.

106 On Washington's fears, see Washington to David Humphreys, 26 Dec. 1786, Washington, *Writings* 29:126.

106 Washington's visit to Germantown described in Deborah Norris Logan, *Memoirs of Dr. George Logan of Stenton*, quoted in Warren, *The Making*, pp. 279–80.

106 For Washington's feeling of anger, see Washington to Hamilton, 10 July 1787, Farrand, *Records* 3:56.

108 Davie's concern expressed in speech of June 30, Madison, *Notes*, pp. 225–26.

109 On departure of Yates and Lansing, see "Robert Yates and John Lansing, Jr., to the Governor of New York," undated, in Farrand, *Records* 3:244–46.

109 "I have conversed . . .": Hamilton to Washington, 3 July 1787, ibid., p. 54.

109 For July 4th activities and speeches, see Warren, *The Making*, pp. 268–70.

111 Franklin's analysis is in his speech of June 11, Madison, *Notes*, pp. 101–2.

113 On Strong's attitude, see his speech of July 14, ibid., p. 293.

113 The "chief thing": Letter from the North Carolina delegates to Gov. Caswell, 18 Sept. 1787, *State Records of North Carolina* 20 (1785–88):777–79.

114 North Carolina so indicated in vote of July 7 on equal suffrage in the Senate, Madison, *Notes*, p. 254.

CHAPTER TEN

The events in this chapter relate to Article I of the Constitution. The relevant clauses are:

Section 2:"[Representatives and direct Taxes shall be apportioned among the several States which may be included within this Union, according to their respective Numbers, which shall be determined by adding to the whole Number of free persons, including those bound to Service for a Term of Years, and excluding Indians not taxed, three fifths of all other Persons.] The actual Enumeration shall be made within three Years after the first Meeting of the Congress of the United States, and within every subsequent Term of ten Years, in such Manner as they shall by Law direct. . . ." The bracketed words were changed by Section 2 of the Fourteenth Amendment, ratified Dec. 6, 1865, which reads: "Representatives shall be apportioned among the several States according to their respective numbers, counting the whole number of persons in each State, excluding Indians not taxed. . . ."

Section 3: "The Senate of the United States shall be composed of two Senators from each State . . . ; and each Senator shall have one Vote. . . ."

Section 7: "All Bills for raising Revenue shall originate in the House of Representatives; but the Senate may propose or concur with Amendments as on other Bills. . . ."

PAGE

116 Morris described his plan in speech of July 6, Madison, *Notes*, p. 245.

116 The committee delivered its report on July 9, ibid., p. 257.

117 "They would not": Morris speech of July 11, ibid., pp. 270–71.

117 Exchange between Gerry and Sherman in speeches of July 14, ibid., pp. 288–89.

118 "The security . . .": speech of Pierce Butler, July 13, ibid., p. 286.

118 "From the nature of man . . .": speech of Mason, July 11, ibid., pp. 264–65.

119 On the origin of the formula, see Robinson, *Slavery in the Structure of American Politics*.

120 "So great is the unanimity": quoted in Warren, *The Making*, p. 279.

120 The caucus is described by Madison in *Notes*, p. 301.

121 "it shews . . .": Madison, in *Federalist Papers*, No. 37, p. 180.

CHAPTER ELEVEN

The events described took place throughout the convention. The clauses relevant to this chapter are in Article I of the Constitution, including:

Section 2: "The House of Representatives shall be composed of Members chosen every second Year by the People of the several States, and the Electors in each State shall have the Qualifications requisite for Electors of the most numerous Branch of the State Legislature.

"No Person shall be a Representative who shall not have attained to the Age of twenty-five Years . . ."

Section 3: "The Senate of the United States shall be composed of two Senators from each State, [chosen by the Legislature thereof,] for six Years . . ." (The bracketed words were changed by Section 1 of the Seventeenth Amendment, ratified April 8, 1913, which reads: "The Senate of the United States shall be composed of two Senators from each State, elected by the people thereof . . .")

"No Person shall be a Senator who shall not have attained to the Age of thirty years . . ."

Section 6: "The Senators and Representatives shall receive a Compensation for their Services, to be ascertained by Law, and paid out of the Treasury of the United States . . ."

PAGE

126 On Madison's concession, see *Federalist Papers*, No. 37, p. 180.

129 "would be as unnatural . . .": Mason speech of July 17, Madison, *Notes*, p. 308.

129 "The evils . . .": Gerry speech of May 31, ibid., p. 39.

129 "should have as little . . .": Sherman speech of May 31, ibid.

129 "If this convention . . .": Rutledge speech of June 21, ibid., p. 167.

131 "Can any man be safe . . . ?": William Blount to Gov. Caswell, 13 Jan. 1787, quoted in Goebel, *History of the Supreme Court*.

131 "What led . . . ?": Mercer speech of Aug. 13, Madison, *Notes*, p. 455.

PAGE

131 "Experience in all . . .": Madison speech of July 21, ibid., p. 338.

131 On the role of "bumbo" in Virginia see Sydnor, *Gentlemen Freeholders*, p. 54.

131 "corrupting influence": Madison, "Autobiography," p. 199.

132 "the grand depository . . .": Mason speech of May 31, Madison, *Notes*, p. 39.

132 "federal pyramid": Wilson speech of May 31, ibid., p. 40.

132 "the people would . . .": Madison speech of May 31, ibid.

133 "There ought to be . . .": Hamilton speech of June 21, ibid., p. 170.

133 "Instability is one . . .": Madison speech of June 12, ibid., p. 106.

134 "would have to travel . . .": Madison speech of June 21, ibid., p. 169.

134 "the wildest ideas . . .": Gerry speech of June 5, ibid., p. 70.

134 "The democratic licentiousness . . .": Randolph speech of June 12, ibid., p. 110.

134 On the Maryland Senate as model see Crowl, "Anti-Federalism in Maryland"; and Madison speech of June 12, Madison, *Notes*, p. 110.

135 "we might be chargeable . . .": Franklin speech of June 26, Madison, *Notes*, p. 198.

136 "Whatever power . . .": Mason speech of June 7, ibid., p. 87.

CHAPTER TWELVE

PAGE

137 "The Great Washington . . .": John Langdon to Joseph Brackett, 1 Aug. 1787, U.S. Constitution Collection, Library of Congress.

138 William Samuel Johnson's recounting in undated letter on the subject of Louisiana's admission to the Union, U.S. Constitution Collection, Library of Congress.

138 On Hamilton and Madison see Hamilton to Edward Carrington, 26 May 1792, Farrand, *Records* 3:366–67.

138 On Maryland's meetings, see "Papers of Dr. James McHenry on the Federal Convention of 1787," in Tansill, *Documents*, pp. 923–52.

139 "I have twice wrote . . .": William Dobbs Spaight to John Gray Blount, 3 July 1787, Independence National Historical Park Collection.

139 "Our business is yet . . .": Oliver Ellsworth to Mrs. Ellsworth, 26 June 1787, Independence National Historical Park Collection.

140 The letters on Johnson's domestic situation are from Elizabeth Ver Plank to S. W. Johnson, 29 May and 25 July 1787, in U.S. Constitution Collection, Library of Congress.

140 "You must be . . .": John Dickinson to daughter, 16 May 1787, Independence National Historical Park Collection.

141 "The crowds . . .": Cutler, *Life, Journals*, 1:271–72.

141 ". . . there is so much . . .": Abraham Baldwin to Joel Barlow, 26 July 1787, Independence National Historical Park Collection.

142 "I was never more . . .": Elbridge Gerry to wife, 26 August 1787, U.S. Constitution Collection, Library of Congress.

CHAPTER THIRTEEN

For the final wording of the enumeration see the Constitution in the Appendix to this book, Article 1, Section 8. On the work of the Committee of Detail and its meaning, see Madison, *Notes*, pp. 385–96; Reardon, *Edmund Randolph*, pp. 110–12; Randolph's notes of committee proceedings in Farrand, *Records* 4:37–51; Crosskey, *Politics and the Constitution*; Kelly, Harbison and Belz, *The American Constitution*, pp. 101–5; Thach, *The Creation of the Presidency*.

PAGE

146   "essential principles only": Mason's copy of Randolph's notes, Farrand, *Records* 4:37.

CHAPTER FOURTEEN

The clauses relevant to this chapter are:

Article 1, Section 9: "The Migration or Importation of such Persons as any of the States now existing shall think proper to admit, shall not be prohibited by the Congress prior to the Year one thousand eight hundred and eight, but a tax or duty may be imposed on such Importation, not exceeding ten dollars for each Person. . . ."

Article IV, Section 2: ["No Person held to Service or Labour in one State, under the Laws thereof, escaping into another, shall, in Consequence of any Law or Regulation therein, be discharged from such Service or Labour, but shall be delivered up on Claim of the Party to whom such Service or Labour may be due."] The bracketed words were superseded by Section I of the Thirteenth Amendment, ratified Dec. 6, 1865, which reads: "Neither slavery nor involuntary servitude, except as a punishment for crime whereof the party shall have been duly convicted, shall exist within the United States, or any place subject to their jurisdiction."

On the politics of slavery in the 18th century see Jordan, *White Over Black*; Davis, *The Problem of Slavery*; Robinson, *Slavery in the Structure of American Politics*. Lynd, "The Compromise of 1787," tries to make the case for an elaborate deal linking the events concerning slavery in the convention with the Confederation Congress' actions on the Ordinance of 1787; the evidence is unconvincing.

PAGE

148   "Forty Dollars Reward," "Twenty Dollars Reward": *Pennsylvania Packet,* 6 Aug. and 24 Aug. 1787.

149   The petition of the Society for Promoting the Abolition of Slavery is dated June 2, 1787, and is contained in the Tench Coxe Papers in U.S. Constitution Collection, Library of Congress.

149   On the number of slaveholding delegates, see Davis, *The Problem of Slavery*, p. 100.

149   "A very strong paper": Tench Coxe to Madison, 31 March 1790, Farrand, *Records* 3:361.

150   Pinckney speech of July 23, Madison, *Notes*, p. 355.

150   Description of mansion by St. Julien Ravenal, quoted in Rogers, *Charleston*, p. 68.

151   For description of South Carolina delegation and political situation in that state, see Zahniser, *Charles Cotesworth Pinckney*, especially p. 89.

PAGE

154 On Mason's slaves see his will, March 20, 1773, in Mason, *Papers* 1:160. For description of Gunston Hall see remembrance of his son, in Rowland, *The Life of George Mason*, pp. 98–100.

158 "These things": Morris speech of Aug. 22, Madison, *Notes*, p. 507.

158 "I found . . .": Martin's "Genuine Information," Farrand, *Records* 3:210–11.

CHAPTER FIFTEEN

For the main provisions on the judiciary see Article III of the Constitution in the Appendix. Also see:

Article I, Section 8: "The Congress shall have Power . . . To constitute Tribunals inferior to the supreme Court . . ."

Article VI: "This Constitution, and the Laws of the United States which shall be made in Pursuance thereof; and all Treaties made, or which shall be made, under the Authority of the United States, shall be the supreme Law of the Land; and the Judges in every State shall be bound thereby, any Thing in the Constitution or Laws of any State to the Contrary notwithstanding."

Article I, Section 10: "No State shall enter into any Treaty, Alliance, or Confederation; grant Letters of Marque and Reprisal; coin Money; emit Bills of Credit; make any Thing but gold and silver Coin a Tender in Payment of Debts; pass any Bill of Attainder, ex post facto Law, or Law impairing the Obligation of Contracts, or grant any Title of Nobility.

"No State shall, without the Consent of the Congress, lay any Imposts or Duties on Imports or Exports, except what may be absolutely necessary for executing its inspection Laws; and the net Produce of all Duties and Imposts, laid by any State on Imports or Exports, shall be for the Use of the Treasury of the United States; and all such Laws shall be subject to the Revision and Controul of the Congress.

"No State shall, without the Consent of Congress, lay any duty of Tonnage, keep Troops, or Ships of War in time of Peace, enter into any Agreement or Compact with another State, or with a foreign Power, or engage in War, unless actually invaded, or in such imminent Danger as will not admit of delay."

The debates on the judiciary occurred intermittently throughout the convention. The best account of the origin of the judiciary is in Goebel, *History of the Supreme Court* 1:164–250. See also Swindler, "Seedtime of An American Judiciary: From Independence to the Constitution"; Berger, *Congress v. The Supreme Court*. Boudin, in *Government by Judiciary*, makes the case, unconvincingly, against the Supreme Court's broad power of judicial review. In support of the proposition that the convention clearly wanted judicial review of congressional statutes, see Patterson, "James Madison and Judicial Review."

PAGE

162 "the security of private rights . . .": Wilson speech of June 16, Madison, *Notes*, p. 126.

163 On the Court of Appeals for Capture and its origin see Swindler, "Seedtime," p. 513. For account of the case of the *Active*, see Smith, *James Wilson*, pp. 124–27.

163 "dispersed throughout . . .": Madison speech of June 5, Madison, *Notes*, p. 72.

PAGE

163 "The people . . .": Pierce Butler speech of June 5, ibid., p. 73.

164 "would disgust . . .": Morris speech of July 17, ibid., p. 305.

164 Martin's motion of July 17, ibid., pp. 305–6.

165 Martin explained in "Reply to the Landholder," 19 March 1788, in Farrand, *Records* 3:286–87.

166 "As to the Constitutionality . . .": Martin speech of July 21, Madison, *Notes*, p. 340.

167 "If the whole . . .": Commonwealth v. Caton, Court of Appeals of Virginia, 1782, in James Bradley Thayer, *Cases on Constitutional Law* (Cambridge, Mass.: Charles W. Sever, 1894), pp. 59–64.

167 On the Rhode Island case, see Trevett v. Weeden, Superior Court of Judicature of Rhode Island, 1786, ibid., pp. 73–78.

168 The prohibitions were discussed intermittently throughout the convention.

168 "This is a favorable . . .": All the paper-money speeches quoted were made on Aug. 16, Madison, *Notes*, p. 471. The U.S. Supreme Court nevertheless upheld the issuance of currency by the government in a series of Civil War–era cases.

169 For descriptions of acts against judges, see Brunhouse, *Counter-Revolution*, p. 103, and Roberts, "Sectional Problems in Georgia."

CHAPTER SIXTEEN

PAGE

171 "We are informed . . .": Quoted in Warren, *The Making*, p. 198.

171 "We hear . . .": Quoted in Howell, *History of Georgia*, p. 425.

172 "Nothing as yet . . .": In Warren, *The Making*, p. 237.

172 "Whatever measure . . .": In Kaminski and Saladino, *Documentary History* 1:135.

172 The hint appeared in *The Pennsylvania Gazette*, 15 Aug. 1787, as well as in papers in other cities. For fuller accounts of the Osnabrück episode see Kaminski and Saladino 1:171; Hamilton, *Papers* 4:236; and Dunbar, *"Monarchical" Tendencies*.

173 On Hamilton's investigation, see Hamilton to Jeremiah Wadsworth, 20 Aug. 1787, Wadsworth to Hamilton, 26 Aug. 1787, and David Humphreys to Hamilton, 1 Sept. 1787, in Hamilton, *Papers* 4:236–41.

173 "The report of . . .": Sydney to Lord Dorchester, 14 Sept. 1787, in Farrand, *Records* 3:80–81.

174 The McHenry–Mercer exchange is reported by McHenry in his notes in Tansill, *Documents*, pp. 933–34. For Martin's response see "Daniel Carroll: Notes and Correspondence" in Farrand, *Records* 3:319–22.

CHAPTER SEVENTEEN

For the provisions dealing with the executive branch see Article II of the Constitution in the Appendix. The debates in convention on the executive branch took place intermittently from June through September. My understanding of their meaning comes primarily from Thach, *The Creation of the Presidency.*

PAGE

176 "Twenty years": King speech of July 24, Madison, *Notes,* p. 358.

176 "energy, dispatch . . .": Wilson speech of June 1, ibid., p. 46.

177 "*stand the mediator* . . .": Wilson speech of July 17, ibid., p. 307.

177 "foetus of monarchy": Randolph speech of June 1, ibid., p. 46.

177 "considered the executive . . .": Sherman speech of June 1, ibid.

177 "strictly executive . . .": Wilson speech of June 1, ibid.

178 " . . . general notoriety": Ibid., p. 48.

178 "Nor, Entre Nous . . .": Pierce Butler to Weedon Butler, 5 May 1788, Farrand, *Records* 3:301–4.

179 "It is essential . . .": Madison speech of July 19, Madison, *Notes,* p. 327.

180 "I perceive with pleasure . . .": Wilson speech of July 19, ibid., p. 326.

180 Dickinson's account is from Dickinson to George Logan, 4 Nov. 1802, quoted in Flower, *John Dickinson,* pp. 246–47, and also available in U.S. Constitution Collection, Library of Congress.

CHAPTER EIGHTEEN

The clauses relevant to this chapter are:

Article I, Section 8: "The Congress shall have Power . . . To exercise exclusive Legislation in all Cases whatsoever, over such District (not exceeding ten Miles square) as may, by Cession of particular States, and the acceptance of Congress, become the Seat of the Government of the United States, and to exercise like Authority over all Places purchased by the Consent of the Legislature of the State in which the Same shall be, for the Erection of Forts, Magazines, Arsenals, dock-Yards, and other needful Buildings;—And

"To make all Laws which shall be necessary and proper for carrying into Execution the foregoing Powers, and all other Powers vested by this Constitution in the Government of the United States, or in any Department or Officer thereof."

Article VII: "The Ratification of the Conventions of nine States shall be sufficient for the Establishment of this Constitution between the States so ratifying the Same."

Article I, Section 7: "Every Bill which shall have passed the House of Representatives and the Senate, shall, before it become a Law, be presented to the President of the United States; If he approve he shall sign it, but if not he shall return it, with his Objections to that House in which it shall have originated, who shall enter the Objections at large on their Journal, and proceed to reconsider it. If after such Reconsideration two thirds of that House shall agree to pass the Bill, it shall be sent, together with the Objections, to the other House, by which it shall likewise be reconsidered, and if approved by two thirds of that House, it shall become a Law. . . ."

Article II, Section 4: "The President, Vice President and all civil Officers of the United States, shall be removed from Office on Impeachment for, and Conviction of, Treason, Bribery, or other high Crimes and Misdemeanors."

Article V: "The Congress, whenever two-thirds of both Houses shall deem it necessary, shall propose Amendments to this Constitution, or, on the Application of the Legislatures of two-thirds of the several States, shall call a Convention for proposing Amendments, which, in either Case, shall be valid to all Intents and Purposes, as part of this Constitution, when ratified by the Legislatures of three-fourths of the several States, or by Conventions in three-fourths thereof, as the one or the other Mode of Ratification may be proposed by the Congress: Provided that no Amendment which may be made prior to the Year One thousand eight hundred and eight shall in any Manner affect the first and fourth Clauses in the Ninth Section of the first Article; and that no State, without its Consent, shall be deprived of its equal Suffrage in the Senate."

PAGE

185   For background on Gerry see Billias, *Elbridge Gerry*.

185   For Gerry's objections to the clause on the seat of government, see his speech of Sept. 5, Madison, *Notes*, p. 581; to the "necessary and proper" clause, speech of Sept. 16, ibid., p. 652; to lack of ban on standing army, speech of Aug. 18, ibid., p. 481.

186   "Entre nous . . .": This and all the letters quoted here are Gerry to Mrs. Gerry, U.S. Constitution Collection, Library of Congress.

187   On the formation of the coalition of dissidents see "Luther Martin's Reply to the Landholder," 14 March 1788, Farrand, *Records* 3:281–86, and Billias, *Elbridge Gerry*, p. 193.

187   "I'll be hanged": "Papers of Dr. James McHenry on the Federal Convention," Tansill, *Documents*, p. 952.

187   "bound hand and foot": Mason speech of Aug 30, Madison, *Notes*, pp. 549–50; "an experiment . . .": Mason speech of Sept. 7, ibid., p. 600; "I would sooner chop . . .": Mason speech of Aug. 31, ibid., p. 566.

188   "considered the system . . .": "Luther Martin's Reply to the Landholder," 14 March 1788, Farrand, *Records* 3:282.

189   The vote on ratification by nine states took place Aug. 21, Madison, *Notes*, p. 565.

192   The vote on the veto override took place Sept. 12, ibid., p. 629.

192   "Treason . . . will not . . .": Mason speech of Sept. 8, ibid., p. 605. Vote took place same date.

192   "The President may . . .": Randolph speech of Sept. 15, ibid., p. 646. Vote took place same date.

193   Complaints of Gerry, Hamilton and Madison in speeches of Sept. 10, ibid., p. 609. Vote on Madison substitute on same date.

193   "should become oppressive . . .": Mason speech of Sept. 15, ibid., p. 649. Vote on Gerry–Morris proposal on same date.

194   Clause on equal suffrage and slavery voted on Sept. 15, ibid., p. 650.

195   Their defense was set forth repeatedly in ratification debates. For background see Rutland, *Birth of the Bill of Rights*.

196   "A bill of rights . . .": Jefferson to Madison, 20 Dec. 1787, in *The Papers of Thomas Jefferson*, ed. J. P. Boyd (1958), Vol. 12, pp. 438–42.

CHAPTER NINETEEN

PAGE

197   On Morris as the author see Gouverneur Morris to Timothy Pickering, 22 Dec.
      1814, Farrand, *Records* 3:419–20; and Madison to Jared Sparks, 8 April 1831, ibid.,
      pp. 498–99.
199   On the semicolon, see "Albert Gallatin in the House of Representatives," 19 June
      1798, ibid., p. 379. Also see Boardman, *Roger Sherman*, p. 257.
202   On the tactic of having Franklin move the proposal, see Madison's observation in
      his *Notes*, p. 654.

CHAPTER TWENTY

For excellent accounts of the ratification debates see Rutland, *The Birth of the Bill of Rights;*
Main, *The Anti-Federalists;* Storing, *What the Anti-Federalists Were For.* For primary docu-
ments see Kaminski and Saladino, eds., *Documentary History of the Ratification of the
Constitution.*

PAGE

210   "I would advocate . . .": Jefferson to Col. William S. Smith, 2 Feb. 1788, quoted
      in Rutland, *Birth*, pp. 129–30.
212   On Morris' death, see Mintz, *Gouverneur Morris*, p. 240.
213   On Martin's demise, see Clarkson and Jett, *Luther Martin*, pp. 294–303.
214   "Considering the peculiarity . . .": Madison's will quoted in Madison, *Notes*, p. ix.

SELECTED
BIBLIOGRAPHY

I. BOOKS

Ames, Fisher. *Works of Fisher Ames*, 2 vols., edited by Seth Ames. Boston: Little, Brown and Co., 1854.

The Annals of America, Vol. 3, *1784–1796: Organizing the New Nation*. Chicago: Encyclopaedia Britannica, Inc., 1968.

Bailyn, Bernard. *The Ideological Origins of the American Revolution*. Cambridge, Mass.: The Belknap Press of Harvard University, 1967.

———. *The Origins of American Politics*. New York: Vintage Books, 1967.

Bancroft, George. *History of the Formation of the Constitution of the United States of America*, 2 vols. New York: D. Appleton, 1885. Reprint ed., Littleton, Col.: Fred B. Rothman and Co., 1983.

Barry, Richard. *Mr. Rutledge of South Carolina*. Freeport, N.Y.: Books for Libraries Press, 1942.

Beard, Charles A. *An Economic Interpretation of the Constitution of the United States*. Reprint ed., New York: The Free Press, 1965.

Berger, Raoul. *Congress v. The Supreme Court*. Cambridge, Mass.: Harvard University Press, 1969.

Bezanson, Anne, Blanch Daley et al. *Prices and Inflation During the American Revolution: Pennsylvania, 1770–1790*. Philadelphia: University of Pennsylvania Press, 1951.

Billias, George A. *Elbridge Gerry*. New York: McGraw Hill, 1976.

Billington, Ray Allen. *Westward Expansion: A History of the American Frontier*. New York: The Macmillan Co., 1974.

Boardman, Roger Sherman. *Roger Sherman: Signer and Statesman*. Philadelphia: University of Pennsylvania Press, 1938.

Boudin, Louis B. *Government by Judiciary*, Vol. I. New York: William Goodwin, Inc., 1932.

Bowen, Catherine Drinker. *John Adams and the American Revolution*. Boston: Little, Brown and Co., 1950.

Boyd, William K. *History of North Carolina*, Vol. II, *The Federal Period, 1783–1860*. Chicago and New York: Lewis Publishing Co., 1919.

Brant, Irving. *The Fourth President: A Life of James Madison*. Indianapolis and New York: The Bobbs-Merrill Co., 1970.

————. *James Madison*, 6 vols. Indianapolis: The Bobbs-Merrill Co., 1941–61.

Brodie, Fawn M. *Thomas Jefferson: An Intimate History*. Toronto, New York and London: Bantam Books, 1974.

Brown, William G. *The Life of Oliver Ellsworth*. New York: The Macmillan Co., 1905.

Brunhouse, Robert L. *The Counter-Revolution in Pennsylvania, 1776–1790*. New York: Octagon Books, 1971.

Burnett, Edmund Cody, ed. *Letters of Members of the Continental Congress*, 8 vols. Washington: Carnegie Institute, 1936.

Burns, James MacGregor. *The American Experiment: The Vineyard of Liberty*. New York: Alfred A. Knopf, 1982.

Channing, Edward. *A History of the United States*, Vol. III, *The American Revolution, 1761–1789*. New York: The Macmillan Co., 1927.

Clarkson, Paul S., and R. Samuel Jett. *Luther Martin of Maryland*. Baltimore: Johns Hopkins Press, 1970.

Collins, Varnum Lansing. *The Continental Congress at Princeton*. Princeton, N.J.: The University Library, 1908.

The Columbian Magazine or Monthly Miscellany, Containing a View of the History & Manners & Literature & Characters of the Year 1787, Vol 1. Philadelphia: T. Seddon, W. Spotswood, C. Cist & J. Trenchard.

Crosskey, William W. *Politics and the Constitution in the History of the United States*. Chicago: University of Chicago Press, 1953.

Crowl, Philip A. *Maryland During and After the Revolution: A Political and Economic Study*. Baltimore: Johns Hopkins Press, 1943.

Coulter, E. Merton. *A Short History of Georgia.* Chapel Hill: University of North Carolina Press, 1933.

Cutler, William Parker, and Julia Perkins Cutler. *Life, Journals and Correspondence of Rev. Manasseh Cutler, LL.D,* 2 vols. Cincinnati: R. Clarke and Co., 1888.

Davis, David Brion. *The Problem of Slavery in the Age of Revolution, 1770–1823.* Ithaca and London: Cornell University Press, 1975.

Dunbar, Louise B. *A Study of "Monarchical" Tendencies in the United States from 1776 to 1801.* Urbana: University of Illinois, 1923.

Ernst, Robert. *Rufus King: American Federalist.* Published for the Institute of Early American History and Culture at Williamsburg, Va. Chapel Hill: University of North Carolina Press, 1968.

Farrand, Max, ed. *The Records of the Federal Convention of 1787.* Revised ed., 4 vols. New Haven: Yale University Press, 1966.

The Federalist Papers, with an introduction and commentary by Garry Wills. New York: Bantam Books, 1982.

Ferris, Robert G., ed. *Signers of the Constitution: Historic Places Commemorating the Signing of the Constitution.* Vol. XIX of the National Survey of Historic Sites and Buildings. Washington, D.C.: U.S. Department of the Interior/National Park Service, 1976.

Flexner, James Thomas. *George Washington: Anguish and Farewell, 1793–1799.* Boston and Toronto: Little, Brown and Co., 1972.

———. *Washington: The Indispensable Man.* A Signet Book. New York: New American Library, 1984.

Flower, Milton E. *John Dickinson: Conservative Revolutionary.* Charlottesville, Va.: University of Virginia Press, 1983.

Franklin, Benjamin. *Benjamin Franklin's Autobiographical Writings,* edited by Carl Van Doren. New York: Viking Press, 1945.

Fulford, Roger. *Royal Dukes: The Father and Uncles of Queen Victoria.* London: Collins, 1973.

Furnas, J. C. *The Americans: A Social History of the United States, 1587–1914.* New York: G. P. Putnam's Sons, 1969.

Goebel, Julius, Jr. *History of the Supreme Court of the United States,* Vol. I, *Antecedents and Beginnings to 1801.* New York: The Macmillan Co., 1971.

Hall, Van Beck. *Politics Without Parties: Massachusetts, 1780–1791.* Pittsburgh: University of Pittsburgh Press, 1972.

Hamilton, Alexander. *The Papers of Alexander Hamilton,* Vols. 3 and 4, edited by Harold C. Syrett and Jacob E. Cooke. New York: Columbia University Press, 1962.

Handlin, Oscar, and Lillian Handlin. *A Restless People: Americans in Rebellion, 1770–1787*. Garden City, N.Y.: Anchor Press/Doubleday, 1982.

Henderson, H. James. *Party Politics in the Continental Congress*. New York: McGraw-Hill, 1974.

Hill, Roscoe R., ed. *Journals of the Continental Congress*, Vol. 33. Washington: U. S. Government Printing Office, 1936.

Hunter, Robert, Jr., *Quebec to Carolina in 1785–1786: Being the Travel Diary and Observations of Robert Hunter, Jr., a Young Merchant of London*, edited by Louis B. Wright and Marion Tinling. Reprint ed., San Marino, Calif.: The Huntington Library, 1943.

Jensen, Merrill. *The New Nation: A History of the United States During the Confederation, 1781–1789*. New York: Alfred A. Knopf, 1950.

Johnson, Amanda. *Georgia: As Colony and State*. Atlanta: Walter W. Brown, 1938.

Jordan, Winthrop. *White Over Black: American Attitudes Toward the Negro, 1550–1812*. Published for the Institute of Early American History and Culture at Williamsburg, Va. Chapel Hill: University of North Carolina Press, 1968.

Kaminski, John P., and Caspare J. Saladino, eds. *The Documentary History of the Ratification of the Constitution*, 4 vols. Madison: State Historical Society of Wisconsin, 1983.

Kelley, Josph J., Jr., *Life and Times in Colonial Philadelphia*. Harrisburg, Pa.: The Stackpole Co., 1973.

Kelly, Alfred H., Winifred A. Harbison and Herman Belz. *The American Constitution: Its Origins and Development*. New York and London: W. W. Norton and Co., 1983.

Ketcham, Ralph L. *James Madison: A Biography*. New York: The Macmillan Co., 1971.

Krooss, Herman E. *Documentary History of Banking and Currency in the United States*. New York: Chelsea House Publishers, 1969.

Lettieri, Ronald John. *Connecticut's Young Man of the Revolution: Oliver Ellsworth*. Hartford, Conn.: The American Revolution Bicentennial Commission of Hartford, 1978.

Lopez, Claude-Anne, and Eugenia W. Herbert. *The Private Franklin: The Man and His Family*. New York: W. W. Norton and Co., 1975.

Madison, James. *Notes of Debates in the Federal Convention of 1787, reported by James Madison,* with an introduction by Adrienne Koch. Athens: Ohio University Press, 1966.

————. *The Papers of James Madison,* edited by William T. Hutchinson and William M. E. Rachal, Vols. 1 and 9. Chicago: University of Chicago Press, 1962.

Main, Jackson Turner. *The Anti-Federalists: Critics of the Constitution, 1781–1788.* New York: W. W. Norton & Co., 1961.

Mason, George. *The Papers of George Mason, 1725–1792,* edited by Robert A. Rutland, 3 vols. Chapel Hill: University of North Carolina Press, 1970.

Masterson, William H. *William Blount.* Baton Rouge: Louisiana State University Press, 1954.

May, Henry F. *The Enlightenment in America.* New York: Oxford University Press, 1976.

McCaugley, Elizabeth P. *From Loyalist to Founding Father: The Political Odyssey of William Samuel Johnson.* New York and London: W. W. Norton and Co., 1979.

McCormick, Richard P. *Experiment in Independence: New Jersey in the Critical Period, 1781–1789.* New Brunswick: Rutgers University Press, 1950.

McDonald, Forrest. *Alexander Hamilton: A Biography.* New York and London: W. W. Norton and Co., 1979.

Miller, Helen D. Hill. *George Mason: Gentleman Revolutionary.* Chapel Hill: University of North Carolina Press, 1975.

Mintz, Max M. *Gouverneur Morris and the American Revolution.* Norman, Okla.: University of Oklahoma Press, 1970.

Mitchell, Broadus. *Alexander Hamilton,* 2 vols. New York: The Macmillan Co., 1957–62.

Munroe, John A. *History of Delaware,* 2nd ed. A University of Delaware Bicentennial Book. Newark: University of Delaware Press, 1979, 1984.

Nettels, Curtis P. *The Emergence of a National Economy, 1775–1815.* Vol. 2 of the Economic History of the United States Series. New York: Holt, Rinehart and Winston, 1962.

Nevins, Allan. *The American States During and After the Revolution, 1775–1789.* New York: The Macmillan Co., 1924.

Oberholtzer, Ellis P. *Robert Morris, Patriot and Financier.* New York: The Macmillan Co., 1903.

O'Connor, John E. *William Paterson: Lawyer and Statesman, 1745–1806.*
New Brunswick, N. J.: Rutgers University Press, 1979.

Onuf, Peter S. *The Origins of the Federal Republic: Jurisdictional Controversies in the United States, 1775–1787.* Philadelphia: University of
Pennsylvania Press, 1983.

Peterson, Merrill D. *Thomas Jefferson and the New Nation.* New York:
Oxford University Press, 1970.

Polishook, Irwin H. *Rhode Island and the Union.* Evanston, Ill.: North-
western University Press, 1969.

Rakove, Jack N. *The Beginnings of National Politics: An Interpretive History of the Continental Congress.* New York: Alfred A. Knopf, 1979.

Reardon, John J. *Edmund Randolph: A Biography.* New York: The Macmillan Co., 1974.

Robinson, Blackwell P. *William R. Davie.* Chapel Hill: University of
North Carolina Press, 1957.

Robinson, Donald L. *Slavery In the Structure of American Politics, 1765–
1820.* New York: Harcourt Brace Jovanovich, 1972.

Rogers, George C. *Charleston in the Age of the Pinckneys,* 2nd ed. Columbia: University of South Carolina Press, 1980.

Rossiter, Clinton, *1787: The Grand Convention.* New York: The Macmillan Co., 1966.

Rowland, Kate M. *The Life of George Mason, 1725–1792, Including His
Speeches, Public Papers and Correspondence,* with an introduction by
General Fitzhugh Lee. New York: G. P. Putnam's Sons, 1892.

Rush, Benjamin. *Medical Inquiries and Observations,* 4 vols. Reprint ed.,
New York: Arno Press and The New York Times, 1972.

Rutland, Robert Allen. *The Birth of the Bill of Rights, 1776–1791.* Revised ed., Boston: Northeastern University Press, 1983.

Schoepf, Johann David. *Travels in the Confederation, 1783–1784,* trans-
lated and edited by Alfred J. Morison. Reprint ed., New York: Bert
Franklin, 1968.

Secor, Robert, John M. Pickering et al., eds. *Pennsylvania 1776.* University Park and London: Pennsylvania State University Press,
1975.

Smith, Charles Page. *James Wilson, Founding Father, 1742–1798.*
Chapel Hill: University of North Carolina Press, 1956.

Sparks, Jared. *The Life of Gouverneur Morris,* with selections from his
correspondence and miscellaneous papers, 3 vols. Boston: Gray and
Bowen, 1832.

Steiner, Bernard. *The Life and Corrrespondence of James McHenry, Sec-*

retary of War Under Washington and Adams. Cleveland: Burrows Press Co., 1907.

Storing, Herbert J. *What the Anti-Federalists Were For.* Chicago and London: University of Chicago Press, 1981.

Strayer, Joseph Reese, ed. *The Delegate from New York or Proceedings of the Federal Convention of 1787 from the Notes of John Lansing, Jr.* Port Washington, N.Y.: Kennikat Press, 1967.

Swiggett, Howard. *The Extraordinary Mr. Morris.* Garden City, N.Y.: Doubleday, 1952.

Sydnor, Charles S. *Gentlemen Freeholders: Political Parties in Washington's Virginia.* Westport, Conn.: Greenwood Press, 1982.

Szatmary, David P. *Shays' Rebellion: The Making of an American Insurrection.* Amherst: University of Massachusetts Press, 1980.

Tansill, Charles C., ed. *Documents Illustrative of the Formation of the Union of the American States.* Washington, D.C.: U. S. Government Printing Office, 1927.

Thach, Charles C., Jr. *The Creation of the Presidency, 1775–1789: A Study in Constitutional History.* Johns Hopkins University Studies in Historical and Political Science. Baltimore: Johns Hopkins Press, 1922.

Tucker, St. George. *Blackstone's Commentaries: With Notes of Reference to the Constitution and Laws of the Federal Government and the Commonwealth of Virginia,* Vol. I, 1803. South Hackensack, N.J.: Rothman Reprints, Inc., 1969.

Van Doren, Carl. *Benjamin Franklin.* New York: Viking Press, 1939.

———. *The Great Rehearsal; The Story of the Making and Ratifying of the Constitution of the United States.* New York: Viking Press, 1948.

Warren, Charles. *The Making of the Constitution.* Boston: Little, Brown and Co., 1928.

Washington, George. *The Diaries of George Washington,* Vol. V, July 1786–December 1789, edited by Donald Jackson and Dorothy Twohig. Charlottesville: University of Virginia Press, 1976.

———. *The Washington Papers: Being Selections from the Public and Private Writings of George Washington,* edited by Saul K. Padover. New York: Harper & Brothers, 1955.

———. *The Writings of George Washington from the Original Manuscript Sources, 1745–1799,* edited by John C. Fitzpatrick, vols. 27–29. Prepared under the direction of the United States Bicentennial Commission and published by the authority of Congress. Washington, D.C.: U.S. Government Printing Office, 1931–44.

Watson, John F. *Annals of Philadelphia and Pennsylvania in the Olden Time.* Philadelphia: Edwin S. Stuart, 1884.

White, Henry C. *Abraham Baldwin.* Athens, Ga.: The McGregor Co., 1926.

Williams, Francis Leigh. *A Founding Family: The Pinckneys of South Carolina.* New York and London: Harcourt Brace Jovanovich, 1978.

Wood, Gordon S. *The Creation of the American Republic, 1776–1787.* New York and London: W. W. Norton and Co., 1969.

Young, Alfred F. *The Democratic Republicans of New York: The Origins, 1763–1797.* Published for the Institute of Early American History and Culture, Williamsburg, Va. Chapel Hill: University of North Carolina Press, 1967.

Zahniser, Marvin R. *Charles Cotesworth Pinckney, Founding Father.* Published for the Institute of Early American History and Culture at Williamsburg, Va. Chapel Hill: University of North Carolina Press, 1967.

II. ARTICLES

Crowl, Philip A. "Anti-Federalism in Maryland, 1787–1788." *William and Mary Quarterly* 3rd ser., IV, no. 4 (October 1947):446–69.

Fisher, Louis. "The Efficiency Side of Separated Powers." *Journal of American Studies* 5, no. 2 (August 1971):113–31.

Gerlach, Larry R. "Toward 'a More Perfect Union': Connecticut, the Continental Congress, and the Constitutional Convention." *The Connecticut Historical Society Bulletin* 34, no. 3 (July 1969):65–78.

Goddard, Henry P. "Luther Martin: the Federal Bulldog." *Maryland Historical Society Fund Publication No. 24.* Baltimore, 1887.

Higginson, Stephen. "Letters of Stephen Higginson, 1783–1804." *American Historical Association Annual Report, 1896.* 1 (1897):704–841.

Hutson, James H. "Country, Court and Constitution: Anti-Federalism and the Historians." *William and Mary Quarterly* 3rd ser., XXXVIII, July 1981:337–67.

———. "The Creation of the Constitution: Scholarship at a Standstill." *Reviews in American History,* December 1984:463–77.

———. "John Dickinson at the Federal Constitutional Convention." *William and Mary Quarterly* 3rd ser., XL, April 1983:256–82.

————. "Pierce Butler's Record of the Federal Constitutional Convention." *The Quarterly Journal of the Library of Congress*, Winter 1980:64–75.

————. "Robert Yate's Notes on the Constitutional Convention." *The Quarterly Journal of the Library of Congress*, July 1978:173–81.

Lynd, Staughton. "The Compromise of 1787." *Political Science Quarterly* 81, June 1966:225–50.

Madison, James. "James Madison's Autobiography," edited by Douglass Adair. *William and Mary Quarterly* 3rd ser., II, April 1945:191–209.

Main, Jackson T. "Government by the People: the American Revolution and the Democratization of the Legislatures." *William and Mary Quarterly* 3rd ser., XXIII, July 1966:391–401.

————. "Political Parties in Revolutionary Maryland, 1780–1787." *Maryland Historical Magazine* 62, no. 1 (March 1967):1–27.

Munroe, John A. "Reflections on Delaware and the American Revolution." *Delaware History* XVII, no. 1 (Spring–Summer 1976):1–11.

Paterson, William. "Papers of William Paterson on the Federal Convention, 1787." *American Historical Review* 9, January 1904:310–40.

Patterson, C. Perry. "James Madison and Judicial Review." *California Law Review* 28, no. 1 (November 1939):22–33.

Roberts, Lucien E. "Sectional Problems in Georgia During the Formative Period, 1776–1798." *The Georgia Historical Quarterly* XVIII, no. 3 (September 1934):207–27.

Roche, John P. "The Founding Fathers: A Reform Caucus in Action." *American Political Science Review* 55, December 1961:799–816.

Swindler, William F. "Seedtime of an American Judiciary: From Independence to the Constitution." *William and Mary Law Review* 17, no. 3 (Spring 1976):503–21.

Ulmer, S. Sidney. "The Role of Pierce Butler in the Constitutional Convention." *The Review of Politics* 22, no. 3 (July 1960):361–74.

Wright, Benjamin F. "The Origins of the Separation of Powers in America. *Economica* 13, May 1933:169–85.

III. NEWSPAPERS (PHILADELPHIA)

The Independent Gazeteer, 18 May–14 August 1787.
The Pennsylvania Journal and the Weekly Advertiser, 10 March–15 September 1786.

The Pennsylvania Mercury, 28 June–17 August 1787.
The Pennsylvania Packet, 16 May–23 August 1787.

IV. MANUSCRIPT COLLECTIONS, UNPUBLISHED

Independence National Historical Park Collection, Philadelphia.
U. S. Constitution Collection, Library of Congress.

INDEX

ABOUT THE AUTHOR

Fred Barbash is deputy national editor of the *Washington Post* and covered the Supreme Court for the *Post* from 1980 to 1985. He has covered state, local and national government for the *Post*, after beginning his newspaper career at the *Baltimore Sun*.